I X 4/08✓ 2/09

THE HISTORY OF
KOREA

THE HISTORY OF KOREA

Djun Kil Kim

The Greenwood Histories of the Modern Nations
Frank W. Thackeray and John E. Findling, Series Editors

Greenwood Press
Westport, Connecticut • London

Library of Congress Cataloging-in-Publication Data

Kim, Chun-kil, 1940–
  The history of korea / Djun Kil Kim.
    p. cm. — (Greenwood histories of the modern nations, ISSN 1096–2905)
  Includes index.
  ISBN 0–313–33296–7 (hardcover : alk. paper)
    1. Korea—History. 2. Korea (South)—History. I. Title. II. Series.
  DS907.18.K5247   2005
  951.9—dc22   2004021180

British Library Cataloguing in Publication Data is available.

Library of Congress Catalog Card Number: 2004021180
ISBN: 0–313–33296–7
ISSN: 1096–2905

First published in 2005

Greenwood Press, 88 Post Road West, Westport, CT 06881
An imprint of Greenwood Publishing Group, Inc.
www.greenwood.com

Printed in the United States of America

The paper used in this book complies with the
Permanent Paper Standard issued by the National
Information Standards Organization (Z39.48-1984).

10   9   8   7   6   5   4   3   2   1

Contents

Series Foreword

The *Greenwood Histories of the Modern Nations* series is intended to provide students and interested laypeople with up-to-date, concise, and analytical histories of many of the nations of the contemporary world. Not since the 1960s has there been a systematic attempt to publish a series of national histories, and, as editors, we believe that this series will prove to be a valuable contribution to our understanding of other countries in our increasingly interdependent world.

Over thirty years ago, at the end of the 1960s, the Cold War was an accepted reality of global politics, the process of decolonization was still in progress, the idea of a unified Europe with a single currency was unheard of, the United States was mired in a war in Vietnam, and the economic boom of Asia was still years in the future. Richard Nixon was president of the United States, Mao Tse-tung (not yet Mao Zedong) ruled China, Leonid Brezhnev guided the Soviet Union, and Harold Wilson was prime minister of the United Kingdom. Authoritarian dictators still ruled most of Latin America, the Middle East was reeling in the wake of the Six-Day War, and Shah Reza Pahlavi was at the height of his power in Iran. Clearly, the past 30 years have been witness to a great deal of historical change, and it is to this change that this series is primarily addressed.

With the help of a distinguished advisory board, we have selected nations whose political, economic, and social affairs mark them as among
the most important in the waning years of the twentieth century, and for
each nation we have found an author who is recognized as a specialist in
the history of that nation. These authors have worked most cooperatively
with us and with Greenwood Press to produce volumes that reflect current
research on their nations and that are interesting and informative to their
prospective readers.

The importance of a series such as this cannot be underestimated. As a
superpower whose influence is felt all over the world, the United States
can claim a "special" relationship with almost every other nation. Yet
many Americans know very little about the histories of the nations with
which the United States relates. How did they get to be the way they are?
What kind of political systems have evolved there? What kind of influence
do they have in their own region? What are the dominant political, religious, and cultural forces that move their leaders? These and many other
questions are answered in the volumes of this series.

The authors who have contributed to this series have written comprehensive histories of their nations, dating back to prehistoric times in some
cases. Each of them, however, has devoted a significant portion of the
book to events of the last thirty years, because the modern era has contributed the most to contemporary issues that have an impact on U.S.
policy. Authors have made an effort to be as up-to-date as possible so that
readers can benefit from the most recent scholarship and a narrative that
includes very recent events.

In addition to the historical narrative, each volume in this series contains an introductory overview of the country's geography, political institutions, economic structure, and cultural attributes. This is designed to
give readers a picture of the nation as it exists in the contemporary world.
Each volume also contains additional chapters that add interesting and
useful detail to the historical narrative. One chapter is a thorough chro-
nology of important historical events, making it easy for readers to follow
the flow of a particular nation's history. Another chapter features bio-
graphical sketches of the nation's most important figures in order to hu-
manize some of the individuals who have contributed to the historical
development of their nation. Each volume also contains a comprehensive
bibliography, so that those readers whose interest has been sparked may
find out more about the nation and its history. Finally, there is a carefully
prepared topic and person index.

Readers of these volumes will find them fascinating to read and useful
in understanding the contemporary world and the nations that comprise

it. As series editors, it is our hope that this series will contribute to a heightened sense of global understanding as we embark on a new century.

Frank W. Thackeray and John E. Findling
Indiana University Southeast

Preface

Today, a comprehensive Korean history book for the general English-speaking public is rarely found, while books on the histories of China and Japan are numerous. One reason for this, I believe, is the language barrier. Language is more than a mere tool for communication; it is the first aspect one must master of learning another culture. The problem lies not in a simple need for more communication between the West and Koreans, but in the walls built by two dissimilar cultural paradigms. No matter how deeply a native English-speaker delves into Korean studies, he or she cannot climb every one of these barriers. Likewise, no matter how fluently a native Korean-speaker can master English, he or she would still face limitations.

As a native speaker of Korean, I have had the same difficulties in writing a Korean history in English. Fortunately, many of these problems were solved when I was invited to Brigham Young University during the 2003–2004 academic year. Professor Mark Peterson, the Korean-studies director of the Department of Asian and Near Eastern Languages at BYU, with whom I have shared a decades-old friendship, provided me with an environment for my writing project. I greatly appreciate his wholehearted support and his contributions for two chapters, including one on Confucianization, which is his specialty. At Mark's suggestion, I taught Korean-history classes during these two semesters. The classes provided me with much inspiration on how to translate Korean-history terminology into refined English concepts. Moreover, through these classes, I met one Jeffrey Ehlers, a student talented in writing, who, as a research assistant funded by BYU, helped me in editing my English draft.

Many thanks also go to Ms. Ginny Kim, assistant legal counsel at Pratt and Whitney, who, out of her own interest in Korean history and with her amazing editorial skills, helped to refine the text for a mere friend of her father. In addition, I am really fortunate to have met Sarah Colwell, assistant editor at Greenwood, who aptly guided a foreign author unfamiliar with American publication processes. I am thankful for her kindness.

I owe a great deal to many scholars for their guidance and review. Professor Noh Tae-don of Seoul National University guided me in selecting recent studies by Korean historians and meticulously reviewed chapters 2 and 3. Professor Yi Tae-jin, also of Seoul National University, provided me with several of his works, which proved to be indispensable. He further reviewed chapters 4 and 5. Professor Lew Young Ick of Yonsei University encouraged and advised me in the initial stages of this project and also read chapter 6. Professor Choe Chungho of Ulsan University shared many valuable ideas on Korean contemporary history and read chapters 7 and 8. And, once again, I thank Mark Peterson for his careful reading of all chapters.

The idea for this book had been incubating in my mind since the early 1970s, when the late historian Ch'ŏn Kwanu wrote a series of articles entitled *Streams of Korean History* in a monthly magazine. His articles inspired me to shape the outline of Korea's antiquity period found in this book. While studying for my master's at Seoul National University, I was fortunate to have his guidance in reading eighteenth-century documents in classical Chinese, including monographs of Korean *sirhak* scholars.

Professor Lee Man Gap, who taught me sociology at Seoul National University, enlightened me on his marginal-group theory by interpreting the transition periods in Korean history under which social change was always initiated by a marginal group beneath the ruling class. I am very grateful for his interest in this project and his encouragement. Professor Kim Jae-On of Iowa University tutored his old classmate at SNU with the reoriented perspective on Korean history he had acquired from American sociology. Many thanks for his guidance and for his reading the introduction and other chapters.

I have been blessed with generous financial assistance from both Myong Ji University and the SBS Foundation. Dr. You Young Koo, chairman of the Myong Ji Educational Foundation, who has collected thousands of books on Korea published in various foreign languages throughout the centuries, enthusiastically supported me in adding one more book to his precious archive. I am grateful to Chairman Yoon Seyoung of the SBS Foundation, who has a special interest in the public education of Korean history and culture throughout the world.

Dr. Lee Hong Koo, former prime minister of the Republic of Korea and ambassador to the United States, encouraged me in writing this book. I am further grateful for his reading the last chapter. Mr. Kim Young Soo, former minister of culture, used all of his influence to support this project. Without his passionate interest, this book would have never been written. I also thank Dr. Son Chu-whan, former minister of information, for his fervent support of my plans.

I must confess my motivation to write a Korean history book is due in part to the memory of my grandfather Hyŏn Sangyun, a harbinger of modern studies on traditional Korean thought, including Confucianism. More thanks go to my father, Kim Chae Yul, who collected many clippings from newspapers and magazines on issues in studies on Korean history. With this book, I hope to teach the past, both its good and bad aspects, to my grandsons Geunmok and Geunbaek, who will grow up to shape a new history in Korea. Finally, I thank In Woo, my wife, who has endured her fumbling spouse for nearly four decades in what was not always the good life.

Timeline of Historical Events

8000–2000 B.C.E.	Comb-patterned pottery people inhabit Manchuria and the Korean peninsula
2000–1000 B.C.E.	Migration of plain-pottery people from the north of China to Manchuria and the Korean peninsula; agriculture civilization begins
ca. 1000 B.C.E.	Bronze Age: T-type bronze dagger used in Manchuria and the Korean peninsula
1000–300 B.C.E.	The kingdom of Old Chosŏn, founded by Tan'gun, the priest-king
ca. 700 B.C.E.	Rice cultivation begins on the Korean peninsula
ca. 300 B.C.E.	Iron Age in Manchuria and the Korean peninsula; Chinese script introduced
194 B.C.E.	Wiman Chosŏn dynasty begins
108 B.C.E.	Wiman Chosŏn conquered by Han Chinese forces; Han Wudi establishes four prefectures, including Lelang

100 B.C.E.–100 C.E.	Ancient kingdoms of the Han-Ye-Maek people, such as Puyŏ, Koguryŏ, Paekche, Mahan, Silla, and Kaya, appear in Manchuria and the Korean peninsula
313	Koguryŏ conquers Lelang, the last Han prefecture
372	Introduction of Buddhism to Korea
414	Koguryŏ King Kwanggaet'o stele erected
427	Koguryŏ moves its capital to Pyongyang
527	Silla adopts Buddhism
562	The Three Kingdoms period begins: Koguryŏ, Paekche, and Silla
612	Koguryŏ's Ŭlchi Mundŏk defeats the Sui Chinese invaders on the Salsu River
648–50	Silla-Tang alliance established by Kim Ch'unch'u
654	Kim Ch'unch'u enthroned in Silla as King Muyŏl
660	Fall of Paekche
668	Fall of Koguryŏ; Silla unifies the Korean peninsula
699	The Han-Ye-Maek kingdom of Parhae founded
727	Silla monk Hech'o writes a travelogue in India
751	Pulguksa temple and Sŏkkuram grotto constructed in Kyŏngju
828	Chang Pogo establishes the Maritime Command on Ch'ŏnghaejin Island
918	Koryŏ dynasty founded by Wang Kŏn
926	Parhae conquered and destroyed by the Khitan
936	Koryŏ reunifies the Korean peninsula, including some parts occupied by Parhae
958	*Kwago,* the civil-service examination system, adopted
1018	Kang Kamch'an thwarts the Khitan invasion
1135	The monk Myoch'ŏng incites a revolt
1145	The *Samguk sagi,* the oldest existent Korean historiography, compiled by Kim Pusik

1170	Military junta stages coup; takes power over Koryŏ
1196	Rule of the Ch'oe House
1231–32	First Mongol invasion; the court flees to Kanghwa
1234	First printing of a book by movable metal type
1251	Second Tripitaka Koreana built in the Haeinsa temple
1264	Peace treaty with the Mongols
1274	Yuan overlordship; Yuan-Koryŏ expedition to Japan
Late 1200s	Neo-Confucianism introduced; *Samguk yusa* authored by the monk Iryŏn
1356	Yuan overlordship ends
1364	Mun Ikchŏm introduces cottonseeds to Korea
1377	Ch'oe Musŏn develops gunpowder
1388	Yi Sŏnggye begins his coup on the Wihwado Islet
1392	Chosŏn dynasty founded by Yi Sŏnggye
1394	Capital moved to Seoul
1440	King Sejong advances the kingdom's northern border to the Yalu and Tumen Rivers
1446	King Sejong officializes hangul, the Korean alphabet
1469	*Kyŏngguk taejŏn*, the royal state code, compiled
1498, 1504, 1519, 1545	Series of literati purges
1592–98	Imjin War, or the Hideyoshi Invasion
1636	The Manchu Invasions
1653	Hendrik Hamel drifts ashore on Cheju Island
1678	*Sangp'yŏng t'ongbo*, Korean metal currency, cast
1712	Stone designating Korea's northern border with China established on Mt. Paektu
1784	First Korean catholic convert baptized in Beijing
1801	First execution of Catholics
1811–12	Rebellion of Hong Kyŏngnae in a northwestern province

1860	Foundation of Tonghak by Ch'oe Cheu
1862	Popular uprising in Chinju
1863	Hŭngsŏn Taewŏn'gun rises to power
1866	American merchant ship USS *General Sherman* burned on the Taedong River; battle with French warships
1871	Battle with American warships
1876	Ports opened to Japan with the Kanghwa Treaty
1882–86	Friendship treaties with the United States, the United Kingdom, Germany, Italy, Russia, and France
1883	*T'aegŭkki*, the national flag, adopted
December 4, 1884	Kapsin Coup staged by Kim Okkyun
January 1894	Tonghak armed uprising; Kabo Reforms
1894–95	Sino-Japanese War
August 1895	Queen Min slain by Japanese assassins
February 1896	King Kojong takes refuge in the Russian legation
April 1896	The Independence Club established; *Tongnip Sinmun*, first newspaper published in hangul, inaugurated
October 1897	Taehan Empire proclaimed
October 1898	Independence Club organizes Joint Meeting of Government and People
1904–5	Russo-Japanese War
November 1905	Korea becomes a protectorate of Japan
June 1907	Emperor Kojong sends three representatives to the second International Peace Conference in The Hague
July 1907	Emperor Kojong abducted
1907–10	Korean guerrilla volunteer resistance against Japanese occupation army
July 1909	Japanese resident-general Ito Hirobumi assassinated by An Chunggŭn
August 1910	Korea annexed to Japan

1910–19	Japanese military rule
March 1, 1919	Mansei movement; Korean Declaration of Independence read
April 1919	Provisional Government of the Republic of Korea founded in Shanghai
1920	Japanese cultural rule begins
April 1920	Two Korean-language newspapers, *Dong-A Ilbo* and *Chosun Ilbo*, founded
April 1925	Korean Communist Party founded in Seoul
June 1926	Mass demonstrations for independence
1936	Japanese institute assimilation policy in Korea
1939	Japanese Government-General decrees that Koreans are to adopt Japanese surnames
1943	Koreans drafted into Japanese army for the Pacific War
August 9, 1945	Soviet 25th Army begins occupation of northeastern Korea
August 15	Korea liberated from colonial rule with the surrender of Japan
August 16	Committee for the Preparation of Korean Independence organized
September 6	People's Republic of Korea proclaimed in Seoul
September 8	Lieutenant General John R. Hodge, commander of U.S. 24th Corps, lands in Inchon
October 14	Soviet Civil Administration holds Soviet-style hero's welcome for Kim Il Sung in Pyongyang
February 1946	U.S. Army Military Government in Korea organizes Representative Democratic Council of South Korea; Soviet Civil Administration organizes in North Korea the Interim People's Committee headed by Kim Il Sung
March 20	First U.S.-USSR Joint Commission held in Seoul
August	North Korean Workers' Party founded
September–October	South Korean communists instigate nationwide sabotage and insurrection in Taegu

February 1947	U.S. Army Military Government in Korea organizes South Korean interim government and appoints chief civil administrator
May 21	Second U.S.-USSR Joint Commission resumed in Seoul
July	Assassination of Yŏ Unhyŏng, moderate leftist leader in South Korea
February 1948	Korean People's Army organized in North Korea
March	UN General Assembly organizes UN Temporary Commission for Korea to implement general elections
April 3	Antielection insurrection by communists on Cheju Island
May 10	UN-supervised general elections held in South Korea
July 17	South Korean constitution adopted by National Assembly
August 15	Republic of Korea established in South Korea; Syngman Rhee elected president
September 9	Democratic People's Republic of Korea established in North Korea; Kim Il Sung appointed premier
summer 1949	Korean Workers' Party founded in North Korea
June 25, 1950	North Korean People's Army invades South Korea; UN Security Council adopts resolution that condemns the North Korean action; Korean War begins
June 27	U.S. president Truman dispatches U.S. forces
September 15	General MacArthur launches Inchon landing
October 19	Chinese Volunteer Army crosses Yalu River and joins the war
July 27, 1953	Armistice signed between North Korea and UN forces
August	Kim Il Sung purges the South Korean Workers' Party faction
1957	Kim Il Sung launches Five-Year Economic Plan and finishes purging of old factions in the Korean Workers' Party
April 19, 1960	Student demonstrations in South Korea oust President Syngman Rhee

October	Kim Il Sung personality cult established
May 16, 1961	Major General Park Chung Hee stages coup in South Korea
1962	South Korean military junta launches First Five-Year Economic Development Plan
October 1963	Park Chung Hee elected fifth president of the Republic of Korea
June 1965	South Korea normalizes diplomatic relations with Japan
1971	Saemaul Movement begins in South Korea
July 4, 1972	North-South Communiqué and establishment of the North-South Coordinating Commission
August	Red Cross talks between the North and South begin
October 17	Yusin (Revitalization) constitution adopted in South Korea
October	Kim Il Sung becomes president by new North Korean constitution
August 1973	Kim Dae Jung abducted in Japan
February 1974	Kim Jong Il becomes "the Party Center," heir apparent to the North Korean president
October 1979	Anti-Yusin student demonstration in Pusan
October 26	Assassination of Park Chung Hee
December 12	Chun Doo Hwan stages military coup in South Korea
May 18, 1980	Kwangju uprising
September	Chun Doo Hwan elected president under the Yusin constitution
October	Sixth Congress of Korean Workers' Party confirms the future succession of Kim Jong Il as North Korean leader; Kim Il Sung proposes a new reunification formula for the two Koreas
October 1983	Assassination attempt by North Korean terrorists on the life of Chun Doo Hwan by a bombing in Burma

September 1985	First meeting of families divided between North and South by the Korean War
June 10, 1987	Large-scale demonstration in Seoul for direct presidential election
June 29	President Chun Doo Hwan accedes to the demonstration's demands for democratization
August	North Korean bombing of Korean Air flight 747
December	Roh Tae Woo elected president by popular vote
September 1988	24th Summer Olympics held in Seoul
1989	The *New York Times* reports the existence of a nuclear power station in Yŏngbyŏn, North Korea
1989–92	South Korea establishes diplomatic relations with Hungary, the Soviet Union, and China
September 17, 1991	The two Koreas join the UN as individual members
December 13	North-South high-level talks sign the Basic Agreement on Reconciliation, Non-Aggression, and Cooperation of Exchanges
December 18, 1992	Kim Young Sam elected South Korean president
July 8, 1994	Death of North Korean leader Kim Il Sung
October	Agreed Framework between the United States and North Korea signed
September 1996	South Korea becomes a member of the Organization for Economic Cooperation and Development
summer 1997	Asian financial crisis hits South Korea
December 3	First International Monetary Fund bailout of South Korea
December	Kim Dae Jung elected president of South Korea
June 13–15, 2000	First inter-Korean summit meeting between Kim Dae Jung and Kim Jong Il in Pyongyang

1

Introduction

MISPERCEPTION OF KOREA

The world is largely unacquainted with Korean history. Often Korea has been mistaken as a part or a mere replica of China. Much of this confusion was the result of a lack of knowledge or interest in Korea. Compared with China and Japan, Korean studies are rare and fairly new. However, Korea has recently attracted worldwide attention due to its emerging role on the international scene. Sometimes the situation or events on the Korean peninsula have been misunderstood by the world because they are often approached without historical and cultural background to interpret them. For instance, it is curious how the isolated Stalinist regime of North Korea can be so resilient while millions of their people starve. Furthermore, it is also curious how the younger generations of South Korea, who have benefited the most from the economic growth and political democratization secured by U.S. military deterrence, can be so anti-American as well as antiglobalization.

How, then, do we approach Korean history? When we say *Korean history,* we have to include the origins of Korean civilization before Korea as an identity had even been created. In other words, Korean history should not be geographically limited to the boundaries of modern-day Korea. We should extend the scope of our perspective up from northern China, Manchuria, and the Korean peninsula and down to the Japanese archipelago. Over the millennia, various ethnic groups who migrated in waves into this vast region shaped what would later become the Korean tradition. Extending the geographical scope of Korean history does not necessarily mean we are expanding the historical territory of the Korean people, as Korean nationalist historians have done throughout the centuries. But our purpose here is to explore the history of Korean tradition and its identity in the East-Asian world setting.

If we take a look at history, although there had been trade between West Asia and the Near Eastern worlds via the silk roads, we see that East Asia had its own order and an independent world system until the Europeans set it in disarray in the nineteenth century. Just like the Mediterranean region under the Roman empire in ancient times, it was more than a Chinese empire—it was a world. This world centered on the concept of *tianxia*, meaning "all lands under heaven" in Chinese. Be that as it may, East Asia was not just a stagnated region throughout its millennia of history, as Eurocentric social scientists often claimed. Far from Karl Marx's argument that the so-called Asiatic mode of production remained "traditional, backward, and stagnant" until the arrival of the West, this world was in fact vibrant and progressive.

The Korean people, like the Gallic people in the Roman empire, shaped their own history and tradition within this world. Given that Korea was situated in the periphery, it was only natural that it took longer to experience civilization in each stage of development. Likewise, the Gallic and Celtic peoples in the Roman periphery underwent periods of uncivilized society. At any rate, Korea was one of the few nations, like Vietnam and Japan, that created and maintained their own identities in this China-centered cosmos. This meant that Korea's culture and society had to progressively adapt and evolve to avoid becoming absorbed by the massive entity of China. Moreover, throughout its history, Korea was affected by both internal and external influences, as was any other society.

Therefore, we should look at Korea's history with a universal approach. Unfortunately, this has rarely been done. Above all, Korean tradition has not been sufficiently explained to the world in view of its crucial role in East-Asian history—as compared, for example, with Japan. Korean history, its premodern history in particular, has been perceived by various scholars both inside and outside Korea from different perspectives, thereby lending itself to controversy and misinterpretation. It has often been misunderstood and sometimes even deliberately distorted and fabricated by foreign historians and missionaries as well as by native scholars and journalists. In recent decades, and even now, some political leaders of both China and the two Koreas have exploited the study of Korean history to serve their own political purposes, as did the Japanese colonialists in the past.

Language barriers amplified these misperceptions of Korean history in the English-speaking world. One reason is that human nature makes it difficult to comprehensively explain Korean history from an objective perspective and without indulging in any particular argument. Nonetheless, by comparing it with other traditions in East-Asian civilization, we would like to explore here the origins of the Korean tradition established in its premodern period and its impact on Korea's modern history. Though lukewarm, previous studies on Korean history have shown progress during the last four decades at home and abroad. Here in this book, we try to selectively update those recent scholarly works that could help us with an objective perspective. Sometimes we deemed it necessary to provide criticism on certain native claims or outside arguments we felt were unreasonable or irrational.

WHAT DOES KOREA OFFER TO THE WORLD?

What does Korea offer to the world? What unique contributions have Koreans made to human civilization? Although Korea has been overlooked in many regards, mostly because of its entering the twentieth century as a colony of another country, Korean contributions to humankind have been substantial. Many things about Korean history are unique, unparalleled in other civilizations. In this book we will examine Korea's history, its contributions to the world, and the pain, as well as the glory, that has come its way. In some ways Koreans overestimate their role in the history of nations, but in several other ways they have not recognized some of their greatest accomplishments as well as they should.

For example, Koreans see themselves as a small, sometimes oppressed country. They are surrounded by large powerful countries—China to the west, Japan to the east, Russia to the north. Add American involvement in the last century, and Korea seems to be a small country surrounded by giants. There is a saying in Korean: "When whales fight, shrimps get their backs broken." They see themselves as shrimps when compared to China, Japan, Russia, and the United States. In actuality, however, Korea is larger than many European countries—a bit smaller than Germany, England, and France, but larger than Italy, Spain, Portugal, and all of Scandinavia. In terms of population, Korea ranks 16th, and in terms of land area, it ranks 83rd. In regards to economy, South Korea alone has the 11th-largest

GDP in the world and is the 12th-largest trading nation. Today South Korea, the world's 38th-richest country, is the sixth-most wired country in the world, with 15.5 million people using the Internet. Moreover, the Korean language is spoken by 75 million people worldwide: 48 million in South Korea, 22 million in North Korea, and another 5 million in expatriate communities in China, Japan, Russia, the United States, Canada, Europe, and South America. It ranks 13th in number of speakers worldwide.

Korea, as an independent nation-state, well understood its role in the East-Asian world system. Thanks to its traditional diplomacy, known as *sadae kyorin* (*sadae:* attendance on the great; *kyorin:* goodwill to neighbors), the Korean people have lived mostly in peace and stability on their peninsula since the seventh century. Throughout these 1,500 years, Korea was ruled by only three dynasties. These dynasties were so uniquely resilient that they suffered and survived through the two considerably devastating wars to occur on the peninsula in its premodern history: the Mongol and Japanese invasions in the thirteenth and sixteenth centuries, respectively. Moreover, the shift between these dynasties took place in a comparatively smooth process once the peninsula was united.

Korea faced a serious challenge in the nineteenth century when a new world system overwhelmed the traditional East-Asian world order. The transitional span between premodern and modern was exceptionally short for Korea. It had less than a decade to reform itself in order to survive in the new paradigm. This entailed bewilderment and tragedy both for the ruling class and the people. Furthermore, the turmoil of the twentieth century sits large in the minds of contemporary Koreans. Korea failed to maintain its independence while modernizing itself and entered the new century as a colony of the Japanese. In 1895, Japan defeated the Qing dynasty in a war that left Korea without its longstanding ally, China. In 1905, Japan defeated Russia in another war and began to dominate Korea, controlling all of the country's external relations in an arrangement that designated Korea as a protectorate. Then, in 1910, Korea was annexed to the Japanese empire.

Another decisive moment in Korean history came in 1945, as a shift in the world-system paradigm occurred once more. Liberation from the Japanese came with the defeat of Japan in World War II, but the liberated Korea was temporarily divided in an agreement between the United States and its then ally, the Soviet Union. The Cold War froze the division, creating two separate governments: the Democratic People's Republic of Korea in the North and the Republic of Korea in the South. The two rival political bodies initially fought each other with their military might, supported by their allies, during the Korean War. However, even the tragedy of millions of victims in this war did not bring both sides together for unification. Thus, the two Koreas have confronted each other and competed with their different ideologies for last five decades. During the Cold-War period, Korea was indeed an experiment of the two rival systems of communism and capitalism. Thus, Korea failed to enter the new world system as the single national entity it had maintained throughout the 15 centuries of its history.

Therefore, one of the greatest tragedies of Korean contemporary society is that the country, which should be one country, is divided. And the division was not created by Korea itself, but by outside powers. Most Koreans hope for the day of reunification.

HOW OLD IS KOREAN HISTORY?

On a test in a Korean-history class, one might see the following question: "When did Korean history begin?" The answers, in multiple-choice format, might include (a) 10,000 years ago; (b) 5,000 years ago; (c) In the year 2333 B.C.E.; (d) 2,000 years ago; (e) In the year 414 C.E.; (f) In the year 668 C.E.; (g) About 350 years ago; and (h) In the year 1948. With such a range of answers, it would be unexpected that the best answer to the question might be the next option, (i) All of the above. Each choice is indeed the correct answer depending on the criteria used to define the starting point for Korea's history. We shall examine each answer.

10,000 years ago

This answer is taken from the archaeological perspective. There are some 400,000-year-old vestiges of people from the Paleolithic period in Korea and Manchuria, but it is unclear whether they have a direct line down to today's Koreans. There are also a few Mesolithic sites found on the peninsula, but it was not until the Neolithic period that there was a continuous settlement in the region. Ten thousand years ago, these Neolithic people left evidence of their lifestyle in the form of stone tools and pottery. Such can be called the beginning of the Korean people, though some would argue that since these evidences are not written records, they cannot be called history, but rather fall into the category of prehistory.

5,000 years ago

This is the answer the most commonly provided by Koreans themselves, yet it is probably the least justifiable based on the data we have.

The dating given in one of the most revered myths in Korea, the Tan'gun myth, places the beginning of Korea's history at a few hundred years less than 5,000 years. However, the way it is rendered in Chinese characters rounds the number off to the year "half a 10,000." There are numerous publications and other references to Korean history being 5,000 years old. Some of the Korean desire to have an old history is due to a similar concern, that older is better, found in China. In the myth, Tan'gun founded the first Korean kingdom named Chosŏn in the 50th year of the first emperor of China, thereby making Korean history almost as old as elder brother China.

In the year 2333 B.C.E.

This year is the actual date offered in the Tan'gun foundation myth. It is based on a fifteenth-century Korean historiography that counted back to the exact year in the reign of the first Chinese emperor. In South Korea, this Tan'gun calendar had been used since 1945, until they adopted the Christian era in the early 1960s.

2,000 years ago

Around 2,000 years ago, Korea, or parts of what was to become Korea, began to take shape and appear in the Chinese records. In a sense, this is the first truly historical record of Korea, although it was not written within Korea's historical boundaries or in the Korean language, but rather in China in classical Chinese. During this period, the ancient Korean kingdoms, such as Koguryŏ, Puyŏ, Paekche, Silla, and Kaya, appeared in Manchuria and the Korean peninsula. They began in Manchuria but are clearly Korean, or proto-Korean, in language and culture.

In the year 414 C.E.

The first significant record written in Korea was dated 414 and is written on a large stele 6.27 meters tall and about 2 meters wide on each side. The text is a detailed account of the reign of king Kwanggaet'o of Koguryŏ, one of Korea's precursor kingdoms. His name means "to expand and open the territory," and indeed, his kingdom eventually covered a large portion of both Manchuria and the Korean peninsula.

In a sense, one can say that Korean written history began with this "document." It is certainly the first record of significant data written by Koreans in Korea. Here, however, is an interesting problem. The location of the monument is in today's Chinese territory, just across the border, north of the Yalu River. Still, it is clearly the record of a non-Chinese people. Though Korea was not yet a unified entity on the peninsula, and one may insist on calling the people of Koguryŏ proto-Korean, the Kwanggaet'o Stele is a significant document of people who would one day become Korea.

In the year 668 C.E.

In the year 668, a kingdom named Silla conquered Koguryŏ, unified the peninsula, and created the Great Silla period. It may be argued that this was the beginning of Korea. It was certainly a landmark in Korean history, for from that time forward the whole Korean peninsula has been considered one country—even at the present, with two governments dividing it. Indeed, all Koreans still consider the division to be merely a temporary phenomenon and expect reunification to someday take place.

Great Silla controlled most of the peninsula, but not all of it as defined by the present-day borders of the Yalu and Tumen Rivers. A state that was mostly Korean and extended far into the north, called Parhae, controlled the rest. Still, the Korean peninsula was mostly under the control of one government from 668 on.

About 350 years ago

Most people would not think of Korean history as starting only 350 years ago, yet social history and religious history saw remarkable changes in the late seventeenth century that were the culmination of a long Confucianization process. Confucianism had been in Korea since the Three Kingdoms period, but it never reached the state of saturation, where the principles of Confucianism were thoroughly adopted, until just over 300 years ago.

These changes that developed in the latter half of the seventeenth century and into the eighteenth century were those things that made the Korean family system so distinct. The very features that most Koreans cite as the unique features of the traditional family, such as the dominance of the lineage organization, primogeniture, the primary role of the eldest son and the line of descent from eldest son to eldest son over generations, patrilocal marriage patterns, ancestor worship controlled by the eldest son to the exclusion of daughters, and several other features of the patriarchal family system were not present prior to the mid-seventeenth century.

In the year 1948

Nearly no one would argue that Korean history began in 1948 with the creation of the current governments in the North and South, yet that is exactly what we claim when we speak of American history as being 200 years old. This assumption of American history is based on the political development of the current government and implies a perspective that ignores many important events. Jamestown and Plymouth were both 400 years old and Harvard University is about 375 years old, yet many still claim that American history has lasted for only 200 years.

And to say that American history began with European settlements ignores the history of native Americans both post-Columbus and pre-Columbus. If one were to take the same perspectives on American history as on Korean history, one can certainly find archaeological evidence that takes American history back several thousand years. It is all a matter of perspective.

Therefore, the best answer to the question on the test in our Korean-history class is probably "All of the above." Each answer has some validity, but, more importantly, one should realize that each claim for the antiquity of one's history is based on certain values. In North America, youth is highly valued. Americans often say, "We are a young country." We exaggerate the dates available and choose the youngest, the political founding of the United States. In East Asia, however, age and seniority are valued, and we see the date is exaggerated to the oldest date possible.

How old, then, is Korean history? Although it is probably the worst date as far as objective evidence is concerned, the most common answer today is 5,000 years old. But other answers are possible depending on one's perspective.

HALF ISLAND

Korea occupies the Korean peninsula. The Korean word for peninsula means, literally, "half island." Koreans have named the seas on its three sides the East Sea, the South Sea, and the West Sea. However, on most maps, the West Sea is called the Yellow Sea, and the East Sea is called the Sea of Japan. Therefore, the Korean government has waged a campaign with mapmakers around the world to have the Sea of Japan changed to the Korean term, the East Sea.

The surrounding seas and the land-link to the north have played important roles in Korean history. The flow of cultural items in East Asia was generally from west to east, from China to Korea and on to Japan.

The majority of such contact and the transmission of new ideas and items between China and Korea were overland; the continuation of the line to Japan was, of course, by sea. There was important contact between China and Korea by sea as well. For example, in the 660s, the Silla kingdom made an alliance with Tang China against Paekche and Koguryŏ, other kingdoms on the peninsula, when the Silla envoy traveled to China by sea. And of course, the massive invasion of Korea by Japanese soldiers in the 1590s was a naval landing. Naval battles were important parts of the Sino-Japanese War of 1894, and the Russo-Japanese War of 1905 was fought mostly on water. MacArthur's famous Inchon landing turned the tide of the Korean War in 1951.

Throughout Korean history, Korea was prosperous when it exploited the sea. During the eighth and ninth centuries, Great Silla dominated the Yellow Sea, the East China Sea, and the Korea Strait with trade between China and Japan. Koreans created their own communities on the Sandong peninsula as well as on the mouth of the Yangzi River. Chang Pogo, a Silla sea lord, once monopolized the East Asian maritime trade. In the late tenth century, Wang Kŏn arose from a powerful maritime merchant family to found the Koryŏ dynasty. However, it was not until the Chosŏn dynasty compromised and accepted the maritime ban instituted by Ming China in the fifteenth century that Korea became isolated and self-absorbed.

In the latter half of the twentieth century, trade via the oceans became tremendously important. Given that Korea has been divided into two since 1948, South Korea became virtually an island nation, with its northern border blocked by the heavily fortified Demilitarized Zone. South Korea has achieved its impressive economic growth only by oceanic trade with the world. Meanwhile, the North Korean economy has grown stagnant after it began isolating itself when its socialist brother countries renounced their ideologies.

MOUNTAINS AND RIVERS

Korea's topography is characterized by mountains, which occupy about 70 percent of the territory. The peninsula is a tilted table. The western parts of the peninsula contain wide coastal plains and fertile valleys nestled between small mountains, while the east coast is marked by narrow farming areas along the coast with high mountain ranges within sight of the oceans. The mountain ranges run in one major direction, from north to south. This geological backbone of the peninsula, known as the Great Range of Paektu, runs from the northern Mt. Paektu, with its height of 2,744 meters, to the 1,915-meter Mt. Chiri in the south. Many summits, such as Mt. Nangnim (with a height of 2,014 meters), Mt. Kŭmkang (1,638 meters), Mt. Sŏrak (1,780 meters), and Mt. T'aebaek (1,546 meters), are located along the Great Range of Paektu.

Consequently, the rivers mostly run from the east to the west. Such major rivers include the Yalu, the Ch'ŏngch'ŏn, the Taedong, the Imjin, the Han, and the Kŭm. Two exceptions are the Naktong and the Tumen Rivers. The Naktong River flows to the south and the Tumen River flows from Mt. Paektu eastward to the sea. The largest population centers, therefore, are located along the lower reaches of the rivers that flow into the Yellow Sea, within the fertile farm areas of the west and the south.

MONSOON CLIMATE

The nature of Korea's climate is defined by its peninsula configuration. Buffered by the Japanese archipelagoes to the east, Korea is more influenced by the northern continent than the ocean. However, Korea belongs to the far northern zone of the east-Asian monsoon belt. It has both a hot, humid summer and a cold, dry winter. During the winter months, strong northwesterly winds created by continental high-pressure air masses over inland Siberia bring cold, dry air to Korea. During the summer, monsoons bring abundant moisture from the ocean and produce heavy rainfalls. About 70 percent of the annual rainfall comes during three months, from June to September. Furthermore, passing cyclonic storms known as typhoons, though their power is usually diminished by the Japanese archipelago, sometimes reach the Korean coasts and add to the rainfalls.

The monsoon climate has made Korea develop its agricultural civilization of rice since the eighth century B.C.E. It makes an idyllic portrait of traditional Korea. Spring comes with the arrival of the swallow, a migratory bird from the south, in the middle of April in the central part of the peninsula. As it rains enough to prepare seedbeds for rice in May, farmers plant rice in the paddies. Thus, spring on the Korean peninsula is the beginning of life. Rice grows during the hot, rainy summer. However, from September to October, the dry, sunny autumn weather ripens the rice. Normally, Korean farmers expect a bumper harvest in autumn unless a typhoon or a harsh drought hits the land. October is the best month of the year, when people celebrate Ch'usŏk, the moon festival. After a short, pretty autumn, a long, dreary winter sets in.

ALTAIC FAMILY

The early settlers that first migrated into the Korean peninsula came from northeast Asia, north of China. In spite of great cultural influence from China over the centuries, the first Koreans did not come from China. The primary evidence of the origins of the Koreans is language. Korean is a member of the Altaic language family, with Turkic, Mongolian, Manchu-Tungus, and Japanese. It is a completely distinct and separate language family from the Chinese family of languages.

There is also other evidence of the Korean people's origin in northeast Asia. These include common elements of myth and early religious symbolism, such as the apparent totems of the bear and tiger as well as the symbols on the early crowns of Silla and Paekche, which had mirrors as well as stones of jade cut into the shape of bear or tiger claws. If one includes the sword, often found with the crowns in burials mound excavations, then one has the three symbols of the Japanese imperial family as well: the sword, the stone, and the mirror. This is one of the threads that run throughout the Altaic region, from northeast Asia through Korea to Japan.

These cultural symbols predate any influence from China, including Buddhism, and are probably part of an early religion that we can call shamanism. *Shamanism* is a Siberian word that describes a religion based on the spiritual powers of the shaman: a priest or priest-king, a leader of the people. The kind of shamanism that exists in Korea today bears many resemblances to that found among other Altaic people.

China's influence came later. But when it did, the impact was nearly overwhelming. With Chinese culture came literacy and the use of Chinese characters, or *sinograms*. Although the native language of Korea was completely different from that of China, Korea was able to adapt the characters to fit Korean words and grammar. The modified form of Chinese, called *idu*, included unique usage of some characters to express Korean grammar and thus made no sense to a Chinese who might try to read it. However, Koreans could additionally read and write sinograms so as to be understandable to the Chinese.

Around the first century C.E., it is believed that two different languages of the Tungusic family were spoken in Manchuria and on the Korean peninsula: the northern Puyŏ group and the southern Han group. As Silla in the south unified Paekche and Koguryŏ, whose languages belonged to the Puyŏ group, the linguistic unification of the peninsula was achieved on the basis of the Silla language, which was believed to be the origin of modern Korean languages. However, interestingly, linguists have found in Korean many vestiges of the Koguryŏ language, now dead.

HANGUL

Korea eventually became one of the rare nations in the world that had its own writing system. The Korean script known as hangul was invented in the fifteenth century under Sejong the Great, the fourth king of the Chosŏn dynasty. The motivation for its invention described by Sejong himself was to enable people to write the Korean language in their own way as well as record the correct sounds of Chinese characters. Despite this, classical Chinese remained more popular for several centuries. However, in the nineteenth century, enlightened harbingers waged a propagation of hangul, publishing the newspapers in this native Korean script. Though hangul's usage was suppressed along with the Korean language during the Japanese colonialist rule, it became the official script in both the North and South after liberation.

Given the two different ways of life in divided Korea for more than five decades, some language differences, vocabulary in particular, as well as some unique regional dialects have been found between North and South. However, Koreans find almost no difficulties in communicating with each other. Modern Korean has six dialects: Central, Northwest, Northeast, Southeast, Southwest, and Cheju. Except for the Cheju dialect, these can be considered merely different accents, rather than true dialects.

Korean is one of the most difficult languages to romanize, given the variety of vowel and consonant phonemes and the complex rules for their realization. It is more difficult than Chinese, and far more so than Japanese. Among the various romanization systems that have been in use since the nineteenth century, the most widely accepted have been the McCune-Reischauer System, created in 1939, and the South Korean Government System, recently revised in 2000. The former has been used in the United States and other Western countries, while the latter has been used in South Korea. Therefore, this book chose the McCune-Reischauer System. However, we use the names of modern public figures as they are commonly known, such as Syngman Rhee, Kim Il Sung, and Park Chung Hee.

2

Early History

MIGRATION WAVES IN ANCIENT EAST ASIA

Tan'gun Chosŏn

Archaeologists estimate that it was between 2000 and 1000 B.C.E. that the ancestors of the Korean people migrated from the north of China to Manchuria and the Korean peninsula. These immigrants brought a late-Neolithic agriculture civilization to the underdeveloped region, conquering the aboriginal *Kammkeramik* (comb-patterned pottery) people. These aboriginals lived by hunting, fishing, and gathering, using simple stone tools. Intermixing with the natives, the waves of immigration later created a more sophisticated Neolithic culture, typified by their plain pottery. The peoples who emerged in this new culture are separately identified in old Chinese historiographies as the Han, Ye, or Maek tribes. For our purposes, we will use the name *Han-Ye-Maek* as a broad term describing these various immigration groups, as there is a consensus among most modern historians that today's Koreans are descended from these peoples. In view of cross-cultural studies of languages and myths, anthropologists categorize them as part of the northern mongoloid race and members of the Tungusic language family.

The Korean foundation myth of Tan'gun Chosŏn is believed to reflect this period of the Han-Ye-Maek people, although we have no existent records of this myth prior to the thirteenth century. Accurate or not, the myth of Tan'gun has been an integral part of Korean identity throughout Korean history. In times of national crises, contemporary intellectuals often invoked this myth to instill patriotism and unify the country. Modern historians, however, have found some historical basis for this myth from studies on mythology and archaeology. In reality, Tan'gun is assumed to be the first shaman-king of Chosŏn, a Han-Ye-Maek chiefdom located in the area of Manchuria and the northwestern part of the Korean peninsula. This Chosŏn state is known by modern scholars as Old Chosŏn to distinguish it from the later Chosŏn dynasty that originated in the late fourteenth century.

The first existent record of Tan'gun the Priest-King can be found in the *Samguk yusa* (*Memorabilia of the Three Kingdoms*), written by the Korean Buddhist monk Iryŏn in the thirteenth century when the Mongols invaded Korea. The author mentioned that the myth was quoted from earlier records now nonexistent. The story from the *Samguk yusa* is as follows:

In the *Wei shu* [*History of Wei*] it is written that two thousand years ago, at the time of Emperor Yao [a legendary emperor in early Chinese history], Tan'gun Wang'gŏm [Tan'gun the Priest-King] chose Asadal as his capital and founded the state of Chosŏn. And in the *Kogi* [*Old Record*] it is said that once upon a time Hwanung, a son of Hwanin, wished to descend from heaven and live in the human world. Learning of his son's desire, Hwanin chose Mount T'aebaek among three great mountains as the most suitable place for Hwanung to bring happiness to all humanity. Hwanin gave Hwanung three heavenly seals and sent him to earth to rule. Hwanung descended from heaven with three thousand followers to a spot under a tree by the Holy Altar atop Mount T'aebaek, where he declared the place as the City of God. He was called Hwanung Ch'ŏnwang [Heavenly King]. Leading the Earl of Wind, the Master of Rain, and the Master of Cloud, he assumed some three hundred and sixty responsibilities including agriculture, life and death, health, punishment, virtue, and vice, and ruled and educated the earth.

At the time, a bear and a tiger dwelling in a cave prayed every day to Hwanung to transform them to human beings. So the Holy King gave them a piece of sacred mugwort and twenty cloves of garlic, saying, "If you eat these and shun the sunlight for one hundred days, you will become human." The bear and the tiger ate the sacred plants and avoided the sun. After only twenty-one days, the bear, who kept the taboo, became a woman, but the tiger, who was careless, failed. Unable to find a mate, the bear-woman prayed again under the Holy Altar tree for a child. Upon hearing her prayer, Hwanung momentarily transformed himself into a mortal state, and lay with her. She gave birth to a son named Tan'gun Wang'gŏm.

In the fiftieth year of Tang Yao [Emperor Yao], year Kyŏng'in in the Chinese calendar, Tan'gun Wang'gŏm made the citadel of Pyong-yang his capital and called his state Chosŏn for the first time. Later, he moved his capital to Asadal on Mount Paegak, and reigned for one thousand five hundred years. In the first year of King Wu of the Zhou dynasty, year Kimyo in the Chinese calendar, Chosŏn was bestowed on Kija [an ancient Chinese sage], and Tan'gun hid himself in Asadal and became a mountain god at the age of one thousand nine hundred and eight. (author's translation)

The Tan'gun myth reflects the archaic concept of statehood in East Asia. Given that a strong kingdom had not yet appeared from the tenth to the fourth centuries B.C.E., Tan'gun, leader of the tribal federation known as Chosŏn, needed this kind of foundation myth to legitimize his authority over the other chiefdoms in Manchuria and the Korean peninsula. Certainly, archaeology has not supported the myth as it is written in the *Samguk yusa*. However, Ch'ŏn Kwanu (1925–91), a modern Korean historian, placed the myth into historical context as follows: In the Tan'gun myth, the story of Hwanung, who came down from heaven with his followers, reflects the migration of a plain-pottery ethnic group called Hwanung from the southern range of the Altai Mountains in Mongolia via northern China to Manchuria and the Korean peninsula. They brought with them a Neolithic civilization of agriculture, which dominated the aboriginal comb-patterned pottery people. Among these natives, the tiger-totem tribe resisted this new wave of immigration, whereas the bear-totem tribe accepted it. With the help of the bear-totem people, the Hwanung tribe created the first ancient state in the region, called Chosŏn and led by the shaman-king Tan'gun. Tan'gun was later succeeded by the next wave of migration led by Kija, who brought an even more advanced bronze civilization.

One can understand the civilization process through ethnic migration in East Asia by comparative studies of mythologies of the various ethnic groups. Thus, foundation myths related to the heavenly gods similar to the Tan'gun myth can be found far later than the Neolithic period in the ancient states of Puyŏ, Koguryŏ, Kaya, and Wa. Each state mentioned above and its corresponding myth matches the chronological order of

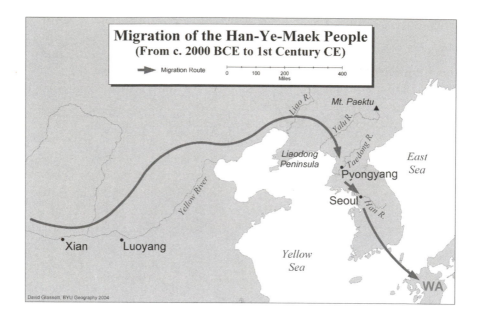

migration of civilization in Manchuria, the Korean peninsula, and the Japanese archipelago. Another interesting character in the Tan'gun myth is the bear-woman who bore Tan'gun the Priest-King. Scholars found that most Neolithic Asian tribes in Siberia and Manchuria shared in worship of the bear as a sacred animal. Thus, we see in this pattern of ethnic worship the migration routes of civilization.

The clearest sources from which we can trace the ethnic waves of migration are archaeological discoveries. The bronze civilization, typified by the T-type bronze dagger, was developed around the tenth century B.C.E., first in the southern part of Manchuria, then later in central Manchuria and the Korean peninsula. This T-type bronze dagger shows unique characteristics distinguishable from both the Siberian Ordos and the Chinese Yellow River bronze civilizations. During the Bronze Age, the tribal territories expanded as population increased due to improved agricultural skills. Around the eighth century B.C.E., rice cultivation started on the Korean peninsula. Also by this time, Old Chosŏn had developed from a tribal chiefdom to an archaic kingdom as consistent waves of ethnic migration from the west continued to bring with them bronze and iron culture. There is no evidence of what writing system was used at this time, but it is likely that these waves of migration also introduced Chinese script (sinograms) to the area.

Chosŏn, as the name of a state, first appeared in a Chinese book written in the fourth century B.C.E., around the time Alexander the Great conquered India. The book refers to diplomatic and trade relations between Chosŏn and the Qi state on the Sandong peninsula in China early in the seventh century B.C.E. This Chosŏn is believed to indicate Tan'gun Chosŏn, which was centered early in the Liaodong-peninsula area in Manchuria. Later, in the fourth century B.C.E., Chosŏn was depicted in Chinese dynasty historiographies as a strong kingdom to the east of Yan, one of the seven states during the Warring States period in China. Old Chosŏn, often at war with Yan, finally moved toward the northwestern part of the Korean peninsula from its old territory in Liaodong after its defeat in the third century B.C.E. By this time, Old Chosŏn is believed to have already reached the stage of iron civilization.

Wiman Chosŏn

North China was in brief turmoil during the late third century and the early second century B.C.E. with the Qin dynasty (221–206 B.C.E.) collapsing and the Han dynasty (206 B.C.E.–220 C.E.) rising. This situation catalyzed migration of the Han-Ye-Maek ethnic groups from territories north of China Proper into the Korean peninsula. Wiman (?–?) was the leader of the last of these migration groups. One can identify him by the description of his Chosŏn style of coiffure and attire in the Chinese historiographies. Interestingly enough, the Old Chosŏn king entrusted him with the charge of defense of the northwestern border against the Han empire, since he was one of the Han-Ye-Maek immigrants from north China that had already been occupying this border area since Old Chosŏn retreated from Liaodong. No sooner had he strengthened his leadership among these frontier tribes than he returned with force to capture the capital of Old Chosŏn and oust the king, in 194 B.C.E.

Wiman (r. 194–? B.C.E.) did not change the name of his new dynasty. Therefore, modern historians believe that Wiman Chosŏn was a confederated kingdom of migrating ethnic groups and native Old Chosŏn tribes. This was the typical political confederation of several autonomous chiefdoms in ancient Manchuria and the Korean peninsula as well as the Japanese archipelago. During the second century B.C.E., Wiman Chosŏn built up its power and conquered parts of the native tribal chiefdoms in the southern Korean peninsula. These tribal chiefdoms are known as the Three Hans: Mahan, Chinhan, and Pyŏnhan. (The word *Han* here is not to be confused with Han China, which is an altogether different character in Chinese.) Han China in its early period established a peace treaty with

Wiman Chosŏn by merely demanding diplomatic kowtowing. However, such a strong kingdom as Wiman Chosŏn was a vital security threat to the emperor in China Proper due to its sensitive geographical vicinity.

ORIGIN OF THE EAST-ASIAN WORLD ORDER

Dong'yi and Han Prefectures

For the ancient East-Asian people, the word *tianxia* (all lands under heaven) meant China Proper and its periphery. This concept of the world did not mean just China as a nation, but as a center of civilization. The one who occupied and controlled this center was believed to have been bestowed with the Mandate of Heaven (*tianming*) and was thereby known as the Son of Heaven (*tianzi*). Qin Shihuangdi (259–210 B.C.E.) proclaimed himself the first emperor of this world after he unified the six warring states in China proper from 230 to 221 B.C.E. He adopted a new title, *huangdi* (emperor), which had previously been used only for deities and mythological rulers in ancient China, although the old ideas of *tianming* and *tianzi* had existed since the Zhou dynasty. This new Qin dynasty was China's first empire, which unified the culture, language, and geography of China Proper.

It was only natural for the Son of Heaven to be concerned about challenges to his sovereignty from any place in the world. Once all rivals were conquered in China Proper, he gave consideration to keeping the East-Asian world order safe from possible threats from China's surrounding states. For example, Qin Shihuangdi began construction of the Great Wall to keep peace for a while from the most immediate threat of the northern nomadic tribes, like the Xiongnu. Since establishment of the Chinese empire, those tribes in the periphery of China Proper were considered to be mere barbarians from the perspective of Chinese ethnocentrism. For example, these barbarians were named pejoratively Dong'yi, Nanman, Beidi, and Xiong, according to the cardinal directions. The Eastern Barbarians (Dong'yi), whose societies were the most civilized among these groups, were thought to be a serious challenge to the Son of Heaven.

However, the Qin dynasty, after only a brief rule of two emperors, was succeeded by the Han dynasty, which lasted for four centuries. As the Roman empire had established *pax Romana* (peace under Roman rule) in the Mediterranean world of antiquity, the Han empire was shaping *pax Sinica* (peace under Han rule) in the East-Asian world. In the second century B.C.E., Han Wudi (156–87 B.C.E.), one of the most dynamic and intelligent emperors in Chinese history, disposed of the Xiongnu in the north and west and then turned his expansionistic ambition to his southern and eastern borders. His intention was to subdue with military might any possible challenger in south China and Manchuria. First, Han expedition forces conquered southern China and northern Vietnam, in 111 B.C.E., and there established three prefectures in order to incorporate the territory into his empire. Three years later, Han Wudi moved his forces to the east but met resistance from Wiman Chosŏn, which eventually fell in 108 B.C.E. after one of its chiefdoms joined the attacking forces. The Han Chinese triumph was possible because the political solidarity of Wiman Chosŏn, which was nothing more than a loose tribal confederation, was not centralized enough to hold back external invasion. In this region, Wudi established four prefectures: Lelang, Zhenfan, Lintun, and Xientu.

Another wave of migration began from northern China to this area as Han China functionaries and merchants settled into these four prefectures. Living in their earthen citadels, these newcomers dominated the native Chosŏn people with their cultural superiority. The Chosŏn people were politically oppressed by the Han officials and economically exploited by the traders, though the former ruling class of Chosŏn now had a chance to taste more advanced ways of life from the center of East-Asian civilization. Moreover, in order to control the prevalent social disorder in the region, the Han rulers multiplied the Hammurabi-like code of law of Old Chosŏn from 8 provisions to approximately 60. Despite these measures, however, severe resistance from the harshly suppressed people made the modification of the Han prefectures inevitable. Furthermore, the prefectures were subject to frequent attacks and external pressures from the neighboring Han-Ye-Maek states. Eventually, the Han empire had to abandon two of them and combine the remaining into one.

Lelang (Nangnang in Korean) was this last prefecture, which had its capital in a county (*xian*) of Chosŏn located in the area of Pyongyang today. Prospering with trade between China and the southern Korean peninsula or the western Japanese archipelago, it lasted until the early fourth century C.E., when it was captured by the kingdom of Koguryŏ. In view of excavated relics, Lelang is believed to be the most advanced political, economic, and cultural center in the region during its four centuries of existence. Rulers of the neighboring Han-Ye-Maek states were naturally impressed by the strength and rich variety of Chinese civilization in Lelang, and traded for useful objects such as superior weapons and iron agricultural tools. The Han Chinese divide-and-rule policy toward the neighboring Dong'yi states, however, did hinder these states' political development in becoming more centralized kingdoms.

Territorial States and Ancient Kingdoms

The Dong'yi, or the Han-Ye-Maek polities, in Manchuria and the Korean peninsula, at the turn of the millennia had grown from loose confederations of tribal chiefdoms to either more centralized territorial states or archaic kingdoms. The names of many of these Han-Ye-Maek kingdoms can be found in the Chinese historiographies compiled during the first century B.C.E. to the third century C.E. These include Puyŏ, Koguryŏ, Ye, Okchŏ, Mahan, Paekche, Koryŏng Kaya, Kŭmgwan Kaya, Silla, and Wa. Lelang, the remaining Han prefecture, was bordered by Puyŏ and Koguryŏ in central Manchuria, and in the Korean peninsula by Ye and Okchŏ to the northeast and Mahan and Paekche to the south. Chinese accounts of these Han-Ye-Maek states varied with political interest in the state described. According to one of the Chinese historiographies, *Sanguozhi Weizhi Dong'yizhuan*, Puyŏ, Koguryŏ, and Mahan were portrayed as states ruled by kings supported by ministers, whereas the other polities in the region remained referred to as loose confederations of tribal communities. Of course, these historiographies cannot be credited as they were literally written. Only for the states with which Han China had good diplomatic relations, such as Puyŏ, was updated and detailed information written. This also includes Koguryŏ, which was located in the areas of former prefectures. Information on other states, such as Mahan and Kaya, which had fewer relations with the Han, was outdated and sketchy.

Despite the persistent military threat from the Han prefectures, some rising kingdoms of the Han-Ye-Maek people in the region were able to grow by conquering relatively underdeveloped neighboring polities. Nonetheless, while the conquered tribal chiefdoms were absorbed into these kingdoms, they were able to keep their rulers as leaders under their new kings for some periods. Among these rising kingdoms, Koguryŏ, Paekche, Kaya, and Silla were prominent rivals.

The kingdom of Koguryŏ, according to legend, was founded in the early first century B.C.E. by Chumong (58–19 B.C.E.), a prince of Puyŏ. Koguryŏ developed from a confederation of five Maek tribes and continued to expand its territory by conquering neighboring chiefdoms like Ye and Okchŏ as well as the Han Chinese prefecture of Xientu. From the early first century C.E., the throne began to be predominantly occupied by one of the Maek tribes, which eventually centralized authority when it began to pass down the kingship through patrilineal succession in the late second century. The new kingdom of Koguryŏ grew in power enough to defy the prefecture of Lelang. However, it suffered a severe defeat in 244 C.E. by expedition forces sent by Wei China, one of the three kingdoms that replaced the failing Han dynasty. Nonetheless, Koguryŏ, after recovering from the temporary loss of its capital by these invading forces, continued to expand its territory in Manchuria and the northern part of the Korean peninsula under the strong leadership of its king and ruling warrior class. Subsequently, Koguryŏ enhanced its economic power by exploiting its conquered people.

The kingdom of Paekche was founded around the first century B.C.E. by Onjo (r. 18 B.C.E.–28 C.E.), the leader of a tribe that migrated from Puyŏ to the Han River area in the central Korean peninsula. In the early first century C.E., Paekche successfully defeated Mahan. At the time, Mahan was a dominant power in the Three Hans region. After its defeat by Paekche, Mahan survived on the southwestern tip of the peninsula until it finally fell completely in the late fourth century C.E. Paekche then absorbed the territory of Daifang, which was reorganized as a new Chinese prefecture in the southern part of Lelang in the early third century C.E. By occupying most of the central western part of the Korean peninsula, Paekche was now able to pursue trade with the southern dynasty of Wu in China (one of the three kingdoms that replaced the Han dynasty) as well as the western part of the Japanese archipelago, where many Paekche people migrated.

Kaya, under the leadership of its legendary founder, King Kim Suro, was a confederation of six Kaya tribal chiefdoms in the Naktong River area of the south-central part of the Korean peninsula. The region had been old territory of the 12 chiefdoms of Pyŏnhan, where iron ore was produced. In the middle of the first century C.E., the six Kayas annexed each other into two independent kingdoms: Koryŏng Kaya in the Upper Naktong and Kŭmgwan Kaya in the Lower Naktong.

Silla emerged in the late fourth century C.E. as a unified kingdom encompassing most of the small polities of Chinhan. The first shaman-chief of Silla was Pak Hyŏkkŏse (69 B.C.E.–4 C.E.), who, according to legend, was found in a large egg by one of the leaders of the six villages in the Kyŏngju area in the southeastern part of the Korean peninsula. After the arrival of a new wave of immigration from Old Chosŏn, which brought iron culture to the area, Silla eventually grew to a confederation from the three major tribal clans of Pak, Sŏk, and Kim. The names of these clans remain as predominant surnames in present-day Korea. Until the fourth century C.E., the chiefs of the new confederation were elected principally by consensus of an aristocratic council. The title of the confederation chief was therefore changed to *nisagŭm* and later *maripkan*, distinguishable from the titles of the former shaman chiefs, *kŏsŏhan* or *ch'ach'aung*. Thus the evolution of these Tungusic titles reflects the expansion of ruling territory.

The first historical reference to the Wa (Wae in Korean) can be found in Chinese and Korean historiographies, which mention "Wa in the East Sea," indicating people in the western part of the Japanese archipelago. Migration from the Korean peninsula to these islands occurred as early as the Three Hans period and brought a more advanced culture to the Neolithic aboriginals. Archaeological and linguistic evidences of this include the facts that the Yayoi pottery culture in Japan from the fourth century B.C.E. shares the same characteristics as plain-pottery culture on the Korean peninsula of the preceding period, and that the primitive Japanese language on the northern Kyushu Island is close to the ancient Koguryŏ language. Immigrants from the areas of Paekche and Kaya, who are believed to have spoken this same language, formed the Wa states there later.

NEW ERA OF EAST-ASIAN DISORDER

Advent of Nomadic Empires

The Chinese have a saying that describes the East-Asian concept of history: "If the world is divided then it will eventually unite. If the world is united then it will eventually divide." This means that a period of peace under one dynasty will inevitably follow with a period of war. During those ages of disorder that followed the decline of a dynasty, therefore, there was not just one Son of Heaven in the world. At times, several dynasties coexisted, and each of these self-styled emperors claimed the Mandate of Heaven for themselves.

At the turn of the fourth century C.E., the East-Asian world entered a new era of disorder when nomadic barbarians in the north of China expanded their power and established 16 "empires" in north China, one after another. This was the result of decay in the Han Chinese order of peace, which began to decline with the division of the Han empire into three dynasties around the early third century. China Proper was again united briefly under the Eastern Jin dynasty, which, however, retreated to the south under pressure of the northern barbarians. Chinese historiographers named these ethnic groups the *wuhu* (five barbarian tribes): (1) the Xianbei in the Mongolian area; (2) the Xiongnu in the Shanxi area of northwest China; (3) the Xie in the Shanxi area; (4) the Tibetan Di in the Sichuan area of west China; and (5) the Tibetan Qiang, also in Sichuan. For more than a century, each of these groups carved themselves altogether 16 self-styled empires, which were continually in and out of conflict with each other.

The first nomadic empire, named the Earlier Yan by historiographers to distinguish from other Yan states, appeared in the mid-fourth century C.E. in the Liao River area in Manchuria, bordered by Puyŏ and Koguryŏ. Because of its close proximity, its interaction with the Han-Ye-Maek kingdoms in the region was crucial. This short-lived (353–70) empire, founded by the Muyong clan of the Xianbei, had occupied that area even before it declared itself a dynasty. In the late third century C.E., this clan had politically developed enough already to adopt a Chinese-style state name, Yan. After securing their eastern borders by subduing Puyŏ and Koguryŏ, they eventually conquered north China, becoming an empire.

During the rise and fall of the nomadic empires in north China, the kingdom of Koguryŏ expanded its territories in Manchuria and the Korean peninsula. After conquering the former Han prefecture Lelang in 313, Koguryŏ became a rising power in the region. Not only did Koguryŏ gain new territory by annexing the old prefecture, but it also advanced its own society by absorbing Lelang's Chinese culture. It was only natural, then, for this now stronger Koguryŏ to conflict with Earlier Yan, the rival power in Manchuria. Eventually, this confrontation came to a head in 342 when Yan invading forces defeated the Koguryŏ army, destroyed its capital, and returned triumphantly with some 50,000 prisoners, including the queen and queen mother. However, after waiting for more than a decade for the Earlier Yan empire to shrink and move its capital from China Proper, Koguryŏ reemerged to advance up to the Liaodong peninsula in 385.

While Koguryŏ dominated Manchuria and the northern part of the Korean peninsula, Paekche expanded its territory in the south by annexing the last of Mahan in 369. At the height of its power, Paekche covered most of the central peninsula and now had a direct connection to the Eastern Jin in south China by sea. The region was now organized into four major opposing forces: Koguryŏ, Paekche, Kaya, and Silla. While in conflict with each other, they allied with forces in China and the Japanese archipelago. Koguryŏ had good diplomatic relations with Silla and the Earlier Qin, which replaced the Earlier Yan in north China, whereas Paekche and Kaya kept close ties with the Eastern Jin and Wa states formed in the northern part of Kyushu Island. In this period, therefore, the East-Asian world was divided into two confronting alliances: Paekche–Kaya–Wa–Eastern Jin, and Koguryŏ–Silla–Earlier Qin.

Buddhism and Development

The new East-Asian world disorder, a result of nomadic barbarians now occupying the center of civilization, had a great impact on the Han-Ye-

Maek people in Manchuria, the Korean peninsula, and the Japanese archipelago. The once peripheral barbarians were now able to experience directly the highest of culture, not as a subjugated people, but as masters. Even those that remained in the periphery, such as the Dong'yi, profited indirectly as equal trade partners. Most of the Han-Ye-Maek kingdoms, therefore, found opportunity to upgrade their political system by standardizing law and instituting Confucian education. Moreover, the Chinese writing system, apparently introduced in the region with the arrival of iron culture, became the essential tool of civilization as these states began to study the Confucian classics and publish their own historiographies.

At this time, a crucial interaction of civilizations occurred in East Asia. Buddhism, a religion shaped in India, was permeating this world on a vast scale. It was first accepted by the barbarians of west China due to their geographical proximity to India, and from there it reached China Proper as early as the late second century. Buddhism, though a very non-exclusive religion, had to coordinate its spiritual territory with the already extant beliefs in China Proper, Taoism in particular. So it was not until 286 that a non-Chinese intellectual in Dunhuang, the ancient center of Buddhism in west China, translated a Mahayana scripture from Sanskrit into classical Chinese. It thereafter underwent a long period of incubation during the Han ethnic dynasties until it found widespread acceptance in the fourth century era of disorder. It was the nomadic dynasties that actively embraced the new religion and promulgated it. The Earlier Qin dynasty (351–394) was especially enthusiastic in promoting Buddhism, considering its Tibetan origins. Thus, Buddhism spread in the East-Asian world mostly by Tibetan or other Tungusic missionaries.

When the Buddhist monk Sundo (?–?), a missionary from the Earlier Qin, arrived in Koguryŏ in 372, he found that shamanism was predominant among the natives. The Koguryŏ king, who was attracted to a new religion more sophisticated than Chinese Taoism or the indigenous beliefs, warmly welcomed him. Among a people already accustomed to shamanism, Buddhism found widespread acceptance as a supplication faith for prosperity and avoidance of woe. Thus in fourth-century Koguryŏ, Buddhism, under royal favor, was set up as a state religion. Paekche followed suit in 384. As a result, small gilt-bronze Buddha icons, which were used as talismans by the Koguryŏ warriors, are seen today in many modern museums. In the National Museum in Seoul, one finds an enchanting statue of a gilt-bronze Maitreya meditating in a half-seated posture, a reflection of Buddhism's flourishing in late-sixth-century Paekche.

Officially accepting Buddhism as a state religion coincided with the Koguryŏ king's eager ambition to systemize edict and decree by Confucian statecraft. He therefore established a Confucian academy to educate the bureaucracy. As its territory rapidly expanded, Koguryŏ needed not only a sophisticated political system, but also a social integration of religion in order to rule its multitribe people. Thereafter, it became a tradition not only for Koguryŏ kings but also for all the rulers in the East-Asian periphery to adopt both Confucianism and Buddhism as convenient political ideology and social morality.

Historians, therefore, use the three following events to measure the political development of states in East-Asian antiquity: the dates of the systemization of edict and decree, the establishment of a Confucian academy, and the introduction of Buddhism. As far as that standard is concerned, Koguryŏ and Paekche were far more advanced than Kaya, Silla, or Wa, which would follow more than a century later. Silla was not to accept Buddhism until 527, and the Yamato Wa until 584. Due to its geographical distance, the Yamato Wa did not institutionalize its legislative system until 701, after the Taika Reform in 654 by the prince Shodoku, the first nonmythological figure in the early Japanese histories.

King Kwanggaet'o

In 1875, a Qing-dynasty magistrate found, by chance, on the site of the ancient capital of Koguryŏ near the upper Yalu River in Manchuria, a great stele on which the dynastic history of King Kwanggaet'o (375–413) was inscribed. Established in 414 by the king's son in order to pay tribute to his father's great conquests, this is the oldest historical document on Korean history that is not found within Chinese historiographies. During his reign (391–413), King Kwanggaet'o's conquered territory was the largest yet in northeast-Asian history. It included the Sungari River to the north, the Liao River valley to the west, the maritime coast to the east, and the Han River valley to the south. Kwanggaet'o is a posthumous name literally meaning "expanding territory." According to his reign title, he was known as the Great King Yŏngnak when he was alive. The fact that this is the first instance of a reign title used in the region means that Koguryŏ was a de facto empire, under which most kingdoms on the Korean peninsula were subdued as tributary states. In 427, during the reign of King Yŏngnak's son, Koguryŏ moved its capital from the upper Yalu River to Pyongyang, a more developed center in the ancient territories of Old Chosŏn and the former Lelang prefecture.

The inscription on the Kwanggaet'o stele describes a total of seven conquests launched from Koguryŏ borders in each of the cardinal directions. These descriptions coincide with historical accounts in the *Samguk sagi*

(*History of the Three Kingdoms*), which was compiled in the twelfth century and is the oldest existent Korean historiography ever printed. The first conquests were directed toward the northern nomadic tribes, the next toward Paekche in the south, then to the tribes in the east, and the last to the Xianbei empire in the west, known as the Later Yan. Because the Han and Liao Rivers were strategically crucial to Koguryŏ's security, the most serious confrontations were against Paekche and the Later Yan. Paekche, once the most powerful kingdom on the Korean peninsula, surrendered to King Kwanggaet'o in 396. Again, at the turn of the fifth century, Koguryŏ fought and defeated the unified forces of Paekche, Kaya, and Wa several times. In 407, the king launched westward and conquered the Liaodong peninsula.

The Mimana Fallacy

According to mythic Japanese historiographies compiled in the eighth century, the Yamato Wa sent expedition forces to the Korean peninsula beginning in 369, conquered Mimana (the Japanese name for Kaya), and established an administration there by 469, later subduing Paekche as a tributary state. This Japanese military outpost was said to last until 562, when Silla annexed Koryŏng Kaya, the last kingdom of the two Kayas. Modern Japanese historians began to write this story as an unmistakable historical fact. The imperialists later used this along with a Kwanggaet'o stele rubbing to justify Japanese colonialism on the Korean peninsula by claiming historical right to that territory, even though the writing on the Kwanggaet'o stele could not support this. Nonetheless, most Japanese-studies scholars abroad have accepted their claims without any scholarly research of their own.

On this issue, however, many questions arise. Considering the various stages of civilization development in East Asia during 360–560, it is difficult to imagine that the underdeveloped Yamato Wa state was able to cross over the sea, conquer the more advanced Kaya kingdoms, and even colonize them for 200 years. It is unlikely that the nascent Yamato regime in the Kinki area in east Japan would have been able to mobilize such large overseas expedition forces given that it first would have had to subdue the polities in west Japan, which were more advanced from the fourth through the sixth centuries. Even if they had been able to overcome such obstacles in Japan, the Yamato Wa forces, armed with old weapons made of iron imported from the Korean peninsula, would then have had to dominate Kaya forces, which were armed with a newer and more sophisticated arsenal. Moreover, because the undersized ships of Wa limited the transportation of troops, how could such a small-scale expedition possibly operate in the vast Naktong River valley?

As discussed earlier, civilization flowed from China Proper via Manchuria and the Korean peninsula to the Japanese archipelago. This was no different in the region for the period 360–560. Compared with the Korean peninsula, which was much closer to civilization's center in China Proper, the Wa states and their people in the archipelago were located at the far end of the East-Asian world. Historically, it is more likely that immigrants from the Korean peninsula, mostly from Kaya and Paekche, would have established polities in west Japan.

Japanese historians often point to the very size of the great tombs found in the Kinki area as proof of the emergence of a strong Yamato Wa confederation state during the third and fourth centuries. The Yamato state, however, remained solely a local power, side by side with the other Wa states on Kyushu Island, until it developed into a central unified kingdom in 645 through the Taika reforms. Thus, it was much later when it established a legislation system (in 701) and moved its capital to Nara (in 710). Nonetheless, it is often argued that the Yamato state was strong enough during the period 350–400 to send military forces to the Korean peninsula. This is because of the discoveries from the eastern Kanto area to western Kyushu Island of the great Kinki-style tombs, which are assumed to be the results of Yamato's growth from east to west. On the contrary, considering that the tombs on Kyushu Island are far older, it is more reasonable that these archaeological discoveries explain the opposite: that the transmigration of civilization was in reality west to east.

Nonetheless, the *Nihonshogi* (*Historiography of Japan*) and the *Kojiki* (*Ancient Records*), the two oldest Japanese historiographies, from the eighth century, depict in detail Yamato Wa's supremacy over such kingdoms as Paekche, Mimana (Kaya), and even Silla. These records state that kings of the Korean peninsula sent tribute to a Yamato Wa emperor, and also meticulously describe Japanese military operations in the Naktong River valley. However, the ruling family of Yamato Wa originated from the Paekche royal family, and at this period they had nothing more than a feudal king. Moreover, given that these Japanese historiographies were compiled later, during the eighth century, when the Yamato court began to promote nationalistic antagonism against Silla for annexing Paekche and Kaya, the Yamato historiographers presumably might have replaced references to the name Paekche with the name Wa in their records. We can find in other Korean historiographies, like the *Samguk sagi*, that these same military operations in the Naktong valley are described as those of Paekche forces, and not of Wa. It is true that Wa forces did appear on the Korean peninsula from time to time during the early centuries, as described in the Kwanggaet'o stele and the *Samguk sagi*. But in these instances they acted as either ally to Paekche or Kaya or as marauding pirates against Silla, not as expedition forces or conquering colonizers.

One explanation for the inconsistencies between Japanese and Korean historiographies is that Japanese historiographers might have sometimes identified Yamato's neighboring states, which were founded by migrants from the peninsula, as those of their originating kingdoms, such as Paekche, Kaya, and Silla. Therefore, although Yamato eventually conquered those states on the archipelago, these Japanese records could be misread to prove that Yamato had actually subdued those same kingdoms on the peninsula. A sword, known as the Ch'ilchido (Sword of Seven Branches) and kept at a Shinto temple in Nara, clearly tells us the tributary relations between Paekche and Wa. On the body of this sword, the few lines of a golden, inlaid inscription are found. Although several characters are not clear, we can read the general message:

> On the sixteenth of the Xth month in the year of *Taehwa* [a possible reign title of either Paekche or the Eastern Jin in the fifth century], the Sword of Seven Branches was forged a hundred times to evade any enemy. This sword of no parallel is fit to be bestowed to a feudal king. Thus, the X [possibly king] of Paekche . . . made this gift for the Wa king to pass on to generations hereafter. (author's translation)

Unlike European feudalism, in East-Asian tributary relationships, the suzerain rulers were the ones to bestow gifts to their feudal lords. Among these gifts, the sword was a popular item because it symbolized military might. In this inscription, it is clear that the Paekche king, who bequeathed the sword, considered the Wa king to be under his overlordship. However, Japanese historians have traditionally interpreted it as the opposite.

Rapid Growth of Silla

Located on the southeastern tip of the Korean peninsula, Silla was a late development in relation to the other kingdoms and, in the beginning, was even weaker than Kaya in its various stages. However, due to an increase in agricultural products with the development of ox-driven plows beginning in the sixth century, Silla grew economically powerful enough to support military conquest of its neighboring polities. At this period, the ruler of Silla changed his title from the old nomadic term *maripkan* (grand chieftain) to the sinogram *wang* (king). Moreover, he designated his kingdom as Silla, paraphrasing from a Chinese idiom meaning "the newer the virtue the broader the rule." Not only did this change of titles symbolize that Silla was developed enough to adopt Chinese civilization, but it also reflected a new concentration of political power for the kingship, which was indispensable for the rapid conquest and expansion of the kingdom.

Silla began as a confederation of six clans under one chief-king, each holding equal influence in a system of councils of which unanimous consent was required for policy decisions. This system was known as the *hwabaek* system. However, with the monarchy's concentration of political power, the Kim dynasty was soon established in the mid-fourth century. Thereafter, the Kim clan monopolized the kingship, and chose their queens only from lineages of the Kim and Pak surnames. Thus, a strict hierarchy of status was developed, with the ruling aristocracy, consisting of the royal lines, at the top, and the bureaucracy of the remaining sur-name clans below. This hierarchy was known as the *kolp'um* system, lit-erally meaning "bone rank." Bone status was reserved only for the royal bloodlines, which consisted of the Holy Bone (*sŏnggol*) and the True Bone (*chin'gol*). Until the mid-seventh century, only those of the Holy Bone, who were strictly descendants of Kims and Paks, succeeded to the throne. True Bone status consisted of the Kim clan, whose maternal lines were other than Pak. Beneath the bone statuses, the bureaucracy was divided into six ranks. The remaining Silla clans, and later ruling classes from conquered states, occupied the upper echelons of these ranks. This bone-rank system strengthened Silla's power by consolidating the ruling elites, embracing the upper classes of conquered states, and successfully controlling the people with a strong grip. Inasmuch as it was an efficient social system, Silla was now able to compete with strong neighbors like Paekche and Koguryŏ.

Buddhism came to Silla during the fifth century when the monk Ado (also known as Mukhoja) arrived as a missionary from Koguryŏ. Unlike in Paekche and Koguryŏ, only the commoners accepted the new religion at first, whereas the conservative aristocracy strongly resisted it. However, the royal family eventually showed interest. In 527, the king finally le-galized Buddhism after the martyrdom of Ich'adon (503–27), the first con-vert among the Silla bureaucracy. According to the *Biographies of the Buddhist Masters*, compiled in the early thirteenth century, Ich'adon con-spired with the king to arrange his own execution and thus create a mir-acle to convert the bigoted aristocracy. The following is an account of the legend.

Ich'adon then made an oath to heaven: "I am about to die for the sake of dharma. I pray that righteousness and the benefits of our religion will spread. If the Buddha is divine, a miracle should occur after my death." When he was decapitated, his head flew to Diamond Mountain, falling on its summit, and white milk gushed forth from the cut, soaring up several hundred feet. The sun darkened, wonderful flowers rained from heaven, and the earth trembled violently. The king, his officials, and the commoners, on the one hand terrified by these strange phenomena and on the other sorrowful for the death of Ich'adon, who had sacrificed his life for the cause of the dharma, cried aloud and mourned. They buried his body on Diamond Mountain with due ceremony. At that time the king and his officials took an oath: "Hereafter we will worship the Buddha and revere the monks. If we break this oath, may heaven strike us dead." Once accepted, Buddhism grew rapidly in Silla as a spiritual backbone for the ruling elite.

Silla was formerly under the overlordship of Koguryŏ in a symbiotic relationship like that of Paekche and Wa. However, Silla now grew confident enough to break from Koguryŏ, whose throne suffered from repeated struggles of succession. Silla began to cooperate with Paekche in absorbing the territories of the weakening Kaya. In 532, it annexed Kŭmgwan Kaya while Paekche subdued the upper Naktong River area. However, the most dramatic advance of Silla occurred later, in 553, when it conquered the Han River valley in the center of the Korean peninsula. Four great stone monuments that the Silla king erected to mark the newly extended borders can still be seen today. This sudden incursion was a serious blow to Silla's former tactical ally Paekche, who had occupied the territory. The king of Paekche was so outraged that he counterattacked in 554 but was slain as Silla won a decisive victory. In 562, Silla finally annexed Koryŏng Kaya, the last of the Kaya kingdoms, and now commanded the two most important rivers on the Korean peninsula, the Han and the Naktong. Although the kingdom of Kaya ended here, its legacy lives on today in the form of a 12-string musical instrument, known as the *kayagŭm,* brought to Silla after Kaya's annexation. For the next century thereafter, the remaining three kingdoms, Koguryŏ, Paekche, and Silla, were locked in triangular warfare, competing for hegemony over the region.

3

Korean Identity

THE END OF THE THREE KINGDOMS

Koguryŏ's 70-year War

In Manchuria and the Korean peninsula, the three kingdoms confronted one another. In 589, the Sui dynasty finally unified China Proper after over 350 years of disunity. This new, short-lived empire preceded the longer-lasting Tang dynasty (618–907). The change in the continental situation portended another East-Asian world order like that of the Qin and Han eras. For a short while, the three kingdoms hurried to send their envoys to the Sui court to respect its diplomatic suzerainty over the East-Asian world. Nonetheless, the recalcitrant Koguryŏ began to be a serious threat to the security of the Sui empire. Koguryŏ had allied with the eastern Turks, who constantly harassed the Sui on its northern border. The first Sui emperor began to war with Koguryŏ in 598, but failed to subdue it. The next Sui emperor, Yangdi, a megalomaniac second only to Qin Shihuangdi, invaded Koguryŏ three times in three consecutive years, starting in 612. The results of this war were disastrous for the Sui, bringing on the end of the dynasty.

According to a Chinese historiography, Yangdi mobilized in his first attack more than 1,130,000 soldiers, army and navy included, from all over the Sui territories. Although ancient Chinese historiographers are given to exaggeration, it was indeed an "expedition of unprecedented scale." At that time, Ŭlchi Mundŏk (?–?), a Koguryŏ minister with strategic military knowledge, pretended to surrender to the Sui forces, thereby inducing them to step deep into Koguryŏ territory. After confirming the enemy had crossed the Salsu River (today's Ch'ŏngch'ŏn River, in the northwestern part of the Korean peninsula), he sent another false message to the enemy general with the following poem in classical Chinese:

> You sought out the stars for superb strategy,
> You pondered the lay of the land with precise calculation.
> Your success in battle is already high;
> Know this is enough, I pray that ye cease. (author's translation)

Flattered and placated by this poem, the Sui general began to withdraw. Ŭlchi Mundŏk attacked the retreating enemy as they recrossed the Salsu River. According to a Chinese record, of a force of 355,000 that crossed the river, only 2,700 escaped. With this grand victory against the foreign invaders, Ŭlchi Mundŏk is known as a national hero in Korean history.

After spending most of its national resources with these unsuccessful expeditions against Koguryŏ, the Sui empire was now challenged by a series of peasant rebellions caused by the resulting harsh taxes. This momentary disorder in China Proper created opportunity for ambitious warlords to proclaim themselves emperor. In 618, Li Yuan, a Sui general, usurped the throne and established the new Tang dynasty. Just as before, the three kingdoms in Manchuria and the Korean peninsula reacted quickly toward the change of dynasties and sent diplomatic envoys. Koguryŏ, the only one of these kingdoms to border the Tang, made the earliest move. For the time being, the two countries remained seemingly at peace. The nascent Tang dynasty was not yet prepared to make any conquering moves of expansion. However, the second Tang emperor, Taizong, who had ushered in a new era of prosperity for the empire, began to extend his ambition to outlying territories. After conquering the eastern Turks in 630 and annexing the various small polities along the Silk Road in 640, he then turned his attention to Koguryŏ.

In 642, a grand magistrate of Koguryŏ named Yŏn Kaesomun (?–666) was charged with the building of a fortified wall on the western border with the Tang. Upon learning of the king's plan to eliminate him out of fear of his political power, Yŏn Kaesomun decided to strike back preemptively. Inviting the king and various political opponents to a feast under false pretense, he proceeded to slaughter them. With his rivals eliminated in this coup d'état, Yŏn Kaesomun handpicked the next successor to the throne and appointed himself as the grand minister plenipotentiary (*mangniji*). Thus, for all intents and purposes, he became the de facto ruler of Koguryŏ.

Koguryŏ's foreign policy, under the dictatorship of Yŏn Kaesomun, tended to be aggressive not only toward the Tang but also toward the other kingdoms on the Korean peninsula. At last having strong leadership after a series of ineffectual kings, Koguryŏ did not easily submit to the reemerging *pax Sinica* order of the Tang. Recognizing Koguryŏ's hard-line stance, Silla eventually approached Koguryŏ, sending its royal envoy Kim Ch'unch'u (604–61), later to become the Silla king, and proposed an allied conquest of Paekche. Yŏn Kaesomun, however, demanded as a precondition of the new alliance the former Koguryŏ territories in the Han River area, which Silla had occupied since 553. The negotiations between the two kingdoms ended in failure, and Kim, who was forcibly detained for two months by Yŏn, was finally allowed to return. Koguryŏ, it seemed, had more interest in an alliance with Paekche. Thereafter, Silla swiftly turned to the Tang for partnership against the now forming Koguryŏ-Paekche coalition.

In 644, Taizong raised an expedition force against Koguryŏ, condemning Yŏn Kaesomun for his brutal murder of the previous king. The invasion failed to reach the capital, Pyongyang, and faced stubborn resistance in various Koguryŏ citadels on the Liaodong peninsula, thereby prolonging the war for a full year. Taizong then changed his strategy into a protracted war against Koguryŏ, maintaining consistent attacks on its border. Koguryŏ, therefore, endured 70 years of war, beginning in 598 with the Sui dynasty, and ending in 668 when it eventually fell to the Silla-Tang alliance.

Leadership in Silla

In 647, the old Silla aristocracy of the weakening *hwabaek* system, fearing the growing power of the throne, attempted to depose the ruling monarch, Queen Sŏndŏk (r. 632–47). This rebellion was suppressed by a rising group of royalists led by Kim Ch'unch'u, who emerged as a powerful political figure in the aftermath. When the queen finally passed away, this royalist group chose her heir, Queen Chindŏk (r. 647–54), the last of the Holy Bone (*sŏnggol*) monarchs.

The most dramatic event in this period was Silla's speedy alliance with the Tang. In 648, Kim Ch'unch'u was sent again as an envoy, this time to China Proper. By promising to wear the Tang style of dress for the Silla bureaucrats upon his return and by leaving one of his sons behind in the Tang capital, Kim Ch'unch'u impressed the emperor, Taizong. In contrast to Yŏn Kaesomun's belligerent attitude toward Tang suzerainty, Kim Ch'unch'u foresaw the advent of the next *pax Sinica* era in the East-Asian world and responded wisely. Due to his success, Kim's political influence in Silla was unchallenged. Thereafter, the Silla court further pleased the Tang emperor by officially using the Tang reign title, a diplomatic concession of deference to Tang's suzerainty. Moreover, the court presented a precious gift: a silk tapestry upon which Queen Chindŏk herself had embroidered the "Song of Great Peace," a poem dedicated to the emperor. Such adroit diplomatic gestures solidified the Silla-Tang alliance.

In the sixth century, Silla institutionalized the *hwarangdo,* a body of youth groups in which members learned traditional values, trained in the military arts and poetry, and nurtured patriotism by touring the country's famous mountains and rivers. Each unit was led by a *hwarang,* a leader from the True Bone aristocracy, such as Kim Ch'unch'u, followed by several hundred young men called *nangdo.* Often, Buddhist monks joined these groups as advisers. The *Samguk sagi,* the twelfth-century Korean historiography, tells us the origin of the *hwarang* as follows:

> The *wŏnhwa* [original flower] first debuted at court in the thirty-seventh year [576] of King Chinhŭng. In the beginning, the king and his officials found it difficult to recruit talented people for service. They let young folk play amongst their peers so that their behavior could be observed and thus the talented among them be selected to official positions. As a result, two beautiful girls, Nammo and Chunjŏng, were selected to lead a group of some three hundred young followers. But the two girls, jealous of their beauty, fought with each other. One day, Chunjŏng lured Nammo to her home and forced her to drink wine until she was intoxicated. She then pushed her into a river. For her crime, Chunjŏng was put to death. The youth group, squabbling amongst themselves, disbanded.
>
> Subsequently, handsome young men, faces made up and beautifully dressed, were selected for service and designated as the *hwarang,* under which followers were gathered like clouds. The members of these groups trained one another in spiritual morality, sometimes enjoying poetry and music or taking pleasure in the mountains and rivers throughout the country. Through these activities, the personal character of each individual could be known and those of integrity were chosen for recommendation to the court.
>
> Kim Taemun, in his *Hwarang segi* (*Annals of the Hwarang*), records: "Wise ministers and loyal officials were hereby chosen, and skillful

generals and brave soldiers were thereby born." (author's translation)

In the early seventh century, the Buddhist priest Wǒn'gwang (542–640) wrote for the *hwarangdo* the "Five Commandments for the Laymen": serve the king with loyalty, attend your parents with filial piety, make your friends out of fidelity, never retreat in the face of battle, and never take lives indiscriminately. Interestingly enough, Wǒn'gwang, who had once studied Buddhism in China Proper, quoted the first three credos of Confucianism among these five commandments (loyalty to king, filial piety to parents, fidelity to friends). Moreover, in urging young men to fight for their nation, he violated the Buddhist creed to kill no living thing. Nonetheless, he conceded that one may kill an enemy in defense of one's country. The *hwarangdo*, endowed with leadership and solidarity between social classes, well portrays the seventh-century spirit of Silla, whose national identity spurred the kingdom in the eventual conquest of the Korean peninsula.

The most famous *hwarang* in the history of Silla was Kim Yusin (595–673), a descendent of King Kim Suro, the legendary founder of the Kǔmgwan Kaya kingdom. Though it had been accepted to the True Bone aristocracy when Silla annexed Kǔmgwan Kaya in 532, Kim Yusin's particular surname differed from the Kim clan of the royal family. In the early seventh century, Kim Yusin was a young *hwarang* who led the most prominent *hwarangdo* of his time, the self-styled *Yonghwa hyangdo* (Disciples of the Dragon Flower Fragrance). He believed himself to be called by heaven to carry out the eventual conquest of the rival kingdoms on the Korean peninsula. As luck would have it, Kim Yusin was a brother-in-law to the rising Kim Ch'unch'u. These two *hwarang* leaders created a partnership that played a great role in the unification of the three kingdoms.

The Fall of Paekche

With the solidification of the Silla-Tang alliance, Paekche, now an isolated kingdom on the southwestern part of the peninsula, felt seriously threatened. Even though Paekche had kept a loose friendship with Koguryǒ, a wedge of Silla territory in the Han River valley between the two made it almost geographically impossible to come to each other's aid. Therefore, Paekche found it necessary in 653 to renew its alliance with the Yamato Wa, which by this time had unified most of Japan. However, to make matters worse for Paekche, Silla's monarchy consolidated its power in 654, when Kim Ch'unch'u assumed the throne and became known as

King Muyŏl, later posthumously honored with the kingly title T'aejong. With the death of the Silla queen Chindŏk, the last Holy Bone monarch, the men Kim dynasty was established. Thus, as the architect of the Silla-Tang alliance became king, Paekche had all the more reason to be wary.

From 655 to 659, Koguryŏ and Paekche began to harass the northern borders of Silla, fearing the southeastern kingdom's growing power. As a response, Silla immediately requested assistance from its ally, the Tang. In 660, the Tang sent by sea an expedition force of 130,000 eastward toward Sabi (today's Puyŏ), the last Paekche capital. Meanwhile, King Muyŏl ordered Crown Prince Pŏbmin, General Kim Yusin, General P'umil, and General Hŭmch'un to advance westward with a force of 50,000. The Battle of Hwangsan Plain was one of the most epic scenes described in the *Samguk sagi*. The Paekche general Kyebaek (?–660), knowing his imminent defeat, slaughtered his own family to spare them from a life of slavery under the conquering enemy. He then led a suicide brigade of 5,000 warriors against the Silla offensive.

General Kim Yusin and his staff marched toward the Hwangsan Plain, where the Paekche general Kyebaek waited in occupation of three strategic locations. Kim Yusin, dividing his forces in three ways, fought four times, but lost every battle. The Silla troops were tired and demoralized. General Hŭmsun said to his son Pan'gul, "For an official, loyalty is utmost, for a son, it is filial piety. If you give your life in this time of crisis, you shall fulfill both." Pan'gul replied, "I hear and obey." He then charged the enemy and fought to death with all his might.

General P'umil called his son Kwanch'ang up to his horse and said to the other generals, "My son is only sixteen years old, but he has a bold spirit. Will he be the very paragon of Silla's troops in today's battle?" "I shall," Kwanch'ang replied. He then mounted his armored horse and with only his lance, charged the enemy. However, he was immediately seized and brought alive before the Paekche general, Kyebaek. Upon the removal of Kwanch'ang's helmet, Kyebaek felt affection for this youth's valor. The general sighed, unable to bring himself to kill the warrior, and said, "We cannot contend with Silla. Even their youth are like this, not to mention their grown men." He released Kwanch'ang alive.

Kwanch'ang returned to his father and said, "It was not because I was afraid of death that I could not slay the enemy general or capture their flag." At this, he drank water with his hands from a well and again rushed the enemy, fighting ferociously. Kyebaek seized him once more and beheaded him, sending the head back tied to the saddle of his horse.

P'umil lifted the head, the blood soaking his sleeve. "My son's face looks so alive," he said. "It is fortunate that he died for his country." Seeing this, the soldiers took heart and resolved to die. Beating their drums and with a great outcry, they charged the enemy. Thus, the Paekche forces suffered a fatal defeat and Kyebaek was slain. (author's translation)

After the collapse of the Kyebaek brigade, the Silla-Tang allied forces reached Puyŏ, which they occupied after a brief but fierce battle, slaying 10,000 Paekche soldiers. The Paekche king and crown prince capitulated to King Muyŏl and the Tang general Su Dingfang. It is said at this time that 3,000 court ladies, in order to escape the invaders, leapt to their deaths in the Paengma River, on which Puyŏ is located. The Tang empire intended to rule Paekche for itself under the commandery it had established. With this foothold on the peninsula, the Tang empire planned to expand its territories even as far as its ally Silla. The Silla king Muyŏl, aware of the Tang emperor's plans, discussed counterstrategy with his officials. In the biography of Kim Yusin in the *Samguk sagi,* an interesting episode was compiled:

Tamigong [the name of an official] suggested, "If we disguise our people with Paekche costume and let them pretend to revolt, the Tang army will be sure to attack them. If we take advantage of this and fight with them, we can succeed." Kim Yusin then said [to the king], "This plan has merit, please accept it." The king replied, "The Tang vanquished the enemy for us. If we return the favor by fighting with them, how can heaven help us?" Yusin answered, "The dog is always scared of its master. However, it will bite him if he steps on it. How can we not save ourselves from this crisis? Your highness, permit it, please!" The Tang spied that Silla was prepared to defend itself and returned home by sea, taking only prisoners, including the Paekche king, his ninety-three officials, and twenty thousand soldiers. They left only a garrison in charge of Puyŏ. (author's translation)

Indeed, it was not so easy for the Tang conqueror to rule even the territory of Paekche. Paekche had lost its capital and king to the unexpectedly large-scale Tang expedition and rapid Silla offensive. However, there were still provincial forces to contend with. Furthermore, rescue forces from the

Yamato Wa had arrived, though too late to save the capital. A Paekche prince exiled to Japan returned to assume the title of kingship and lead the resistance for three years against the Silla-Tang occupation forces. In 663, however, the allied forces finally defeated these resistance armies and the Japanese navy. Thus the kingdom of Paekche ended.

The War of Unification

After a successful expedition to Paekche, the Tang's next target was Koguryŏ. In 661, the Tang raised a force of 350,000 to attack Koguryŏ and asked Silla to supply only provisions. Although Silla was mourning the death of King Muyŏl, Kim Yusin nonetheless led the supply troops toward Koguryŏ's capital, Pyongyang. However, Pyongyang proved to be an impregnable fortress in spite of an eight-month siege.

Meanwhile, the Tang annexed the Paekche territory as a province under direct rule, naming one of the Paekche princes as provincial governor. However, the Tang empire's expansionism did not end there but turned its intentions toward its ally Silla. Instituting a policy to purposely degrade Silla's status, the emperor then proceeded to designate the new Silla king, Munmu, with the same title as the Paekche governor. Furthermore, the Tang used its *pax Sinica* overlordship to force the two territories into an alliance of friendship. Silla, though grievously insulted, complied, waiting for the right opportunity to circumvent the Tang's imperial ambition for rule of the peninsula.

When Yŏn Kaesomun, Koguryŏ's omnipotent dictator, died in 666, the way was open for Silla and the Tang to attack. His death left a power vacuum that his sons struggled to fill. The Tang and Silla used this opportunity to advance toward Pyongyang in 668. The sons of Yŏn Kaesomun, unable to resolve their bickering, fell easily before the enemy. Upon the all-out attack of the Silla-Tang alliance forces, Pyongyang was sacked and the Koguryŏ hegemony, once the strongest power in the northeast-Asian region, ended.

After the conquests of Paekche and Koguryŏ, the Tang empire tried to revive the same dominance in Manchuria and the northwestern Korean peninsula held by the previous Han dynasty. In 669, it established the Protectorate-General to Pacify the East in Pyongyang, one of four agencies in the cardinal directions of the empire, each with the purpose of administering the border territories conquered by the Tang. This East Protectorate-General was the largest among them, and covered the old territories of Koguryŏ, with a subordinate office in Paekche. However, the people of Koguryŏ, their king and most of their aristocracy now taken prisoner, resisted the rule that the Tang instituted. Some of the resistance leaders seceded their territories to Silla, where they found a closer ethnic affinity. Others crossed the sea to the Japanese archipelago. Many in Paekche did the same, searching for refuge in the Yamato Wa.

Meanwhile, Silla, taking the opportunity resulting from the Tang's uneasy rule of the peninsula, expanded its territory by absorbing most of former Paekche. The Tang responded with diplomatic pressure and in an attempt to depose the current Silla king, named his brother, who was staying in the Tang capital, the "King of Silla, Supreme Commander of Kyerim [Silla]." War was now inevitable between Silla and the Tang occupation forces. Fortunately, Silla had the advantage. At that time, the Tang emperor was ailing, and the reign of the empire was handed to Empress Wu, who supported a more pacifist policy. Furthermore, the Tang was distracted by the emerging Tibetan power in the west, and therefore could not devote any more resources to Silla than it already had. The Tang forces on the peninsula remained nonetheless formidable. However, in 675, Silla decisively crushed the Tang armies north of the Han River, and in the following year defeated the Tang navy sent as reinforcements, thus effectively driving all occupation forces from the peninsula.

Thus, the Tang was forced to move the Protectorate-General capital from Pyongyang to the Liaodong peninsula in 676. This meant the complete withdrawal of its occupation forces from the area. Unfortunately, King Muyŏl and General Kim Yusin did not live long enough to see their dream of unifying the three kingdoms become a reality. Now it was Great Silla that occupied most of the Korean peninsula. The former territories of the three kingdoms were divided into three provinces each, establishing a total of nine provinces with five different subcapitals. With Kyŏngju, the main capital, located in the eastern tip of the country, these five subcapitals remained as regional centers where the former aristocrats of Kaya, Paekche, and Koguryŏ were accepted into the ruling class of Great Silla.

Although the nation covered only two-thirds of the Korean peninsula, Great Silla is considered the first Korean dynasty, as it included the peoples of Silla, Paekche, and Koguryŏ. For the first time in their history on the peninsula, the Han-Ye-Maek people were now unified under a national identity.

GREAT SILLA IN THE *PAX SINICA* WORLD

Wŏnhyo

The integration of the three kingdoms entailed a Korean amalgamation of three different Buddhist traditions, initiated by Silla Buddhism. Prior to unification, Silla, the latest to convert to this new religion, enthusiasti-

cally nurtured monks and students in order to send them abroad. Mahayana (Great Vehicle) Buddhism dominated seventh-century Silla thanks to the pervasiveness of texts translated from Sanskrit into classical Chinese. Silla Buddhist philosophers, publishing many books and theses, advanced studies on doctrine, of which one of the hottest issues was the discussion on Buddhahood. Ever since the *Nirvana Sutra* was introduced in the early seventh century, the Korean people believed that any person could achieve Buddhahood, as each human being was born with a Buddha nature. However, a new trend from China gave rise to the contention that some human beings were born without this fundamental disposition to become Buddhas. Nonetheless, most Korean scholars rejected this idea. Among these was the Great Master Wŏnhyo (617–86).

Avoiding just one doctrine, Wŏnhyo embraced the various schools of

Buddhism in the three kingdoms and laid the foundation upon which the Korean people of Great Silla could easily accept the precepts of Mahayana tenets. Having never studied abroad, he created a unique Buddhist philosophy that harmonized various doctrinal interpretations and became a great influence in China and Japan. After the unification of the three kingdoms, Wŏnhyo's philosophy contributed not only to national reconciliation between the conqueror and the conquered but also to the popularization of Buddhism among the ruled subjects.

Wŏnhyo, meaning "early dawn," was originally born under the surname Sŏl, a family line of lower rank in the bureaucracy. It was said that he was so brilliant that he needed no teacher before becoming the chief priest of a temple in the capital. Needless to say, he had reached an extraordinary stage of spirituality, and was not bound to the Buddhist commandments. One day Wŏnhyo saw bees and butterflies flitting from flower to flower, and he felt a strong desire for a woman. He walked in the street singing, "Who will lend me an axe that has lost its handle? I wish to cut a heaven-supporting pillar." No one but King Muyŏl understood that his metaphor of "the axe without handle" meant a widowed woman. In one of the Confucian Classics, an axe handle symbolized the male, whereas "heaven-supporting pillar" meant a man destined for greatness in service of the state. The king arranged for a union between the master and his own widowed daughter, Princess Yosŏk, believing the two would produce a great sage. On his way to the princess's palace, Wŏnhyo deliberately fell into a stream. Thus, upon his arrival, the princess ushered the master inside in order to change his wet clothes. That night Wŏnhyo shared her bed. The princess later bore a son, Sŏl Ch'ong (?–?), named after the secular surname of Wŏnhyo. Sŏl Ch'ong grew up a great scholar, standardizing the *idu* script, a system using sinograms to write the Korean language. He was indeed a heaven-supporting pillar of Great Silla.

After breaking the Buddhist commandment of celibacy, Wŏnhyo changed his priest's robe for secular clothes and gave up his reverend title. Taking a gourd mask, which he dubbed "No Impediment" (citing a phrase from the *Avatamska Sutra:* "the absolute man of no impediment may free himself from life and death"), he composed a hymn to espouse this theme and toured village after village in the country, singing, dancing, chanting, and reciting. His popular way of teaching, though peculiar, attracted the poor and illiterate masses in the countryside, effectively enlightening them to Buddhist tenets. His simplistic but to-the-point work, *Arouse Your Mind and Practice,* is willingly recited today by modern Korean Buddhists as a popular self-admonition text for the new convert. The following are some excerpts:

Now all the Buddhas adorn the palace of tranquil extinction, *nirvana*, because they have renounced desires and practiced austerities on the sea of numerous *kalpas*. All sentient beings whirl through the door of the burning house of *samsara* because they have not re-nounced craving and sensuality during lifetimes without measure. Though the heavenly mansions are unobstructed, few are those who go there; for people take the three poisons [greed, hatred, and de-lusion] as their family wealth. Though no one entices others to evil destinies; many are those who go there; for people consider the four snakes and the five desires to be precious to their deluded minds.

Everyone knows that eating food soothes the pangs of hunger, but no one knows that studying the dharma corrects the delusions of the mind. Practice and understanding that are both complete are like the two wheels of a cart. Benefiting oneself and benefiting others are like two wings of a bird ... Hours after hours continue to pass; swiftly the day and night are gone. Days after days continue to pass; swiftly the end of the month is gone. Months and months continue to pass; suddenly next year has arrived. Years after years continue to pass; unexpectedly we have arrived at the portal of death.

... How many lives have we not cultivated? Yet still we pass the day and night in vain. How many lives have we spent in our useless bodies? Yet still we do not cultivate in this life time either. This life must come to an end; but what of the next? Is this not urgent? Is this not urgent? (Excerpts from the translation by Robert E. Buswell, Jr., in *Sources of Korean Tradition: From Early Times through the Sixteenth Century*, vol. 1, New York, Columbia University Press, 1997)

Wŏnhyo's enlightenment still touches our spiritual mind, just as with the people of eighth-century Great Silla. This literary gem of early Korean Buddhism rings in our ears with its enchanting rhymes and biblical rhetoric.

The Rise of Parhae

Since the unification of the Korean peninsula under Silla rule in 676, the Tang empire was not only unable to assimilate the people of the con-quered territory of Koguryŏ but also unable to maintain rule in the region. At the end of the seventh century, the Khitans north of China revolted against the empire, diminishing Tang influence in the western area of the Liao River, where many Koguryŏ and Malgal people had been forcibly relocated. This multiethnic group, led by a former Koguryŏ general, now moved eastward through Manchuria in order to flee completely from the grip of the Tang. Settling in the Mukden River valley in 699, they founded another Han-Ye-Maek kingdom called Parhae (Pohai in Chinese) and immediately sent envoys to Silla and the nomadic Turks in Mongolia. It was only thanks to a power vacuum in the region that a kingdom like Parhae could arise and survive for two centuries.

Parhae has become a controversial issue among modern nationalist historians in East Asia. Given that the kingdom consisted of several different Han-Ye-Maek ethnic groups, the main argument focuses on whether Parhae should be considered a Korean dynasty. Since there is no existent historiography written by Parhae historians, what we know of this kingdom is based on fragmental records from Silla, the Tang, and Japan. According to those records, two ethnic groups were dominant in this kingdom: the remnants of Koguryŏ and the people of Malgal, ancestors of the Manchu. It is believed that the Koguryŏ people were under the direct rule of the Parhae king, whereas the Malgal people were a semi-autonomous group governed by their tribal chiefs, who then submitted to the authority of the monarchy. Therefore, the Koguryŏ people played a leading role in Parhae, while the Malgal tribes were merely subordinates.

Parhae rapidly recovered most of the old Koguryŏ territories and regained some of its prosperity. This created tensions in the East-Asian world for a while, which entailed another rapprochement between Silla and the Tang. However, they could not militarily subdue Parhae, who sought to ally with Japan and other nomadic powers in north China. Therefore, the Tang eventually had to accept the reality of its limited power, and satisfy itself in merely playing the leading role in East Asia.

From the eighth century on, the international situation in the region stabilized under the *pax Sinica* system. Envoys, merchants, and Buddhist monks frequented Tang China, Silla, Parhae, and Japan. Many Korean monks had been crossing the sea to Tang China to further their studies since the early seventh century. Now, however, the Korean monk Hech'o (704–?) traveled twice as far, to the Buddha's land of India. His travelogue, which depicts the eighth-century scenery in India, was found in a Dunhuang cave by the French explorer Pelliot in the early twentieth century.

During this period, Korean trade, both official and private, increased remarkably in terms of scale and variety. It mostly concentrated on China, though it also prospered with Japan. Korean gold artifacts were so popular among high society in Xian that Silla was known as a land of gold even among the visiting Islamic merchants. According to Arabic accounts in the ninth century, it is believed that some of them in fact reached this mysterious country searching for gold. Precious gems imported from Central Asia via the Silk Road and Chinese silk enchanted the ladies of the

Silla aristocracy. Homemade high-quality textiles and herb medicines from Korea were in demand in China and Japan, while books and stationery from China were necessary for Korean intellectuals. The culture of Tang China, at this time flourishing with advanced sciences, religions, and arts, spread among the ruling classes in Silla, Parhae, and Japan.

In the Sandong peninsula, special trade embassies were established for the envoys and merchants of Silla and Parhae. Even a Korean Buddhist temple was opened for the Silla community there. At the mouth of the Yangzi River, a Korean community of a much larger scale, called Sillabang, emerged with the thriving private trade. If we compare the twentieth- and twenty-first-century *pax Americana* with the eighth- and ninth-century *pax Sinica*, Sillabang is reminiscent of today's Korean communities in the United States, such as the Koreatowns located in Los Angeles and New York.

Kyŏngju

The capital of Great Silla, Kyŏngju, like Xian of Tang China and Nara of Japan, was one of the most prosperous cities in the eighth- and ninth-century *pax Sinica* world. The population of this city was estimated as 200,000 households during the eighth century. The people of Kyŏngju included royal families, aristocrats, officials, priests, soldiers, merchants, potters, artisans, entertainers, and slaves. Most of them dwelled in beautifully decorated tile-roofed houses. The royal palaces were surrounded by gardens with artificially designed ponds, while magnificent temples built for Buddhist worship stood downtown and in the suburbs. It is regrettable that most of those splendid structures were destroyed during the most miserable two wars in Korean history: the Mongolian and Japanese invasions of the thirteenth and sixteenth centuries. Only stone sculptures, reliefs, and pagodas survive in the remains of these palaces and temples. However, Kyŏngju was designated in 2000 by UNESCO as a World Cultural Heritage site, citing its royal tombs, its ancient astronomical observatory, and the nearby open museum of Buddhist sculptures. Besides Xian in China and Constantinople in Europe, it is difficult to find such a prosperous city elsewhere on the earth at that point in history.

The *Samguk yusa* describes a ninth-century scene in Kyŏngju as follows:

During the reign of the forty-ninth ruler of Silla, King Hŏn'gang, houses with the tile roofs stood in rows from the capital to the seas, with not a single thatched roof in sight. Music and song flowed in the streets day and night, and wind and rain came in due time throughout the seasons. (author's translation)

The "Song of Ch'ŏyong" is one of the most famous of the popular songs composed with the *idu* writing system at this time. These songs were known as *hyangga*. According to a shamanistic legend in the *Samguk yusa*, Ch'ŏyong, a son of the Dragon of the East Sea, came to the capital to serve the Silla king. The king bestowed him with a title and a beautiful wife. The Demon of Plague, covetous of Ch'ŏyong's wife, transformed into a man and lay with her while Ch'ŏyong was in town. Upon arriving at home, Ch'ŏyong witnessed this adultery and sang a song while dancing:

> In the moonlit capital,
> Carousing far into the night,
> I return home and behold,
> Four legs in my bed.
> Two were mine;
> Whose are the other two?
> Two were once mine,
> But now taken from me; and nothing can I do. (author's translation)

When Ch'ŏyong turned to leave, the demon appeared in his true form, knelt before him, and said, "I lusted after your wife and now I have sullied her. But you did not show me any rage, and I am greatly moved and praise you. I swear that I will not enter any house if I even see the picture of your face." Hereafter, people put pictures of Ch'ŏyong on their gates to protect their houses from plagues and evil spirits.

Ch'ŏyong, a literary character, gives us a typical portrait of the aristocratic lifestyle of the Kyŏngjuans. These were the True Bone (*chin'gol*) aristocrats who had blood ties with the royal family on either the paternal or maternal side. In the process of conquest, the number of the True Bone increased to embrace the ruling families of the conquered kingdoms. These aristocrats enjoyed opulent lives in the capital or subcapitals of Great Silla, served by slaves and supported by their stipend villages.

Buddhist Arts

The eighth century was a golden age as far as Korean Buddhist arts are concerned. In this period, numerous Buddhist temples were constructed in the mountains and downtown Kyŏngju, with halls of Buddha shrines, pagodas, bells, corridors, and so on. Moreover, stone Buddha statues and rock reliefs were plentiful in the ravines and valleys throughout the countryside. Under Buddhism, artisan skills such as architecture, sculpture, painting, and gilding flourished remarkably. The Great Silla period of Buddhist art is characterized by a dynamic expression of vibrant realism.

Pulguksa, meaning "Buddha Land Temple," and Sŏkkuram, a grotto shrine, were constructed in 751 under the personal guidance of Kim Tae-sŏng (701–74), prime minister of Great Silla. These two edifices tell us about the religious enthusiasm and financial power of the ruling aristocracy as well as the sophisticated aestheticism in the architecture and sculptures of Korean artists, as seen in their granite masonry. Citing the Sŏkkuram grotto as a masterpiece in creative artistic achievement and Pulguksa as an unprecedented superior form of architecture, UNESCO designated both of them in 1995 as World Cultural Heritage sites that had remarkably influenced the lives of the Korean people throughout their history.

The Pulguksa temple and the Sŏkkuram grotto are located in the eastern mountains of Kyŏngju. Inside the artificially built grotto, a statue of Sakyamuni Buddha stands eastward so as to meet the first light of the rising sun. Korean Buddhists believe that the Pure Land, or paradise, lies somewhere over the East Sea. Sakyamuni Buddha is surrounded by 12 marvelous reliefs of bodhisattvas. Among them, the most fantastic is Avalokitesvara (*Kwanŭm;* or, in Chinese, *Kwanin*), the goddess of faith in Korean Buddhism, an equivalent to the Madonna in Christianity. One can almost feel the folds of the bodhisattva's dress fluttering in the breeze.

Unlike the Sŏkkuram grotto, the Pulguksa temple lost its original wooden structures during the sixteenth-century Japanese invasion. However, two magnificent three-story pagodas, each 10.4 meters tall, were fortunately preserved in the courtyard. These are named Sŏkkatap (Pagoda of Sakyamuni) and Tabotap (Pagoda of Many Treasures), after the concepts found in the *Lotus Sutra.* They have a contour that is unique among the many other pagodas in the world of the same two concepts. Sŏkkatap is piled with layers of straight square lines, while Tabotap is decorated with delicately carved curves. This is meant to depict simplicity versus complexity and idealism versus realism. The contrast reminds us the spiritual history of the period: the earlier purism and unreserved martyrdom of Ich'adon versus the no-impediment philosophy and flexible harmonization of Wŏnhyo. Interestingly enough, these disparities of thought have continued throughout Korean history, on the political scenes in particular, as we will see in the later chapters.

The Bone-Rank System

In Great Silla, state power gradually strengthened with the institutionalization of tax and corvée labor. The Holy Bone (*sŏnggol*) monarchs had become extinct since the reign of King Muyŏl. The True Bone (*chin'gol*) monarchs, now in power, promoted Confucianism, a political ideology that advocated loyalty to the monarch and thereby further centralized their political power. In the late seventh century, the king established the National Academy, where students were taught the Confucian classics. Sŏl Ch'ong, the sage son of Wŏnhyo, standardized the classics using the *idu* writing system, making them easier for Koreans to read. In spite of this, the propagation of Confucianism only went so far. To further increase their power, the throne institutionalized a Tang government system. Confucian-oriented, this system had effectively curbed aristocracy in China. However, the Silla aristocracy, their prestige and privilege deeply rooted in the bone-rank (*kolp'um*) system, continued to maintain their own hold on power.

Great Silla was indeed a kingdom of the True Bone aristocracy, monopolizing not only the kingship but also the upper echelon of the bureaucracy. No matter how wise and capable, those who had not inherited this status could only be promoted as high as the sixth-rank office, the level directly below True Bone. Traditionally, in Silla, officials were recruited either by testing their archery skills or by recommendation from the True Bone aristocracy. Although the Tang-style test of the Confucian classics was introduced in 788, these recruitment methods remained in practice. Because the youth of the True Bone could easily take office merely by recommendation, most of the students enrolled in the National Academy came from fourth- and sixth-rank families.

Therefore, many talented people looked elsewhere to achieve their ambitions. Some left for the priesthood, while others went to Tang China to be recruited by the court, taking advantage of the more egalitarian opportunities in the *pax Sinica* world. Ch'oe Ch'iwŏn (857–?), described as one of the greatest sages of Great Silla, passed the Tang state examination and thus served as a high-ranking official in the ninth-century Tang government. Nonetheless, upon returning home he could find no other desirable role in the Silla bureaucracy than a sixth-rank official. Disappointed, he retired to the mountains and lived as a hermit, calling himself "Lonely Cloud." As described in the twelfth-century *Samguk sagi*, 4 of the top 10 sages during the Silla dynasty were non–True Bone status, including Ch'oe Ch'iwŏn. Thus, it was the marginal sixth-rank class that would later challenge the True Bone aristocracy in the demise of Great Silla.

This limited social mobility was effective in consolidating national unity when Silla was one of the three kingdoms competing for the hegemony of the Korean peninsula. However, it was ineffective in recruiting a more competent bureaucracy in the expanded territories of Great Silla. Beginning in the late eighth century, this social rigidity initiated domestic political instability. During the last 150 years of Great Silla, as many as 20 kings took the throne in a series of fierce succession struggles during which some of them were killed. One of the more dramatic stories of this period is recorded in the *Samguk sagi*. The hero of this story is Chang Pogo (?–846), a warrior commander, whose name is a sinicized version of Kungbok.

Chang Pogo, a commoner talented in military arts, went to Tang China to become a military officer. Chinese pirates frequented the ninth-century East-Asian sea, raiding Korean merchant ships and marauding Korean coasts. Chang Pogo returned to Silla and suggested to the king to establish a maritime command on the island of Ch'ŏnghaejin, located near the southwestern tip of the peninsula. The king named him a commander of a force of 10,000. Chang Pogo, after eradicating the pirates, proceeded to monopolize the trade between both China and Japan. His Ch'ŏnghaejin command now emerged as a virtual maritime kingdom. Shortly thereafter, for his support of a succession struggle in Kyŏngju among the True Bone aristocracy, he received the title of general and many stipend villages from the new king. However, his ambition did not end there. He desired that his daughter be the queen. Unfortunately, the capital aristocracy found this unacceptable on the pretext of his low social status. They wanted to curb the development of independent power in the provinces. Angry, Chang Pogo attempted to revolt and was assassinated before he could initiate anything. Thus the power of Ch'ŏnghaejin also ended with the life of Chang Pogo.

4

Medieval Korea

WARLORDS

The spread of peasant rebellions in the late ninth century marked a dynamic change in the history of the Korean peninsula. Although caused by heavy taxes, the rebellions coincided with a brief period of turmoil in China Proper that resulted in a retraction of the *pax Sinica* world system under the Tang dynasty. On the peninsula, numerous local strongmen and bandit leaders, having accumulated their own private militias, took advantage of the disorder created by the rebellions and competed against one another for control of the provinces. Thus, as only small territories surrounding the capital were under direct control of the royal government, Great Silla was no more.

The ninth-century Korean warlords emerged from various backgrounds: maritime traders, commandery officers, bandits, Buddhist monks, and local aristocrats. Most of them worked their way up from a lower social status and, once achieving their leadership, called themselves "lord" or "general" and nurtured private forces. The local aristocracies, however, belonged to a marginal group in the ruling class of Great Silla. They consisted of either True Bone groups driven from the capital or local elites of sixth-rank status. This sociopolitical turmoil in late-ninth-century

Silla is comparable to similar periods of unrest associated with the decline of each of the Chinese dynasties. Korea now entered the warring-states period in its history. Just as in the Chinese continent, numerous heroes rose from regional power bases and fought each other for eventual hegemony over Korea.

With respect to premodern Korea, feudalism is one of the most controversial concepts disputed among historians. Debate centers on whether feudalism actually existed in Korea. It certainly did not from a Eurocentric perspective. By the strictest definition, feudalism is a system of contractual relationships between lords and vassals, where lords make grants of fiefs to vassals in return for pledges of military and political services. Throughout Korean history, there are no instances of such contractual relationships as found in medieval Europe. Comparing the local strongmen in ninth-century Korea to European feudal lords, as some did with the feudal kings in the eleventh-to-third-century B.C.E. Chinese Warring States period or of the warlords in fourteenth-to-sixteenth-century C.E. Japan, results in superficial analogies at best. Rather, the relationships between the Korean local strongmen and the peasants they ruled were closer to the relationships between European lords and their subjects. In such relationships, labor service was exchanged for military protection. Thus, the medieval characterization of the ninth-century Korean warlords and their autonomous territories better lies under seignorialism or manorialism, which convey a much broader sense of feudalism.

If Great Silla could be called the Age of Antiquity in Korean history, then which period can we define as the Medieval Age? Conventionally, historians have defined medieval Korea as beginning with the foundation of the Koryŏ dynasty in 918. However, the question of periodization has been another hot issue of debate among historians. The conventional method of periodizing according to dynasties is outdated, as it does not correspond exactly with any substantial socioeconomic change. Usually such changes in history far precede the advent of a new dynasty. Medieval Korea, therefore, should be defined as starting as early as the late ninth century, when the political, economic, and social institutions of Great Silla began to decay. Politically, the kingdom was undergoing a series of succession crises among the True Bone royal family. Economically, state finances were threatened by the swollen number of tax-exempt villages that paid stipends to the aristocracy. Above all, socially, the traditional bone-rank system was crumbling.

At the turn of the tenth century, Kyŏnhwŏn (?–936) and Kung'ye (?–918) had become the most prominent of all the warlords on the Korean peninsula. Kyŏnhwŏn was an exceptionally successful military officer in the southwestern provincial commandery, located in the old Paekche territory. Kung'ye started out as a bandit leader in a central peninsular area that was part of old Koguryŏ. In order to rally the people of their territories, the two proclaimed themselves kings of Paekche and Koguryŏ, respectively. To distinguish from the earlier Three Kingdoms period, modern historians named these new kingdoms Later Paekche and Later Koguryŏ. With Silla, now diminished, still in existence, the Later Three Kingdoms period had arrived.

Wang Kŏn

Wang Kŏn (877–943) came from the central western coast of the peninsula, where his family had been enriched by maritime trade with China. During the decay of Great Silla, he emerged as a powerful local strongman. With the advent of the Later Three Kingdoms period, he joined his territory with Later Koguryŏ and served as a minister and a general to King Kung'ye.

In 918, Wang Kŏn ousted King Kung'ye in a coup d'état and founded the Koryŏ dynasty, choosing his political base Kaegyŏng (today's Kaesŏng) as his capital. The name Koryŏ itself is an abridged form of the word Koguryŏ, and naming it thus is an indicator of Wang Kŏn's ambition to reclaim the vast territories of the former kingdom. Indeed, Wang Kŏn reconstructed Pyongyang, the old capital of Koguryŏ, which had been abandoned by Great Silla. Naming it Sŏgyŏng, or "Western Capital," this resettlement on the former Silla frontier gave Koryŏ impetus to expand considerably northward. These two capitals were believed by Buddhist geomancers to be located in places auspicious for a long-lived kingdom. Compared with other capitals, like Kyŏngju of Great Silla in the southeast and Wansanju, today's Chŏnju of Later Paekche in the southwest, Kaesŏng had a geographical advantage in the center of the peninsula on the Yesŏng River mouth.

In ninth-century Korea, geomancy began to emerge as a widespread element in popular belief. This trend was enhanced by the Sŏn (Qian in Chinese, or Zen in Japanese) master Tosŏn (827–98), who infused geomantic beliefs with Buddhist ideas. In the disorder of the declining Great Silla period, Tosŏn prophesied that one day a sage would receive the mandate of heaven and rise to be a ruler. His geomantic prophecy pointed to Kaesŏng as the location where the future ruler would rise. The place was without question Wang Kŏn's political power base, which the master had frequented. Interestingly enough, Tosŏn mentioned in his prophecy the word "mandate," a term only used by the founders of dynasties in China

Proper. In using this word, he gave legitimacy to the future ruler of reunified Korea. Indeed, Wang Kŏn proclaimed his reign title as Ch'ŏnsu, meaning "mandate bestowed from heaven."

Wang Kŏn's bold proclamation of his own reign title contributed to his legitimacy in ruling Korea. However, most of his successors had to abandon such prestigious technicalities in their titles for a more pragmatic security against whoever dominated China Proper—the Chinese, Khitan, Jurchen, or Mongols. Since the eighth century, the Khitan, a Mongolian tribe, had emerged as a threat to the Tang, eventually founding the Liao dynasty, whose territory included today's Beijing in north China. It was imperative that the new nomadic empire secure the Liao River valley, which was occupied by Parhae. The Malgal tribes, the semiautonomous ethnic groups in Parhae, escaped from the loosened grip of the kingdom to join the new power. In 926, the Khitan, using mobile mounted forces, made a surprise attack on the weakened Parhae, sacked its capital, and forever destroyed its civilization. Thus ended the last dynasty established by the Han-Ye-Maek people in Manchuria.

Remnants of ancient Koguryŏ in Parhae wanted to join Koryŏ after their kingdom fell, believing that Koryŏ would be the genuine successor of Koguryŏ's former glory. Migrating in groups, they were welcomed by Wang Kŏn, who sympathized with them out of his similar Han-Ye-Maek origins. Early tensions between the Khitan and Koryŏ were largely due to the king's hostility toward those who had destroyed Parhae. In 934, Wang Kŏn bestowed his royal surname to the crown prince of the former kingdom as he arrived in Koryŏ with tens of thousands of his people. The migration of Parhae people continued intermittently for the next century thereafter.

Wang Kŏn was an outstanding leader, embracing not only the migrations from the north but also all other powers on the peninsula, even his own rivals. In order to appease the local strongmen, he employed two policies: strategic marriages and the bestowing of the royal surname. He married the daughters of powerful warlords and former Silla aristocrats and thus had 29 wives, 6 of whom were given queen status, with the remaining 23 designated with royal ladyships. High-ranking titles were often bestowed to favored local strongmen along with the royal surname. His strategy contrasted with that of the Later Paekche king, Kyŏnhwŏn, whose policy was to trample Kyŏngju with military might, slaying the Silla king and dishonoring the queen. In 935, Silla at last chose to surrender to Koryŏ, whose leader showed more generosity than that of Later Paekche. Before long, Kyŏnhwŏn himself had to solicit the aid of Wang

Kŏn in order to subdue his own son, who had betrayed him. In 936, Koryŏ finally reunified the Korean peninsula, decisively defeating Later Paekche.

The Ten Injunctions

A new age needed a new dynasty. The social change of the new medieval age in the ninth century made a new dynasty in the tenth century inevitable. After the murder of the last patrilineal descendant of King Muyŏl of Silla in the late eighth century, his successors could no longer sustain their monarchy. Although Koryŏ owed much to Great Silla in terms of political, social, and cultural heritage, its founders promoted various reforms to suit the expectations of the people who had suffered hardships during the warring period.

Given that Wang Kŏn had achieved the reunification of the Later Three Kingdoms by embracing the autonomous regional strongmen and Silla aristocracies, he was now seriously concerned with how his descendants would be able to command and control the powerful ruling classes. Before he died, Wang Kŏn, now posthumously honored with the name of T'aejo, left behind the Ten Injunctions, a set of admonitions for his descendants that were to assure the prosperity of the kingdom. Of the 10 items, 5 relate to the political system with which the kings should rule the state. T'aejo's first concern was how to apply the Chinese political institution model to the reality of Korea.

T'aejo said in his fourth injunction, "In the past we have always had a deep adoration for Tang-style culture, and we have modeled their institutions. But our country is a separate land, and our people's character is different. Therefore, there is no reason to copy it. Also, the Khitans are uncivilized, and their language and customs are strange. Their institutions and manner of dress should never be imitated" (author's translation).

Indeed, most modern historians concede that the Koryŏ political system was distinguishable from that of China, although on the surface it appeared to be a replica of the Tang. For example, in 958, Kwangjong (925–75), a son of T'aejo and fourth king of Koryŏ, institutionalized the Tang-style civil-service exam system (*kwagŏ*) with Korean modifications. While Kwangjong was advised in this by Ssanggi (?–?), a former Chinese envoy to Korea, the Koryŏ exam system was tailored to Korean realities. With this new system, Kwangjong aimed to tame the autonomous local warlords into a civilian bureaucracy loyal to the monarch. Unlike the Tang practice, the civil-service exams were open mainly to the descendants of the capital aristocracy and the local elite, known as *hyangni*, or hereditary local strongmen.

Kwangjong, having witnessed bloody power struggles among the local warlords after the death of T'aejo, was determined to promote his own reform policies for a stronger monarchy. They included: (1) the Slave Investiture Act of 956, through which the state expanded its economic and military sources by the confiscation of private slaves owned by the aristocracy; (2) the reorganization of the royal military forces and their expansion to 300,000 in order to defend against the Khitan military threat; and (3) the replacement of local strongmen and aristocracy by officials appointed by the throne. Introduction of the new government employment system by means of the exam centralized the power of the kingship by creating a new capital bureaucracy that was recruited by merit and not by inheritance. The central bureaucracy consisted of two wings: civilian and military. Together, these were known as the yangban, which literally means "two wings." The reform policies were passed down to Kwangjong's successors, who further degraded the status of the *hyangni* and curbed the power of the capital aristocracy. However, the later kings were not so successful in circumventing their power. Mostly those with strong family backgrounds were eligible to take the exams. Moreover, some candidates were considered to have protected appointment (*ŭm*) privileges that made them exempt. Thus, the Koryŏ yangban, originally meant to be a meritorious aristocracy, inadvertently became a hereditary literati class, known as *munbŏl*.

T'aejo's seventh injunction states, "It is very difficult for the king to win the people's hearts. If you want their hearts, give heed to remonstrance and distance yourself from slander. If you accept remonstrance, you will be a sage king. Though sweet as honey, slander has no credibility and will cease of its own accord. When you make the people labor, lighten their burden and learn the hardships of farming. If thus, you will have the hearts of the people and peace and prosperity in the land" (author's translation).

Ironically, the more powerful the king was in the premodern history of East Asia, the stronger the criticism of his policies. Since the reorganization of the central government after Tang's Three Chancelleries and Six Ministries in 983, the Office of Remonstrance played a crucial role in curbing the king's autocracy. Moreover, any vital state issue was decided by consensus of the Council of High-Ranking Ministers of the Two Chancelleries (*chaech'u*), which also had restraint on the king. This council that participated in and supervised military and legislative affairs was another example of the Korean modification of the Chinese political system. In the eleventh century, this top policy-consulting organization was occupied mostly by the hereditary literati.

The major economic sources of the early Koryŏ aristocracy were the salaries and prebends provided by the state. This salary system was known as the Field and Woodland Rank system (*chŏnsikwa*). Thus, salaries and prebends were systematized based on ranks in the bureaucracy, wherein the size of prebended fields and woodlands were scaled accordingly. The heir of Kwangjong created this method in order to reorganize the old stipend villages and fields owned by the local strongmen and aristocracy.

T'aejo's ninth injunction states, "The salaries for the bureaucracy should be set according to the circumstances of the state. They should not be increased or diminished. The classics say that salaries should be determined by the merits of those who receive them and not by private consideration ... Since our country shares borders with savage nations, always beware of the threat. Take good care of the soldiers; lighten their burden of forced labor; inspect them every autumn; and give honors to the brave" (author's translation).

War with the Khitan

After the fall of the Tang, the Khitan founded the Liao empire in north China during the resulting East-Asian disorder period of the late tenth century. Koryŏ, however, would not accept the legitimacy of this new empire. In fact, Koryŏ was openly hostile toward the Khitan for their destruction of Parhae. For their part, the Khitan desired peace with Koryŏ so that they might turn their attention to attacking China Proper. However, Koryŏ enthusiastically supported the Song dynasty, which formed south of the Liao empire.

Crossing the Yalu River in 993, the Khitan invaded Koryŏ. But they were held back at the Ch'ŏngch'ŏn River, the same line where in 612 the Sui expedition forces had been defeated by the Koguryŏ commander Ŭlchi Mundŏk. Fortunately, the Khitan, worried about their border with the Song to the south, were reluctantly convinced by the Koryŏ general Sŏ Hŭi (940–98) to cease their advance. General Sŏ Hŭi persuaded them to accede to Koryŏ's claim of old Koguryŏ territories south of the Yalu River. He argued two reasons for the claim: (1) Koryŏ is the genuine successor of Koguryŏ, and (2) Koryŏ needed that territory in order to open the way to the Liao for trade and diplomacy. As soon as the invaders withdrew, Sŏ Hŭi annexed the territories and constructed six fortresses on the border of the Yalu River, conquering the Jurchen who inhabited the region.

Discontent with the Koryŏ occupation east of the Yalu River, the Khitan emperor himself again invaded in 1010 and sacked Kaesŏng, the capital, retreating only after the Koryŏ king promised to respect the Liao suzerainty. Later, in 1018, a third large-scale invasion from the Khitan was thwarted by Koryŏ forces led by the general Kang Kamch'an (948–1031). The Khitan thereafter gave up trying to subjugate Koryŏ by force. Thus, a balance of power in East Asia remained for a period between Koryŏ, the Song, and Khitan Liao. During the 30-year war with Koryŏ, numerous Khitan, some who were prisoners of war, immigrated into Koryŏ and formed ethnic communities.

Koryŏ Celadon

In the early twelfth century, a new Jurchen empire named Jin succeeded Khitan Liao, thereby forcing the Song to abandon their northern territories in China Proper and retreat south of the Yanzi River. Despite this, relations between Koryŏ and the Song deepened. The Song needed strong ties with Koryŏ in order to defend against the Jin. Thus, Korean envoys to the Song at this time were not treated as tributary envoys, but as ambassadors from a state of equal diplomatic status. Koryŏ was more interested in trade and cultural exchanges with the Song than security from the Jin threat. Not only did the official trade of envoys increase, but private trade also prospered. In a Song historiography, the population of Koryŏ at this period was recorded as 2.1 million, the first ever totaled population in Korean history. Whereas Korean merchants exported raw materials (such as gold, silver, copper, and ginseng) and manufactured goods (such as golden and silvery artifacts, books, paper, brushes, fans, and flower-patterned mats), Chinese merchants brought silks, books, ceramics, medicinal herbs, perfumes, and musical instruments. On the mouths of two rivers, the Yangzi in China and the Yesŏng in Korea, large commercial communities grew and were often frequented by even Arabic merchants.

In a popular Koryŏ song (*yŏyo*), the narrating voice reminds one of a Korean Madame Butterfly living by the Yesŏng River. One imagines that perhaps a Chinese or an Arabic merchant had had a love affair with a beautiful Koryŏ courtesan during his stay in Kaesŏng. As she came out on the wharf to see her lover off, she sang,

> Do you have to go?
> Do you have to leave?
> How will I live?
> Do you have to leave?
> Grabbing hold, I could stop you;
> But you would resent me so,
> And never again would you come.

So I send you off, my gloomy lord,
Go, but come right back! (author's translation)

Koryŏ celadon, famed for its beauty, was produced at this time of cultural exchange between Koryŏ and the Song. During the mid-tenth century, Korean potters were inspired by Song glazed ceramics. One and a half centuries later, they perfected their own type of glazed celadon, creating a unique "secret color" (*pisaek*) of blue monochrome. A celadon-glazed porcelaneous wine cup and stand with inlaid decoration was found in the tomb of a twelfth-century king. Praising it as the best illustration of the Koryŏ monochrome tradition, Evelyn B. McCune, a Korean art historian, wrote,

The cup is eight-lobed with a spray of chrysanthemums in each. The lip and foot have scalloped edges, repeated in the foot of the saucer. The saucer has a wide, flat rim with a recessed center in which one finds incised fish among waves. Surprises come in the thirteen-petaled chrysanthemum on the flat top of the stand, concealed until the cup is raised, and the thirteen-petaled lotus in the bottom of the cup to be seen only when it is empty. ("Salute to Korea's Rich, Emerging Artistic Heritage," *Smithsonian* May 1979, p. 115)

This celadon wine cup tells us of a highbrow taste for life among the Koryŏ ruling class. Given that it was found in a royal tomb, one can assume its users would have been kings, queens, courtiers, and so on. The ruling aristocracy in medieval Korea was limited in numbers by inheritance. However, compared with Silla, in which only the Kim and Pak families made up the True Bone class, the number of families in power increased. As T'aejo himself had married 29 wives in order to embrace the local warlords, these ruling families continued to increase in numbers through intermarriage with the royal family and among themselves.

According to recent empirical research, there were 29 descendant families that had produced a significant number of high-ranking officials during the early Koryŏ period. Although a few families of Silla True Bone background, such as the Kyŏngju Kims, Kangnŭng Kims, or P'yŏngsan Paks, still inherited the same privileges, the majority of those families in power stemmed from the rising local strongmen, and thus originated from all over the peninsula. Moreover, a few families from the Silla sixth-rank status groups, such as the Kyŏngju Ch'oes, climbed to the upper echelon through the state examination system. Due to their intellectual superiority, they played an important role in the reform policies during the early period of the kingdom.

Buddho-Geomancy

One can catch some glimpses of the religious beliefs, social ideologies, and even some prejudices of the Koryŏ kings when reading the Ten Injunctions of T'aejo. Some items of these injunctions, in particular, are believed to be good indicators of the social ideals of medieval Korea, given that these clear instructions had been by and large passed down and respected by the Koryŏ monarchy throughout the dynasty. Not surprisingly, 4 items of the 10 injunctions relate to Buddhism and geomancy, which dominated the ideas of the Koryŏ rulers.

The first injunction states, "The great achievement in the founding of our kingdom depended upon the favor and protection of the Buddhas. Therefore, the temples of both the Meditation [Sŏn, or Zen] and Doctrinal schools should be erected and monks should be dispatched to administer them" (author's translation).

The second injunction continues, "All the temples and monasteries in this country were founded upon sites chosen by Master Tosŏn by geomantic process of elimination. He said, 'If they are indiscriminately built on locations not chosen by me, the terrestrial force and energy will be sapped and damaged, hastening the decline of the dynasty.' I am greatly concerned that the monarchy, the aristocracy, the queens and ladies, and the courtiers all may wish to build many temples and monasteries in the future in order to seek Buddha's blessings. In the last days of Silla, people competed to randomly build temples. As a result, the terrestrial force and energy was wasted, causing its demise" (author's translation).

The idea that "the king is Buddha" was passed on to the Koryŏ rulers from a long tradition originating in early Silla. Not only did the king strive for Buddhahood, but often princes of the royal family were also sent to enter the priesthood. In confronting the nomadic empires to the north, Koryŏ monarchs tended to seek Buddha's divine intervention. For example, the first Tripitaka Koreana, in the eleventh century, was printed as a devotion to solicit protection from Khitan invasions. Soon after the enormous topography was destroyed by Mongol invaders during the thirteenth century, the court made new ones.

Faithful to the injunctions, the Koryŏ court granted high prestige to the Buddhist clergy with titles and excessive privileges, including tax exemption for the temples and monasteries. Besides state patronage, Buddhism in medieval Korea, like Christianity in medieval Europe, enjoyed economic prosperity with lavish donations and support from both the aristocracy and commoners, which eventually entailed corruption and decadence in the late period of the dynasty. Whereas the Silla aristocracy had justified its bone-rank system based on the Buddhist doctrine of the transmigration of the soul, supporting only the Flower Garland school, the Koryŏ monarchy emphasized the Meditation school, which had remained popular among the commoners. The Korean Meditation school was associated with geomancy and led by the monk Tosŏn, a mentor of Wang Kŏn himself.

The fifth injunction says, "I achieved the great task of founding the dynasty with divine aid from the elements of the mountains and rivers of the Three Hans land. The Western Capital [Pyongyang] in harmony with the element of water, is the source of the terrestrial force of our country as well the land of a ten thousand generation dynasty" (author's translation). Thereafter, T'aejo continued to exhort his royal successors to visit the Western Capital, Pyongyang, four times a year, indicating which months they should reside there for at least 100 days.

He further mentions in his sixth injunction two important religious events that celebrate both Buddhism and geomancy, "I wish the two festivals of Yŏndŭng and P'algwan to be deemed of great spiritual value and importance. The former is to worship Buddha. The latter is to worship the spirit of heaven, the spirits of the five sacred mountains, and the dragon gods of the great rivers" (author's translation). These events, more or less observed throughout the dynasty, eventually evolved into medieval community festivals for agricultural ritual rather than religious worship. Yŏndŭng fell on January 15 according to the lunar calendar, where one then prayed for a prosperous harvest year, celebrating the results at P'algwan in October. The *hyangni* aristocracy, the local elites, used these festivals to enhance their autonomy and solidarity among the people in the provinces. In the eleventh century, these two events became known as international festivals to the northeast-Asian merchants of neighboring countries, who came to Koryŏ for trade.

One of T'aejo's strong prejudices in relation to geomancy is revealed in his eighth injunction, "The mountains and land south of Kongju and the Kongju River [today's Kŭm River] are so treacherous that its inhabitants are treacherous as well. For that reason, if they participate in the affairs of state, intermarry with the royal family and its relatives, and take power, they might overthrow the state, as they resent the loss of their own state during the unification" (author's translation). Interestingly enough, this bigotry was practiced against the people of that area until recently, having been passed down throughout Korean history.

Geomantic Rebellion

The rebellion did not arise from the south as T'aejo had predicted, but first occurred in the capital and then in the north. In the early twelfth century, Koryŏ faced a new issue of security. The Jurchen, rising in the north, had destroyed the Khitan Liao and established the Jin dynasty. Soon after failing to conquer the Jurchen and expand its northeastern territory to the Tumen River, Koryŏ began to suffer from severe conflict within the bureaucracy over foreign policy toward the Jin. In 1126, the pro-Jin power group, headed by the king's father-in-law, attempted a palace coup, which was promptly suppressed.

During this domestic turmoil, a new political group from the northern provinces, in subduing the palace coup, found an opportunity to take power. They took as their mentor the Buddhist monk Myoch'ŏng (?–1135), who advocated a political reform called *ch'ingje kŏnwŏn* (proclaiming an emperor with a reign title). By creating an emperor out of the Koryŏ monarchy, he meant to confront the Jin dynasty in the north. He actively campaigned to move the capital to his hometown of Sŏgyŏng, today's Pyongyang, thereby promoting a northward policy. According to his own geomantic interpretation, Kaegyŏng or Kaesŏng, the capital, had wasted its terrestrial force and energy in fending off the palace coup, whereas the forces of Sŏgyŏng, the Western Capital, were still fresh enough to enhance the kingdom and help expand its territory to the north.

Accepting Myoch'ŏng's suggestion in 1129, the king stayed in Pyongyang for four months, the longest stay yet of the Koryŏ monarchs who frequented there in obeisance of T'aejo's injunctions. The king proceeded to construct a royal palace in the very place Myoch'ŏng had indicated in a geomantic prophesy, which claimed that if the king should build a palace in that spot, Koryŏ would become a great empire, conquering the Jin and the other 36 states of the East-Asian world. However, the Confucian-oriented aristocracy in the capital, who were unconvinced by Myoch'ŏng, did not want to leave their inherited political base. Kim Pusik (1075–1151), leader of the anti-Myoch'ŏng group, opposed the capital-relocation policy, using Confucian rationalism to criticize geomancy as shamanistic and illusionary.

Unable to move the capital, Myoch'ŏng and his group in Pyongyang revolted in 1135. Myoch'ŏng, as leader of the rebels, proclaimed the Great Wi empire. The court immediately responded to news of the revolt, naming Kim Pusik commander of the retaliatory forces. After a yearlong resistance, the rebellion was eventually suppressed. Pragmatic realism won over illusionary idealism. However, the latter ideology was indicative of popular sentiment among the Koryŏ people concerning the rising Jurchen, who had previously been viewed as subject to Koryŏ overlordship. Myoch'ŏng is just one example of idealists throughout Korean history who failed to achieve their naive visions.

After the Myoch'ŏng revolt, the Confucian aristocracy, headed by Kim Pusik, began to lead Koryŏ politics. In the middle of the twelfth century, Kim Pusik was tasked with compiling the *Historiography of the Three Kingdoms*, the *Samguk sagi*, which depicted the ancient history of Korea beginning from Old Chosŏn to Great Silla. The compilation was modeled after the classical historiography *Shiji* (*Sagi* in Korean) of China written by Sima Qian, the Chinese Herodotus. Kim's realistic view of Korean history coincided with the contemporary pragmatic diplomacy of the court, by which Koryŏ recognized the suzerainty of the Jin empire after it had conquered the north of China Proper. He has been criticized by the nationalist historians in modern times as a defeatist who had given up on the northward policy of the Koryŏ dynasty by legitimizing Silla instead of Koguryŏ. However, it is only natural that Kim would glorify Silla given that he was a descendent of the Silla aristocracy. Nonetheless, no one can deny the value of the *Samguk sagi* as the most reliable example of a Korean historiography. In this oldest extant history book written by a Korean, the author attempts to explore Korean identity in the East-Asian world order through its ancient history.

Military Rule

Under the hereditary aristocratic rule of the Confucian *munbŏl*, military officials had been discriminated against. During the frequent wars against the Khitan and the Jurchen, these officials, in spite of their meritorious services, had been neglected in promotions and rewards. It was a tradition in Korea since the Great Silla period to set a civilian as supreme commander over the military, as the court had valued diplomacy and scholarship as a better means to secure peace in the civilized society of the East-Asian world order. Certainly, under the *pax Sinica* world, belles-lettres was a much more important subject for the state exam. Therefore, military men were disdained for their unlettered qualities and thus treated as inferiors among the ruling class with whom neither the royal family nor the aristocratic elites wanted to intermarry.

In 1170, discontented military leaders, headed by Chŏng Chungbu (?–1178), succeeded in a coup d'état. Thereafter, the military power ruled by a junta known as *chungbang* went far beyond the established authority of the monarchy, replacing the throne as they willed. However, the period was marked as a time of disorder, as the early military leadership was challenged by internal struggles among themselves as well as with local revolts and peasant uprisings. It is notable that the 1198 slave insurgency in the capital, though brutally suppressed, aimed to overthrow the strict status system of medieval Korea. Finally, Ch'oe Ch'unghŏn (1149–1219), son of a military general, rose to power after liquidating all his military rivals in 1196. Strengthening his private political army, known as the Sambyŏlch'ŏ, he stabilized Koryŏ politics and established a 62-year-long rule of the Ch'oe House, which became a hereditary shogunate-like autocracy.

Under military rule, some Confucian literati continued to serve the court bureaucracy, while others hid themselves in Buddhist monasteries in the mountains, developing a belles-lettres school of Buddho-Confucianism. The hereditary aristocracy was reorganized considerably by intermarriages between the royal families; those literati officials who remained; and the military, a few of whom were of mixed blood from the slave class. Ch'oe Ch'unghŏn, known as a learned man of statesmanship despite his military family background, invited many Confucian scholar-officials to join his government. Among them, Yi Kyubo (1168–1241) served as the prime minister under the Ch'oe regime. He was recruited by Ch'oe Ch'unghŏn in 1192 when he wrote the epic ballad *King Tongmyŏng* (the posthumous name of Chumong, the founder of old Koguryŏ), in which he praised Koryŏ as the genuine successor of Koguryŏ. A rather romantic visionary, he rejected the rational realism of Kim Pusik's *Samguk sagi*, which had instead underscored the legitimacy of Great Silla's unification of the three kingdoms.

40-Year War with the Mongols

At the turn of the thirteenth century, Chinggis Khan (1165–1227) united all the warring clans and tribes in Mongolia by force; conquered all the polities and kingdoms in Central Asia; and occupied north China, defeating the Jurchen Jin empire. The Mongol relationship with Koryŏ started in 1219 with an alliance against the Khitan, who were now invading the peninsula, taking advantage of the fall of the Jin, their former overlords. During this brief period of diplomacy, conflicts between the two allies swelled after the murder of a Mongol envoy who had demanded unreasonable tribute from Koryŏ. In 1231, the Mongols invaded and reached the capital, Kaesŏng. They withdrew after a peace negotiation, under which Koryŏ recognized Mongol overlordship. The Mongols in turn left officials behind to occupy the northwestern territory.

The heirs of the Ch'oe House, finding Mongol intervention in Koryŏ affairs unacceptable, finally decided to fight against the invaders. In 1232, Koryŏ moved its capital to Kanghwa, an island located off the west coast of the central peninsula, believing that the Mongol forces were weak when it came to fighting over sea. The military regime was able to defend its island capital for almost 40 years against a series of Mongol invasions. However, the Mongol forces rained devastation on most of the Koryŏ mainland, destroying many precious cultural heritages, including the first Tripitaka Koreana, made during previous wars with the Khitan. Led by the exiled island court, the Korean people continued to fight against the invaders in spite of enormous loss and sacrifice, even killing off a Mongol commander in the guerrilla war that ensued. Praying to Buddha for peace, the court endeavored over 10 years to reproduce some 81,137 pieces of woodblock printing plates of the Tripitaka (Buddhist scriptures), completing them in 1251. This second Tripitaka Koreana is still well preserved today in the Haeinsa Temple in South Korea, designated by UNESCO in 1996 as a World Cultural Heritage.

Due to the Koreans' metallurgical skills and the ability to manufacture high-quality paper, it should be noted that Korean printing technology developed remarkably during this period of war. In 1234, a book of ritual ceremonies was said to be printed by the first metallic movable type, more than two centuries earlier than Johannes Gutenberg's 42 lines of the Bible. The oldest book printed with the metallic type now in existence, however, is a Buddhist book of tenets, printed at a Korean temple in 1377 and now preserved at the Bibliothèque Nationale de Paris.

Globalization under Yuan Overlordship

As the war with the Mongols dragged on, the Ch'oe regime on the island capital suffered from financial pressure. Although taxes could be collected by seaways, their grip over the inland territories was nonetheless loosened. In 1258, a palace coup against the fourth heir of the Ch'oe House by another military ruler ended the regime's 62-year-old reign. Shortly thereafter, the new regime quickly sued for a peace negotiation with the Mongols, who had softened their stance. Khubilai Khan (1215–94), now ruler of the Mongol empire, welcomed the peace offer from Koryŏ, a kingdom that had persistently resisted for so long. For him, peace with Koryŏ became a political advantage in the bloody succession struggles among his brothers in the 1250s. Meeting the Koryŏ crown prince in the Mongol capital, Khubilai accepted all the conditions Koryŏ offered, including the continuance of the monarchy and the immediate withdrawal of Mongol forces from the peninsula.

After the peace treaty with the Mongols, the Koryŏ military rulers began to contend with the monarchy, which used Mongol influence to restore the power of the kingship. In 1270, the Koryŏ monarch finally returned to the old capital, inviting Mongol intervention to end the reign of the military rulers, who opposed the Mongols' request for Koryŏ support in their expedition to Japan. As a result, the Sambyŏlch'o, the political army of the military rulers, revolted against the monarchy and continued their anti-Mongol resistance in the south islands until they were suppressed in 1273. Thus, the 40-year war with the Mongols virtually ended the military rule.

In 1271, Khubilai Khan, who had been cultivated by Chinese tutors since his youth, proclaimed his empire the Yuan dynasty, thus sinicizing his reign. In 1274, Koryŏ became known as an in-law kingdom to the Yuan when the Koryŏ king was made to marry a Yuan princess. For eight generations thereafter, the crown princes of Koryŏ were forced to continue this practice of intermarriage with the Yuan imperial family. Under Yuan overlordship, Koryŏ conceded to the Yuan direct rule over its northeastern territory and accepted downgraded titles for the king and chancelleries in the central bureaucracy. Moreover, in 1274, Koryŏ was reluctantly mobilized, forced to build warships and supply troops for a Yuan expedition to Japan. However, Khubilai Khan's first attempt to conquer Japan using the Koryŏ navy was wiped out by a typhoon that the Kamakura shogunate in Japan called the *kamikaze*, or "godly wind." Nonetheless, Khubilai's ambition did not end there. After conquering the last remnants of the old Song dynasty in 1279, he remobilized Koryŏ the year after to prepare for a second expedition against Japan. In 1281, Yuan and Koryŏ forces again launched toward the Japanese archipelago, while the former Song navy sailed around the islands to attack from the west. This time too, the allied expedition forces met again with strong seasonal typhoons, having hesitated for several months on the sea. During these two forced mobilizations, Korean labor and resources were wasted considerably.

Under Yuan overlordship, the Korean people in general suffered severely from the burden of enormous tribute requirements, which included gold, silver, ginseng, medicinal herbs, hunting falcons, and so on. In addition, the Yuan demanded many Korean artisans and women every year. It was a fashion for the polygamous Mongol aristocracy to take a Korean woman as one of their wives. The Mongol overlordship, moreover, resulted in a prevalence of pro-Yuan collaborators in Korea who gained privileges for their cooperation. The character of the Koryŏ aristocracy had changed as it intermarried with the military during the rule of the junta, and now it changed once more with the inclusion of these collaborators. In the provinces, great estates, known as *nongjang*, increased as this new aristocracy seized state lands improperly. The greater the *nongjang*, the less the state taxes on those lands. Ironically enough, most of the Koryŏ kings, though of mixed Mongol blood, showed nationalistic enthusiasm for reform politics and fought against the profiteering collaborators for national interest, using the personal influences of their Mongol mothers in the Yuan court.

As much as the Korean people had paid the price under Yuan overlordship, Korea was able to join the global civilization of the Mongol empire. Compared with the *pax Sinica* periods during the eighth through the twelfth centuries, Korean trade and commerce increased remarkably not only in scale but also in diversity due to new contacts with the Islamic world. These new developments entailed advances in science and technology.

Cotton cultivation had already spread over Yuan China in the thirteenth century. Mun Ikchŏm (1329–98), an envoy to the Yuan, brought back cottonseeds from south China and first cultivated them on Korean soil in 1364. Shortly after, mass cotton production, using the new invention of the wheeled loom, created a revolution of clothing at a time when only rugged hemp cloth, expensive silk, or ramie fabrics were used.

The Yuan further developed gunpowder, invented by the Chinese earlier, in the eleventh century, into powerfully explosive cannons. This technology was learned from the Central Asians conquered by the Mongols. Yuan forces used explosive gunpowder during the Japanese expeditions but kept its production methods secret from Koryŏ. Later, in the fourteenth century, Ch'oe Musŏn (?–1395) learned these methods from a visiting Yuan merchant. Ch'oe was recruited by the Koryŏ court in 1377 in order to produce the gunpowder with which Koryŏ was able to crush the Japanese marauders who frequented the Korean coasts.

In the early fourteenth century, new agricultural technologies, such as irrigation and deep plowing, were introduced to Korea by books on rice cultivation from Yuan China. Interestingly enough, scholars believe from recent empirical studies that a remarkable population growth in Korea occurred beginning in the fourteenth century with a prominent decrease of infant-mortality rates. This was mainly due to new developments in the use of local herb medicines, which led to an increase of books published on the subject. Local herb medicine was studied and promoted mostly by the local *hyangni* literati, who were trained in Confucian studies.

Above all, the most critical change in this period occurred in spiritual circles. As Buddhism disappointed Korean scholar-officials by its decadence due to the hereditary privileges bestowed by the monarchy, they turned more toward Neo-Confucianism. This new philosophy was created a couple of centuries earlier by the Song sage Zhu Xi (1130–1200), who reinterpreted the Confucian classics with a new metaphysical and spiritual perspective in order to counter the sophisticated metaphysics of Buddhism. The thoughts of Zhu Xi dominated intellectual society in the Yuan capital, which some Korean scholar-officials, such as An Hyang (1243–1306) and Yi Chehyon (1287–1367), had frequented in their studies and exchanges with Yuan scholars. An Hyang is credited with being the first ancestor, symbolically, of Korean Neo-Confucianism.

5

Korean Tradition

YANGBAN STATE

Ch'oe Yŏng versus Yi Sŏnggye

The decline of the Yuan dynasty in the fourteenth century had loosened the grip of its dominance over the kingdom of Koryŏ. After Khubilai Khan died in 1294, the empire was weakened by fierce succession struggles within the imperial family and sporadic rebellions of the Chinese people under Mongol rule. By the mid-fourteenth century, China Proper was occupied by several rebel powers, among which Zhu Yuanzhang from south China succeeded in founding a new Chinese empire, the Ming dynasty (1380–1644), driving the Mongols from Beijing back to their homeland. For Koryŏ, the foreseeable disorder in the East-Asian world would be either another crisis or an opportunity to recover its own independence and revive its former glory.

Taking advantage of disorder in the continent, King Kongmin (1330–74), the last king anointed by the Yuan, purged the pro-Yuan aristocracy after creating a new diplomatic relationship with the Ming and restoring by force Koryŏ rule over the northeastern territory that was under the Yuan directorate. The reform-minded king began to confer with a newly rising group of scholar-officials who, unlike the old aristocracy, passed the civil-service exam and were determined to put Neo-Confucian ideology into practice. However, Koryŏ was still plagued by external problems. Chinese rebels from the north, called Red Turban bandits, and Japanese marauders from the south harassed the kingdom incessantly. At one point, Red Turban bandits sacked the capital, Kaesŏng, while continued waves of Japanese marauders made their way inland and devastated vast areas. Internally, the powerful hereditary aristocracy obstructed King Kongmin's radical attempts to reform their corrupt, lavish lifestyles and eventually arranged the assassination of the king himself.

During the turmoil created by the invasions of bandits and marauders, two generals emerged as war heroes: Ch'oe Yŏng (1316–88) and Yi Sŏng-gye (1335–1408). While both of them were renowned for their prowess in the military arts and strategies, they contrasted in their policies as well as personal backgrounds. Ch'oe Yŏng, descendant of the hereditary capital aristocracy, insisted on a northward invasion of the Liaodong peninsula now occupied by a Ming garrison. Yi Sŏnggye, son of a local strongman on the northeastern border, anticipated another *pax Sinica* world order under the Ming and opposed the expedition as impractical. Thus, we have a contrast of two ideologies and political groups: idealistic nationalism versus realistic globalism, and central aristocracy versus local strongmen.

Gaining power after the death of King Kongmin, Ch'oe Yŏng launched forces toward Manchuria in 1388 in spite of Yi Sŏnggye's criticism. A reluctant commander of these forces, Yi Sŏnggye decided to use this irrational expedition as a pretext to replace the old aristocracy. In the summer of that year, Yi Sŏnggye stopped on his way north at Wihwado, an islet on the Yalu River, and instead turned his army south to Kaesŏng. Thus he chose pragmatic realism in respecting the East-Asian world order of the *pax Sinica* system under the Ming, just as Kim Ch'unch'u and Kim Yusin had done in the seventh century under the Tang. Now, like Julius Caesar in the first century B.C.E., he crossed his own Rubicon River. The reform-minded Neo-Confucian scholar-officials in Kaesŏng welcomed Yi Sŏnggye, who had no hereditary political base in the capital. They expected him, as their leader, to eradicate the deep-rooted corruption and irregularities of the capital aristocracy.

Indeed, Yi Sŏnggye, once in power, started land reform in 1391 supported by the Neo-Confucian scholar-official group. He eventually implemented the Rank Land Law, a prebendal land-allotment system. In medieval Korea, land was the major economic source for the state, ruling class, and people. The early Koryŏ land system was in disarray because the powerful aristocracy, both civilian and military, as well as pro-Yuan families had increased their private lands into large-scale tax-exempt estates (*nongjang*). Thus, in the fourteenth century, taxable lands had decreased enough to threaten state finance, military provisions in particular. There was no more available land to be prebended for the salaries of the newly appointed officials. These rising Neo-Confucian scholar-officials, known as *sadaebu*, supported the land-reform policy, whereas most of the hereditary aristocracy opposed it. Under the Rank Land Law, the reformists aimed to redistribute all state land according to the new bureaucratic hierarchy in exclusion of the old aristocracy. For the hereditary aristocracy, this meant the loss of their privileged private lands, of which those not distributed to the new elite would return to the peasantry. Thus the peasantry would be better off and the state would earn more taxes.

The rationalist Neo-Confucian scholar-officials then turned to the Buddhist temples and monasteries enriched by privileged tax exemption and private donations, strongly criticizing their decadence and corruption. To the eyes of the Neo-Confucians, the lavish Buddhist ceremonies sponsored by the throne and the ruling class were merely a waste of resources. Moreover, since the Koryŏ dynasty was founded, the Buddhist priests had not only been protégés of the monarchy but also strong allies of the hereditary aristocracy. Thus, the anti-Buddhist movement of the new power group aimed to end the religion's political engagements in medieval Korea. Yi Sŏnggye and the Neo-Confucian scholar-official groups had thereby finished groundwork for the founding of a new dynasty.

Chŏng Mongju versus Yi Pang'wŏn

Due to his scholarship and martyrdom for his loyalty to the Koryŏ dynasty, Chŏng Mongju (1337–92) became the most prominent among the earlier Neo-Confucian scholar-officials. Although he belonged to one of the hereditary aristocratic families, he was recruited by the civil-service exam and pursued the pragmatic pro-Ming policy, supporting the land reform and anti-Buddhism of Yi Sŏnggye. However, he opposed the shift of dynasties promoted by the pro-Yi group because it betrayed the Confucian principle of *wangdo* (rule of right), which forbade disloyalty to the king. Therefore, he attempted a political coup to crush the pro-Yi plot to change the dynasty, but failed when he was assassinated.

Yi Pang'wŏn (1367–1422), a son of Yi Sŏnggye, was also recruited by the civil-service exam and trained as a Neo-Confucian literati, joining the new scholar-official group that supported his father. He contributed greatly to the changing dynasty by eliminating political opponents and countered Chŏng Mongju's arguments with the Confucian concept of *p'aedo* (rule of might) to rationalize a heaven-mandated shift of dynasties. It is said that Yi Pang'wŏn first attempted to embrace Chŏng Mongju before taking action to assassinate him. Dialogue between the two was encapsulated in two Korean traditional poems called *sijo,* a verse in three tightly structured lines. In entreating Chŏng Mongju for his support, Yi Pang'wŏn recited,

> What does it matter, whether it's this way or that?
> Consider the vines of the arrowroot trees twisted and entangled on Mt. Mansu;
> We could be so entwined and live happily for one hundred years. (author's translation)

And Chŏng Mongju responded,

> Though I die, and die again, and die a hundred times,
> Long after my bones have turned to dust; whether my soul exists or not,
> My heart, ever loyal to my Lord, shall never fade away. (author's translation)

In 1392, supported by the reformist Neo-Confucian scholar-officials, Yi Sŏnggye was enthroned as the founder of the Chosŏn dynasty, which would last until 1910. Though Yi Sŏnggye used military might to launch the coup d'état from the Wihwado Islet, the shift of dynasties was relatively peaceful, unlike the Later Three Kingdoms period or the Warring States eras in China Proper and the Japanese archipelago. The conflict over the dynasty change came through several purges and reforms. Respecting Ming suzerainty, Yi Sŏnggye consulted the Chinese court and decided to name his new dynasty Chosŏn. This was the name of the ancient kingdom of Tan'gun, which, according to legend, was succeeded by the kingdom of the sage-king Kija, a mentor of Confucius himself.

In 1394, he moved to a new capital, Hanyang, located in the center of the Korean peninsula near the mouth of the Han River. He constructed a 17-kilometer wall that connected the four cardinal mountains surrounding the round valley. Behind these walls, palaces, ancestral shrines, offices, stores, and schools were built according to a master plan. The initial population of this walled city began at about 100,000 and eventually doubled by the end of the nineteenth century. Today, old Hanyang has expanded to the vast metropolis of Seoul, with a population of approximately 20 million.

The Architect of the Yangban State

Among the ardent supporters of the shift of dynasties, Chŏng Tojŏn (1337?–98) was prominent for his anti-Buddhist Neo-Confucianism and his master plan for a sociopolitical system in the new dynasty that he modeled after the *Zhou li* (*The Rites of Zhou*), a canonical Confucian work created by the sage-kings in ancient China. He believed that the utopian political system should be based on sovereign king power, but supported by an elite yangban class trained by Neo-Confucianism and practiced in the rites and rituals of the Confucian canon. As a visionary, Chŏng Tojŏn suggested a kingdom ruled by a patrimonial bureaucracy of Neo-Confucian yangban literati, whose power was delegated from a benign monarch. However, he later became victim of a political struggle over royal succession. His assassinator, Yi Pang'wŏn, the third king of Chosŏn (posthumously named T'aejong), was far from a benign monarch. Nonetheless, Chŏng Tojŏn's vision of Neo-Confucian rule was eventually realized in most of the royal successors throughout the dynasty.

In a modern perspective, the Chosŏn dynasty in medieval Korea was an authoritarian monarchy, whose power was more concentrated than that of the previous Koryŏ dynasty. Technically, the Chosŏn king, though a surrogate of the Ming emperor's mandate of heaven, wielded absolute authority over his subjects. However, just as in Chŏng Tojŏn's utopian vision, he delegated his political power to a patrimonial bureaucracy of scholar-officials, known as the yangban. In the provinces, the local elite (*hyangni*) were degraded to mere working-level clerks, known as *ajŏn*, in service of the yangban magistrates dispatched from the capital. To prevent these magistrates from taking root in local power, each was given limited terms of office. Unlike the hereditary vassals in medieval Europe, the Chosŏn yangban were rigorously recruited by the civil-service examination, known as the *kwagŏ*. Despite this, social mobility was limited between classes in various ways, such as the exclusion of the many descendants of concubines, known as *sŏja*, from the exam. A school system was created for yangban and elite commoners both in the capital and the provinces.

Once recruited by the *kwagŏ*, the Korean yangban, loyal to the monarch, served as executors of the delegated monarchical power. In the earlier period of the Chosŏn dynasty, the yangban consisted of merely 10 percent of the total population. Civilian yangban were literati who cared primarily for the cultural humanities rather than administrative professionalism. While they openly disdained economic profiteering, they were nonetheless obsessed with bureaucratic power. The military yangban, unlike the knights of medieval Europe, were merely one wing of the bureaucracy under civilian supreme commanders. Both civilian and military yangban made their living solely by salaries and allowances. Unemployment for them meant downfall. Therefore, many were desperate to pass the *kwagŏ*, through which they could achieve their status and prestige. In history, however, one can see that many high-ranking officials were chosen from political or military groups that supported the king's policies. For instance, long lists of yangban who were rewarded with the title of merit subjects, known as *kongsin,* were usually drawn up after political coups.

Though the Chosŏn political system was based on the ideal that the king was responsible for the life of the people, a Confucian interpretation of the parent-child relationship, most of the real politics throughout the dynasty's history tended to follow the interests of both the monarchy and bureaucracy in power. However, there was enough freedom in the yangban bureaucracy for debate and criticism on policies to curb the king's autocracy. The Chosŏn king was obliged every day to study the Chinese classics or Korean history and debate issues and policies with his scholar-officials. The words and behavior of the king were recorded exactly by an official court historian in order to be later judged according to Confucian morality by future readers. The king was forbidden to read what the historian had written about him. The articles were only available for others to read after the king had passed on. These records were compiled in the *Annals of the Chosŏn Dynasty* (*Chosŏn wangjo sillok*), which still exist today thanks to a dispersed storage of these volumes.

In fact, not all the kings were sagely and learned enough to fit the Confucian ideal of leadership. However, the fourth king of the Chosŏn dynasty, known as Sejong the Great (1397–1450), was an extraordinary monarch who achieved some of the best works of the yangban state of medieval Korea.

Sejong the Great

King Sejong was enthroned in 1418, when East Asia was prospering in the *pax Sinica* world system under the Ming. By this time, Chosŏn had well prepared for this season of prosperity with its newly architected politico-economic systems based on Neo-Confucian ideals. Sejong had an attentive father, T'aejong, who eliminated any political obstacles for his heir. Though not the eldest son, Sejong was fortunate as well to have passive elder brothers who conceded the throne in favor of their younger sibling. Moreover, he was surrounded by the efficient military officials who were previously trained by his father and would expand Chosŏn territories to the north.

As a sage-king, Sejong the Great restored an old Tang-style royal think tank known as the Chiphyŏnjŏn (Hall of Worthies), where he debated and discussed policies and issues with a score of brilliant young scholar-officials. One of the great tasks of this think tank was creating the Korean script. Known as hangul, this is the alphabet still used by Koreans today. Hangul is a unique writing system of phonetic signs. In the preface of his proclamation of hangul in 1446, one can read King Sejong and his scholar-officials' consciousness of national identity:

> The Korean language is different from that of Middle Kingdom [China]. One cannot communicate with sinograms. Therefore, the people, though they have something to say, are mostly unable to express themselves. In taking compassion on those people, here are newly made scripts of twenty-eight letters. Let the people learn them with ease and use them in everyday life. (author's translation)

The development of hangul is just one example of how Sejong the Great helped define the territory, language, and culture of fifteenth-century Chosŏn into the traditions of the Korea we know today.

Indeed, Sejong published a plethora of books translated into hangul on such subjects as a eulogy of the royal ancestors, Confucian ethics, Buddhist scriptures, agriculture, and sericulture. Publishing flourished due to the remarkable improvement of metallic type and printing technology. Given that literacy was restricted to the ruling elites in premodern society, to invent a writing system easily learned by the common subjects was a revolutionary idea. Furthermore, Sejong sponsored the invention of astronomical instruments such as rain gauges, water clocks, and observatory instruments. All these inventions and publishing developments were in relation to Sejong's interest in the promotion of agriculture.

The estimated population of fifteenth-century Korea was 5–6 million, a remarkable increase in comparison with the previous century. This was due to continued exploitation of local herb medicines and progress of agricultural technologies. However, the state only counted 4 million in the censuses it took every three years. A considerable number of people are assumed to have escaped from the list to avoid taxes. Common independent farmers or tenants of yangban-owned land made up the majority of the population. Though both of these paid taxes to the state, the tenants were further burdened by rent to the yangban. The other third of the population were slaves, known as *nobi,* both state- and privately-owned.

In medieval Korea, land was the major economic resource. King Sejong created a reserve of about 5 million bushels of rice, with which he launched military campaigns to the northern border with the Jurchen and south across the sea against the Japanese. In 1434, Sejong dispatched expedition forces to construct six fortresses along the Tumen River. Later, he sent another expedition force to the northwestern border to establish four prefectures along the Yalu. Thus, today's North Korea's border with China is still fixed along these two rivers. Before the northern campaigns, however, Sejong dispatched forces in 1419 to the Japanese island of Tsushima, where there was located a base of marauders. The expedition was planned and carried out by Sejong's father, the retired T'aejong.

Korean diplomacy in the *pax Sinica* world system under the Ming was dualistic, as expressed in the doctrine of *sadae kyorin* (*sadae:* attendance on the great; *kyorin:* goodwill to neighbors). The concept of *sadae kyorin* was nothing new. It had been around since the time of Great Silla. It was only given a name when Yi Sŏnggye rose to power. Here, "attendance on the great" referred to Korea's relationship with Ming China, while "goodwill to neighbors" defined trade with the Jurchen, Japan, Ryukyu, and Namman (Nanman in Chinese), which included Siam (Thailand) and Java.

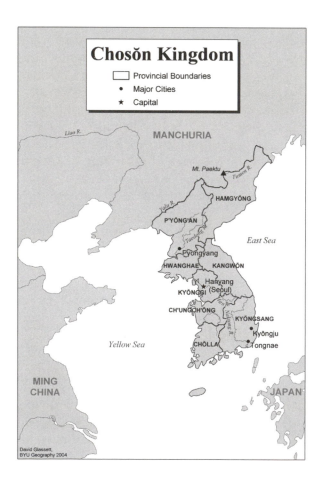

Some of these states paid tribute to the Korean court, while Chosŏn itself paid tribute to Ming China. These nominal tribute relationships were a form of trade. Chosŏn received gifts from the Ming for its tribute, while the same held true of the relationship of Korea's neighbors with the Chosŏn court. Chosŏn bestowed court ranks on the Jurchen chiefs on the Manchurian border as well as on the lord of Tsushima, who usually mediated Korea's relationship with Japan. The Chosŏn court bestowed Korean ranks to the Ryukyu kings as well. In the capital of Ryukyu Island, there was a small Korean enclave that engaged in trade with Siam and Java.

The Literati Purges

Unlike Sejong, his grandson Tanjong (1441–57) was ill-fated to have an ambitious uncle, Prince Suyang (1417–68), who eventually usurped the throne. Organizing a palace coup, Prince Suyang eliminated most of his political rivals, including his own brothers and his nephew king as well. Posthumously known as Sejo, he was enthroned in 1455. King Sejo contributed to the consolidation of the Chosŏn-dynasty monarchy with his great achievements. He began codifying previous legislations into the State Code (*Kyŏngguk taejŏn*), completed later under his grandson's reign. The State Code describes not only the basic power system of the monarchy but also the Confucian-oriented socioeconomic structure of yangban society.

However, the political shift of Prince Suyang's coup became a great issue among the Neo-Confucian yangban, who were divided into two groups: those who supported the coup and those who opposed it. To the former, Sejo's succession of the throne by might not only lacked political legitimacy but also violated the Neo-Confucian concept of the rule of right. The latter supported the rule of might, believing that for the prosperity of the kingdom the weak throne needed a change toward a more vigorous monarch. Again here, one sees the contrast of idealism versus realism.

Six loyal scholar-officials, who opposed Sejo and attempted to overthrow him, were put to death. Another six left the court and hid in the countryside. People named the former the Sayuksin (Six Dead Loyalists) and the latter the Saengyuksin (Six Living Loyalists). These loyalist groups, as years went by, were regarded compassionately by the people, while the supporters of the coup fell into disrepute. In the late fifteenth century, a new group of yangban literati, sympathetic to the loyalists, rose to take their place. Many scholar-officials educated in the southern provinces were able to enter the court by the civil-service exam thanks to royal encouragement of provincial education. Most of them were taught by retired scholar-officials who advocated the Neo-Confucian concept of rule of right. Chŏng Mongju, who did not cooperate with the changing of the dynasty in the late fourteenth century, was esteemed among them as a role model. These new scholar-officials were known as *sarim*, or rustic literati, because they had emerged from the countryside.

The *sarim* entering the court from the provinces threatened the vested interests of the royal family and the capital aristocracy, consisting of officials who had been rewarded with the title of "merit subject" after the coups. The latter wanted to maintain the established order of politics. During the early sixteenth century, the conservative capital yangban were able to defeat the progressive *sarim* through a series of literati purges in 1498, 1504, 1519, and 1545. The 1498 literati purge was instigated by an article in the annals of the previous king, written by an official historian who belonged to the *sarim*. In this article, he had quoted a poem of his deceased mentor, which implied that Sejo's rise to the throne was illegitimate. Thus Sejo's heir, to protect his legitimacy, brutally purged this writer-historian and his group of rustic literati.

In sixteenth-century Korea, due to trade with Ming China and Japan as well as a new beginning in village market commerce, the private landownership of the extended royal family, the capital aristocracy, and the rustic yangban continued to increase. This led to the eventual dissolution of the earlier Rank Land Law. These private lands were either tilled by the landowner's slaves or rented to commoner tenants for as much as 50 percent of the harvest. The commoners were further burdened with taxes and obligated military service. Therefore, they eked out an even more difficult living than the slaves, who were exempt from these burdens.

In this age of medieval Korea, Cho Kwangjo (1482–1519), a leader of the reform-minded *sarim*, attempted once more to realize the Neo-Confucian dream of the rule of right. His reform movement, however, was brutally suppressed in the 1519 literati purge. The capital aristocracy feared their merit-title rewards would diminish under his reform policies. Disappointed in the central politics and economically exploited, the people in the countryside began to rebel while supporting various bandit groups. Im Kkŏkchŏng (?–1562), leader of one of these bandit groups, harassed travelers along the major roads connecting the capital and northwestern provinces for three years. Himself a son of a butcher, a base status in Neo-Confucian society, Im led a bandit group comprised of people from various social classes like slaves, commoner peasants, and even fallen yangban.

The Literati Cliques

Some of the rustic yangban, who were discouraged by the series of literati purges, abandoned central politics and hid themselves in the mountains, studying and teaching Neo-Confucianism. They opened private academies known as *sŏwŏn*, which were a sort of Neo-Confucian monastery. Since the first *sŏwŏn* was established in 1543, they increased remarkably to more than 100 by the late sixteenth century. By the seventeenth century, there were more than 700, and in the latter part of nineteenth century, they numbered more than 1,000. As the yangban educated there began again to participate in court politics, the *sŏwŏn* turned into political power bases of the *sarim*. Nonetheless, the *sŏwŏn*-trained Neo-Confucian scholars concentrated more on metaphysical studies of cosmic principles and human nature than on the practical statecraft of power and prosperity. They believed that adherence to the rule of right, which could only be understood through metaphysical understanding of the cosmos and mankind, would make the state thrive and prosper. Though Neo-Confucianism had started in China, it was now exploding in Korea.

Three scholars were prominent in this apogee of Korean Neo-Confucianism: Sŏ Kyŏngdŏk (pen name Hwadam; 1489–1546), Yi Hwang (pen name T'oegye; 1501–70), and Yi I (pen name Yulgok; 1536–84). In the Neo-Confucian metaphysical approach to the cosmos and mankind, Hwadam, with his philosophy on the primacy of material force (*ki*, or *qi* in Chinese), influenced most of the yangban based in the central region of the peninsula near his hometown, Kaesŏng. Meanwhile, T'oegye advocated the primacy of principle (*i*, or *li* in Chinese). His followers were based in Andong in the rustic southeastern region. However, Yulgok, based in the capital region, synthesized the two, advocating a dualism of principle and material force.

In the latter half of the sixteenth century, the rusticated yangban, trained in these numerous private academies in the provinces, reemerged at court through the civil-service exam. They organized into literati cliques known as *pungdang* and strove against each other for political hegemony. However, these cliques, which were first classified by their *sŏwŏn* connections, later factionalized further according to their political interests. In 1575, the first two groups of literati cliques were called the Easterners and the Westerners, according to the location of their leader's houses in the capital. Generally, most of the Easterners were the followers of T'oegye, the advocate of *i*, whereas the Westerners were followers of Yulgok, who promoted both *i* and *ki*. When Yulgok passed away in 1584 after failing to reconcile the two cliques, the court became dominated by the Easterners. However, they were soon fractioned into the Southerners and the Northerners. Clashing for political initiative, all three literati cliques thereafter continued until 1863 to branch off in all directions.

The Imjin War

Toward the end of the sixteenth century, a new Jurchen hero named Nurhachi (1558–1643), later the founder of the Qing dynasty, united numerous tribes in Manchuria and began to threaten the East-Asian world order under the Ming. Meanwhile, on the Japanese archipelago, another hero, Toyotomi Hideyoshi (1536–98), subdued most of the warlords in Japan and began to harbor a naive ambition of conquering the continent. In order to satisfy the warlords, Hideyoshi planned to invade the Korean peninsula and divide the territory among them. Since the Japanese depended on grain, linen, and cotton obtained from Korea, Hideyoshi first asked Chosŏn to resume trade, which had been suspended after insurrections by Japanese merchants in Korean ports. When he received only a lukewarm response from Chosŏn, he then threatened invasion if the court did not let him make use of Korean roads for Japanese expedition forces in attacking Ming China. Needless to say, the Korean court, loyal to the Ming suzerainty, rejected his demands. Hideyoshi eventually mobilized a force of approximately 200,000. In the spring of 1592, the year *Imjin* according to the Chinese zodiac, the invaders landed in Pusan, the southeastern port of Korea. The Imjin War had started.

The kingdom of Chosŏn at the time was unprepared for this war. Enjoying a comfortable peace under the *pax Sinica* system, Koreans had neglected national defense. The yangban and slaves were exempt from military service, and the enlisted commoners were thus demoralized by this inequality. Moreover, Korean soldiers lacked sufficient training. By contrast, the Japanese forces were well trained and had much experience from the century-long warring-states period in Japan. Moreover, they were armed with musket rifles that had been obtained from Portuguese merchants during the sixteenth century. In terms of military forces and weapons, Korea, except for its cannons, was far inferior to Japan.

The Japanese forces soon crushed with overwhelming power the hastily organized Korean defenses. Only three weeks after landing, they reached and sacked the capital Seoul. After a series of defeats, the Korean king, who escaped with his court to the northern border on the mouth of the Yalu River, appealed to the Ming emperor to send reinforcements. However, the Ming wavered for months before deciding to send troops to punish the invaders for violating the *pax Sinica* East-Asian order. After sacking Pyongyang and occupying the northeastern coast of the peninsula, the Japanese generals offered to negotiate for peace, giving unfair conditions from their position as victors. The Chosŏn court rejected their demands.

With the Japanese forces occupying the major roads connecting the main citadels like Seoul and Pyongyang, many yangban literati in the vast countryside began to organize volunteer guerrilla forces. Although they were not trained as warriors like the Japanese samurai, their instilled sense of Confucian loyalty to the monarchy drove them on in war against the invaders. In fact, the national crisis brought by the Imjin War would be an opportunity for the Korean people to strengthen their solidarity under yangban leadership. Although the army of the central government was consistently defeated, the volunteer guerrilla militias, mostly peasant commoners led by the yangban, dealt substantial blows to the Japanese. As the war was prolonged, other local government forces, cut off from the court, began to join the resistance.

Yi Sunsin

Heroes always appear whenever crises arise in history. An unknown admiral, one of the four navy commanders assigned to the southern coast, played a decisive role in defending the kingdom of Chosŏn. Yi Sunsin (1545–98), born in a waning yangban family, was one of the few military officials who had prepared themselves for national emergencies. Previously, to circumvent Japanese piracy, he had invented wooden warships clad with iron (called the Turtle Ships for their shape), which now became a powerful tool against Toyotomi Hideyoshi's navies. Given that the Japanese forces largely depended upon overseas supply lines to their home archipelago, Admiral Yi's relentless naval battles certainly disrupted the Japanese expedition on the peninsula. Through four major clashes, Admiral Yi's fleet defeated most of the Japanese navies by luring them into the many narrow bays along the southern coast of the peninsula. Indeed, Admiral Yi's military prowess so impressed the sixteenth-century invaders that the later Japanese supreme naval commander during the 1904–5 Russo-Japanese War performed ceremonial rites to him as a war god before he was to meet the Russian Baltic fleet in the Korea Strait.

In the beginning of 1593, the Ming eventually sent a full-scale dispatch of troops to recapture both Pyongyang and Seoul. Yu Sŏngnyong (1542–1607), a Korean prime minister who eventually recommended the king nominate Yi Sunsin as a naval commander-in-chief of the southern coast, returned to Seoul and wrote in his memoir the miserable scene he found there:

> The Japanese had already abandoned the capital the day before. I entered the walled city, following the Ming troops. I saw the people who had remained there. Less than one percent of the population had survived, and they were so sick and starved that they looked like ghosts. The weather at that time was very hot. The corpses of both men and horses, scattered here and there, gave out such a strong stench that people passed by hurriedly, covering their noses. All the houses and buildings, private or public, were completely gone. Only a few that were used as the quarters of the enemy were still standing at the bottom of Mt. Namsan in the east side of South Gate. The buildings including the Royal Ancestral Shrine, the three palaces, the belfry, and all the government offices and schools, which used to be in the north above the main street, were burned to ashes. The Residence of the Little Princess was able to survive because it was occupied by Ukida Hideiye, the commander of the Japanese expedition forces. (author's translation)

After an exchange of wins and losses, the Ming and the Japanese forces began to consider peace negotiations. Thanks to the Korean navy's dominance, the Japanese forces withdrew to the southeastern coast, and the Ming troops advanced southward to confront them. In the summer of 1593, a truce was declared so that diplomacy between the Ming and Japan could get underway. However, Toyotomi Hideyoshi, a megalomaniac in his own right, would not duly honor the Ming suzerainty, whereas the Ming court, for its part, would not acknowledge the rising independent power of Japan. The negotiations broke down, and in 1597 the war resumed.

For the Japanese generals, Yi Sunsin, now the commander-in-chief of all navy forces on the southern coast, was a serious obstacle. Thus they plotted to alienate Yi Sunsin. Sending a spy, they provided misinformation to the Chosŏn court about the location of the Japanese forces. The court then ordered Admiral Yi to attack that location. However, Yi, skeptical of the information, disobeyed. The court then fired Yi Sunsin from his post and imprisoned him. Thus, the Korean navy, which Yi had finally succeeded in organizing earlier in the war, was again set in disarray. Without navy support, the Chosŏn-Ming forces on land were pushed back to the capital by the Japanese. Desperate, the Chosŏn court finally decided to reinstate Yi Sunsin as navy commander-in-chief, who upon his release discovered that the Korean navy had only 12 warships left. On the 15th day of the ninth month in 1597, before he launched this tiny fleet to meet the 55 ships of the enemy, he wrote in his diary,

> At a staff meeting, I told all the captains, "Common military practice states that if you fight to die, you shall live, and if you try to live, you shall die. It also says that if one man guards a narrow passage he can fend off a thousand soldiers. This is our situation. If you disobey even the least of my orders you shall be punished without mercy according to military law." They gave me their solemn promise. (author's translation)

Indeed, Admiral Yi fought to die. He defeated the 55 enemy ships with his mere 12 and survived. Yi Sunsin regained the command of the sea with the support of the newly arrived Ming navy. On land, the enemy retreated to the southeastern coastal area as a cold winter closed in. The next year in 1598, Toyotomi Hideyoshi died. The Japanese invaders had no choice but to withdraw from the Korean peninsula. Chasing the retreating enemy on the sea, Yi Sunsin again fought heroically, burning hundreds of Japanese warships and killing numerous soldiers. Unfortunately, he was caught by a stray bullet from the retreating enemy, and thus passed away a great figure in Korean history.

After the War

The Imjin War devastated most of Korea, killing hundreds of thousands of Korean people. Tens of thousands were taken prisoner, and arable lands, houses, palaces, temples, and numerous precious cultural heritages were destroyed. The war, though tragic, was one of the few interactions between Korea, Japan, and China in the secluded premodern history of East Asia. This period, like the Mongol invasions in the thirteenth century, marked an enormous trafficking of population on the Korean peninsula. More than 200,000 Japanese troops as well as another 220,000 Chinese troops traversed Korean soil. The Ming troops, in particular, consisted of various ethnic groups from the continent. As their stay prolonged, a few of them, marrying into the populace, settled on the peninsula. Many Japanese prisoners of war became naturalized subjects by Korean marriages as well and formed their own communities. Many Korean people moved abroad, too. Most of those who married the Ming troops left Korea with their Chinese spouses for the main continent. Tens of thousand of Koreans were brought to the Japanese archipelago as prisoners of war. Many of these returned after the peace settlement between Chosŏn and the Tokugawa shogunate that had succeeded the hegemony of Japan after Toyotomi Hideyoshi's death. However, most of these prisoners stayed in the archipelago, while a few were sold to Portuguese merchants as slaves in Southeast Asia and Europe.

Among the Korean prisoners of war, many scholars and artisans were honorably received by the Japanese warlords, who rewarded them with official posts, salaries, and stipend lands. Japanese Neo-Confucianism in the seventeenth century is largely indebted to the Korean scholar prisoners of war, who became tutors of the warlords and the shoguns. Following the counsel of their Buddhist-monk advisers, some warlords collected many books about Neo-Confucianism, agriculture, and medicine during their occupation of Korean territory. Most of these books were reprinted in Japan after the war by printing technology obtained from Korean prisoners.

Among the artisans, the potters in particular were welcomed and highly compensated by the warlords. Since the earlier centuries, Japanese marauders had especially targeted Korean ceramics in their pillaging. The ceramics, used as mere vessels in Korea, were valued as precious treasures in Japan, where only wooden vessels were common. Given that the Zen Buddhist tea ceremony became a fashion among the Japanese ruling class, ceramic tea instruments were thought of as a sort of art collection. Thus, the Japanese warlords, when invading Korea, kept their eyes open for Korean potters and their technology, as well as raw material for producing ceramics.

In Korea, as Koryŏ celadon began to wane, porcelain known as *punch'ŏng* (*mishima* in Japanese) was developed with the establishment of the Chosŏn dynasty. While the former, with its unique color of blue monochrome, reflects the feminine taste of the sophisticated Koryŏ aristocracy, the latter, with its gray-blue or gray-yellow engravings, represents the dynamic and masculine temper of the early Chosŏn yangban. From the late fifteenth century, another type of porcelain was produced with the development of native glazes. These are the typical Chosŏn white porcelains known today, on which blue or red figures are gracefully engraved on a gray-white background.

Japanese warlords brought back not only the potters and the earthen materials of Korean soil but also the kilns themselves. After the war, Japanese ceramic manufacturing advanced remarkably thanks to those captured Korean potters. Today their descendants on Kyushu Island have proudly inherited the ancestors' ceramic artisanship. Indeed, the Imjin War was a ceramic war.

The Manchu Invasions

At the turn of the seventeenth century, the Jurchen Manchu, under Nurhachi, strengthened their hegemony in Manchuria and north China, taking advantage of the ailing Ming dynasty, which was harassed on all sides by the Mongols in the north; the Turks in the west; Europeans (such as the Portuguese) in the south; and finally, the Japanese in the east. After conquering the Liaodong peninsula in 1616, Nurhachi proclaimed the state of Later Jin, taking the name of the former Jurchen empire. Thus he was in a position to contend with the Ming and threaten Chosŏn. Among the literati cliques of the Chosŏn court after the Imjin War, the dominant and pragmatic Northerners chose a smart policy of neutrality toward the conflict between the Manchus and the Ming. However, the Westerners' clique soon overthrew the king in a coup d'état and turned to a more orthodox Neo-Confucian policy that insisted on loyalty to the Ming. As Korea became openly anti-Manchu, the Later Jin invaded the peninsula in 1627 on the pretext that the political coup was illegitimate. The Chosŏn court, overpowered by the invaders, negotiated for peace. Though the court did not officially recognize the Later Jin suzerainty, it was forced to accept their superiority on a diplomatic level.

By the time Hwang Taiqi succeeded his father Nurhachi, the Manchus had grown strong enough to conquer China Proper. Hwang Taiqi, later given the posthumous title of Taizong, changed the name of his empire in 1636 to the Qing and demanded that Chosŏn recognize his suzerainty. When the Westerner-dominated court rejected these demands, Taizong attacked Korea that very same year. He himself led a force of 100,000, consisting of Manchus, Mongols, and even Koreans who had previously surrendered to the Qing. Within five days, the capital was sacked. The king and the court escaped to a small fortress in the mountains and resisted for 45 days. Finally, the king surrendered. Humiliated, he was made to kowtow before Taizong during a ceremony in which he grudgingly accepted the *sadae* relationship with the Qing.

Recovery

The Imjin War had resulted in a change of government in Japan and in China, but Korea, the greatest victim of the war, did not see a change of dynasty. This factor of dynastic resilience is an important feature of Korean history that is seen repeatedly. Whereas the Japanese were driven off, with tremendous aid and expense, from Ming China, the Manchus came and left quickly, staying only long enough to secure a pledge of loyalty from the Korean court. Moreover, the devastation wrought by the Manchus was minimal compared to that of the Japanese. Ming China, which came to the aid of its "younger brother," Korea, suffered the heaviest political casualties. Weakened by the war effort against Japan and the incompetence of the emperor, the Ming court was toppled by the Manchus in 1644.

Surprisingly enough, the Korean people, who saw their king kowtowing to the haughty barbarian conqueror, did not show disdain toward their incompetent monarch and the ruling yangban class, but instead turned their strong animosity against the invaders. During the Imjin War as well, though the people suffered disappointment when their king abandoned the capital and fled to the north, they fought in the resistance under yangban leadership. There is no other reason to explain the people's support of such a weak ruling class but for the Neo-Confucian value of loyalty.

Moreover, the people's predisposition to xenophobia was revitalized after the two invasions from the neighboring "barbarians." After the Manchu invasion, the people's reaction is implicit in how they idolized three literati heroes who were executed by the invading forces for their anti-Manchu stands. Furthermore, specific plans for northward expeditions against Qing China, though not implemented, were promoted by the next king, who, as one of princes, had been imprisoned by the Manchus.

The pride and prejudice of the Korean people reconfirmed the traditional foreign-policy doctrine of the Chosŏn dynasty: *sadae kyorin*. *Sadae* (attendance on the great) meant that Koreans felt a moral obligation toward their "elder brother," Ming China, who had saved Korea from the Japanese invasion. Koreans outwardly practiced *sadae* to the Qing dynasty after the fall of the Ming, but inwardly they began to believe that they, not the Qing, were the true legitimate heirs of East-Asian civilization, even using the reign title of the last Ming emperor until the nineteenth century.

As for the *kyorin* (goodwill to neighbors) side of the doctrine, the Chosŏn court was satisfied to resume its traditional protocol of diplomatic superiority toward Japan. The protocol dictated that the Japanese envoy, the Tsushima lord, was not allowed to enter the capital, but made to stay at the Wa House in Pusan while his letters from the shogun were delivered. On the other hand, the Chosŏn court would send its envoy directly to Edo, the capital of the shogunate. This diplomatic policy would last until the nineteenth century, when the East-Asian world order would again collapse.

CONFUCIANIZATION

Quiet Change

The years after the Japanese and Manchu invasions, most of the seventeenth and eighteenth centuries, are dismissed by many scholars as uneventful, given that stability and progress were the quiet hallmarks of the period. It is interesting to note that in 1712 Korea erected a monument on Mt. Paektu, which came to be seen as the spiritual home of Korea, and in a sense, the symbol of the origin of the people. This important mountain peak, the highest point in Korea, was on the border with China. And although it is considered an important symbol, the border was never clearly defined and was thus the subject of some dispute with China. From this point in the eighteenth century, however, Korea's claim to the southern half of the mountain, which is the headwaters of the two rivers that form the kingdom's northern borders, the Yalu and the Tumen, has been well established.

Below a quiet political surface in the seventeenth and eighteenth centuries, many important changes took place. Some changes were tied to national and international events, while others were the product of a quiet evolution of society. Some histories dismiss the seventeenth century as simply a time of slow recovery from the two invasions. While that is true, that economic and social recovery took place, there were other things going on that were independent of the wars.

The seventeenth and eighteenth centuries, then, while overlooked by some as uneventful, were truly the hallmarks of the Chosŏn period. They were periods of peaceful progress. The Chosŏn dynasty was marred by the Japanese and Manchu invasion in the late sixteenth century and was eventually toppled by the foreign influence that began in the late nineteenth century, but the majority of the long, 514-year dynasty was characterized by great periods of peace, stability, and progress on a number of fronts.

Debate over Ritual and Confucian Family Life

During the reign of King Hyojong (1619–59), an event occurred that seemed inconsequential at the time but was to have a lasting impact on Korean society. The incident was a debate over ritual. According to Confucian ritual texts, the degree to which one mourns for the passing of a relative is defined by the duration of the mourning period. For instance, *sadaebu*, or scholar-officials, were to mourn for the passing of their parents for three years. The issue at court was complicated. The king's stepgrandmother had died. One literati clique at court argued that the king should mourn for three years; the other argued that one year of mourning was appropriate. The division at court was led by two senior scholar-officials. Song Siyŏl (1607–89) and the Westerners' clique on one side argued for one year of mourning, whereas Hŏ Mok (1595–1682) and the Southerners argued for three years. The Southerners won the debate and thereby secured positions in the court for members of their party, and the Westerners were left out.

To understand the depth of the impact of the ritual controversy at the court, we need to examine what was happening in the wider society. In the latter half of the seventeenth century, the Neo-Confucian revolution that helped launch the Chosŏn dynasty nearly three centuries earlier finally revolutionized the family. Prior to the mid-seventeenth-century household, matters could be characterized as pre-Confucian in many ways. For example, Confucian texts prescribe that ceremonies for the ancestors are the responsibility of the eldest son. The inheritance was also prescribed by primogeniture. But the earlier Korean practice was to divide the inheritance equally between the sons and the daughters, and the ceremonies were conducted on a rotational basis, with each sibling, male or female, oldest or youngest, taking turns hosting the ceremonies. This was in spite of the fact that the ritual texts said the eldest son had the responsibility alone.

The evidence for transformation from these earlier practices is found in inheritance documents from the late seventeenth century. In one, for example, the siblings that were dividing the inheritance after the death of the parents wrote that henceforth daughters were no longer to host the ceremonies. It said that somehow Korea had lost the way of the sages—it assumed that in the golden age of antiquity, Korea had done it right, had practiced primogeniture, but over the centuries had fallen into an uncivilized pattern of rotating the ceremonies between the siblings. The document then said that with the current division of property, daughters would no longer be given an amount equal to the sons, but rather they would be given one-third as much. The explanation was that since, by the ritual texts, sons mourned for three years at the passing of a parent, and daughters mourned for only one year, the daughter should have one-third as much property. The document went on to say that the daughters should no longer take a turn in the hosting of the ceremonies. In subsequent generations, the daughters' inheritance was reduced to zero (although one could argue that the dowry given a daughter at marriage became a kind of inheritance).

Another aspect of the Confucian transformation of Korea can be seen in the practice of adoption. As daughters lost their rights to inheritance, Korea borrowed another custom from China to solve the problem of not having a son—adopt the son of a brother or cousin, someone from the same bloodline. In the early Chosŏn period, a man without a son might adopt an heir, but the heir might have come from the mother's side of the family as much as from the husband's. And if a man had daughters in the first half of the Chosŏn dynasty, he did not have a need to adopt. In the latter half of the dynasty, he would certainly arrange to adopt a nephew. At this time, the percentages of families involved in adoptions rose to over 15 percent of the population, a figure close to the percentage of people in the population who did not naturally have a son. In other words, everyone who could adopt did adopt.

As with adoption and inheritance, other aspects of family life changed with this process of Confucianization. Marriage patterns that were once more flexible and pragmatic became almost completely patrilocal. That is to say, in the early half of the Chosŏn dynasty, newly married couples would in some cases live with the bride's family, in some cases with the groom's family, and in some cases they would set up a residence in a new place. After the transformation, the ideal case was to marry and live at the home of the groom, and the daughter-in-law would come from outside the village.

This practice led to the development of the single-surname villages that are so commonly found in Korean rural areas. These features of the Confucianization were particularly true of the upper class, the yangban *sadaebu*, although the lower classes eventually came to emulate the upper-class ideals to the extent that they could. In the case of villages becoming dominated by a single-surname group, a single lineage or clan, this was the mark of a yangban village. Mixed surnames in a village meant that it was the village of commoners. When one asks the residents of the typical single-surname village when the village was founded, the answer is often in the seventeenth century.

In fact, the development of the lineage itself was one of the features of the Confucianized society of the later Chosŏn period. These patrilineally organized lineage groups became the dominant feature of society. The organization was represented in a document, often in multiple volumes of a printed genealogy. The genealogy came to be a document that recorded the male descendants in some detail for all generations possible but only listed the daughters as marrying out to a particular household of another lineage group. The daughters' descendants were usually not recorded at all, but an exception was made if one of their sons, or sometimes a grandson, achieved a prominent position in the government; otherwise, the daughters' line ended with the notation of whom she married.

Printed genealogies of the early Chosŏn period were not like that at all. Rather, since all descendants were equal, sons and daughters and their lines of descent were kept in full detail. Thus, the Andong Kwŏn genealogy of 1476, the earliest such document extant, contained over 10,000 names, but only a minority of them were named Kwŏn. In posttransformation documents, they did not list the surname with each entry because everyone obviously had the same surname.

The clan or lineage (or, perhaps more accurately, the patrilineage) came to groups of people thought to be related to one another. As such, it was a group of men related to men through male ties. Wives came from outside, did not change their surnames, and, although buried with their husbands, were not considered members of the lineage. Daughters married out and were not considered members of their natal lineage. A man with grandchildren would consider those of his surname (that is, members of the patrilineage) as his real grandchildren, whereas those born to his daughters had different surnames, were not considered part of the lineage, and were called *oeson*, or "outside grandchildren." If a man had three grandchildren by only his daughters, when asked if he had any grandchildren, he would most likely say no.

Causes of Change

In various ways—inheritance, adoption, marriage, clan organization, village structure, and even the popular genealogy—we see that the social life of Koreans changed radically in the late seventeenth century. There were probably three causes for the change to take place at that time. First was the natural development of Confucianism and Neo-Confucianism. Confucianism had been around since the fifth century or so, and its influence had gradually grown. Neo-Confucianism created a new following when it was introduced in the late fourteenth century. And gradually it came to play a greater role in society and ideology.

These changes in society were probably a result of population pressures. We know that the population of Korea was growing, and that sometime in the seventeenth century it reached a kind of saturation point where population density began to push the limits of the productivity of the land. Prior to the seventeenth century, a bad year or famine did not necessarily mean death. However, after the seventeenth century, there were several cases where bad harvests meant starvation. In other countries, too, growth in population has led to changes in inheritance and social practices.

The final cause of change may have been that revealed by the ritual controversy at court mentioned above. Underlying the great concern over proper ritual in the late seventeenth century was the fact that the Ming dynasty had fallen and had been replaced by a non-Chinese, barbarian Manchu dynasty. Korea, under the Chosŏn court, had considered itself the "younger brother" of "elder brother" China. Placing the international relation in familial terminology was one of the manifestations of a Confucian orientation to the world. With the demise of Ming China, without an older brother, and with the court of China Proper in the hands of barbarians, Korea felt the impetus to step up and become the standard-bearer of Confucianism in the world. Korea's identity, based on such a strong Confucian view of the world, left it with no choice but to become the standard of orthodoxy.

These factors all came together to make late Chosŏn the most ideal Confucian society ever to exist at any time or any place on this planet. It became much more orthodox than China had been at any point in its history. Perhaps it was a function of scale. China was so large that there was always room for differing belief systems. Korea was a perfect size, smaller than China, to become thoroughly orthodox and thoroughly committed to Confucian ideal.

Yŏngjo

The eighteenth century was remarkably stable. There were only three kings that ruled in the hundred years from 1700 to 1800. One ruled for the first quarter century, one ruled for the middle half century, and one ruled for the last quarter century. Yŏngjo (1694–1776), who ruled for 52 years, from 1724 to 1776, was the longest-reigning king of the Chosŏn dynasty. His reign was remarkable, and in all regards was probably the most notable of the Chosŏn kingdom, second only to Sejong the Great. His otherwise sterling reign was marred by two events, one small and in dispute, and one large and tragic.

The minor event, and somewhat in dispute, surrounded Yŏngjo's rise to the throne. He succeeded his half brother, who died under somewhat suspicious circumstances at the age of 36 after only three years on the throne. Since Yŏngjo was the beneficiary of this untimely death, suspicions naturally arose that Yŏngjo had poisoned his brother. But the case was never proven and did not result in the dethronement of the king, as was the case when King Kwanghaegun (1575–1641) was dethroned in part because of the murder of his stepmother.

The second case was complicated and painful. Yŏngjo's heirs to the throne were limited. He had only two sons, and one died young, leaving only one son as candidate for crown prince. He was known as Prince Sado (1735–61). Sado was apparently a victim of a mental disorder. His behavior was violent at times and derelict at others. His violence was unleashed on servants and occasionally resulted in deaths. His dereliction was marked by leaving the palace for questionable purposes, such as sexual misbehavior. Yŏngjo, in his attempt to train and correct his wayward son, tried several things, including even abdicating and turning the throne over to Sado to see if that would make him more serious about his role. It did not. Thus, Yŏngjo retook the throne and tried other methods to prepare Sado.

Finally, Yŏngjo saw no other alternative but to eliminate his son. Yŏngjo had a grandson who indeed became his successor and is known as Chŏngjo (1752–1800). Therefore, with an heir secured, Yŏngjo decided the kingdom would be better off without Sado. Yŏngjo first ordered his son to kill himself. Sado refused and begged for another chance. Finally, on a certain day in August of 1761, Yŏngjo dressed in his military uniform and marched into the courtyard of the crown prince's section of the palace. Yŏngjo again demanded that Sado do the honorable thing and kill himself. He again refused and begged for his life. Yŏngjo then did an unusual thing: he called for the servants to bring in a rice chest. A large wooden chest was hauled in, and Sado was ordered to climb inside.

The witnesses were not sure what the king had in mind and did not imagine that Sado would never be allowed to crawl out of the chest. However, eight days later, Sado died. At one point a servant of Sado squeezed some grains of rice through the cracks in the wooden chest. Yŏngjo heard of it and had the servant executed. Yŏngjo intended for Sado to die of starvation or suffocation. It appeared that in the king's mind, any means of death that would draw the blood or mar the body of a royal person would be unacceptable, with the exception of suicide. The witnesses of this tragedy included the crown prince's wife, Lady Hyegyŏng (1735–1815). As the mother of Chŏngjo, who at the time was only nine years of age, she was concerned that the way the death of Sado would impact the reign of her son. She thus wrote a series of memoirs chronicling the death of her husband.

When Yŏngjo died, at the age of 80, the throne was inherited by Chŏngjo, who was by then 24. Chŏngjo lamented the death of his father and chose to believe that it was not the fault of his grandfather but rather the result of the actions of a segment of the bureaucracy. Chŏngjo, therefore, revived Yŏngjo's *t'angp'yŏng* (impartiality) policy and recruited scholar-officials from all literati cliques.

Sirhak

Thus, in the eighteenth century young scholar-officials, who had been taught by creative literati mentors, began to enter the court. A new brand of philosophy, known as *sirhak*, or "practical learning," had been developed since the seventeenth century, mostly by the off-court scholars, such as Yu Hyŏngwŏn (1622–73) and Yi Ik (1681–1763). These scholars had urged practical reforms of Confucian statecraft, criticizing the established policies based on the orthodox Neo-Confucianism. Yu Hyŏngwŏn is known as the harbinger of this school of thought, with his mammoth writings on these ideal reforms. For example, he suggested a new recruiting system in the educational institutions based on recommendation. Many of these scholars argued that the examination system should be revised to include practical administrative matters, not merely the classics and philosophy, as was the case at the time. Whereas this new approach to philosophy attracted many thinkers and writers, in the end, the tradition won and the exams were not revised. Moreover, the *sirhak* advocates were sometimes considered heterodox and on the fringe.

In 1776, Chŏngjo, known as the sage-king, established the Kyujangkak, a royal academy, at the palace. Like Sejong the Great, he recruited brilliant young scholars there and charged them to advise him personally in policy decisions. Chŏng Yagyong (1762–1836) became one of Chŏngjo's favorite scholar-officials. Chŏng, who inherited the mantle of the *sirhak* from Yu Hyŏngwŏn and Yi Ik, further developed this school of thought in the nineteenth century with his newly obtained knowledge of Western science, which had been creeping into Korea in the late eighteenth century by Korean envoys to Beijing.

Chŏngjo wanted to demonstrate his filial piety to his father, Prince Sado, by constructing a fortress near his father's tomb to the south of Seoul. The citadel, known as Hwasŏng Fortress in today's city of Suwŏn, was recently restored according to the 10-volume work printed with metal type, *Records of the Hwasŏng Fortress Construction.* The site was designated as a World Cultural Heritage by UNESCO in 1997. The architect of this fortress was Chŏng Yagyong, who had applied the scientific knowledge of the contemporary *sirhak* thinkers. Chŏngjo frequently visited the citadel while he worshipped his father's tomb nearby. An eightfold screen painting of the royal procession to Hwasŏng and the memorial ceremonies for Prince Sado can now be seen at the National Museum in Seoul.

MERCANTILISM

There were many economic changes in society in the late seventeenth century. Merchant activities were prospering. Men who had been merely tax agents, moving goods from the countryside to Seoul, started to prosper with extra trade associated with tax goods. Furthermore, a monetary reform helped to move the market system forward. Traditional markets stood every five days in major towns in the country, which numbered more than 1,000 in the mid-eighteenth century. Particularly, these markets near the ports, due to their large-scale transactions, contributed to the rise of brokers, warehousemen, innkeepers, and moneylenders. As a result, wholesalers on a national scale appeared in major commercial centers like Kaesŏng, Pyongyang, Ŭiju, and Tongnae. Ŭiju, a northwestern city on the mouth of the Yalu River, and Tongnae, a southeastern city, became the international trade ports with the Manchus and Japan.

Trade had previously been conducted on the basis of barter, and taxes had been paid in goods such as rice; bolts of cloth; and specialty items, including gold, fur, and ginseng. However, the government began to mint coins in 1678. Copper coins, with the Chinese characters *sangp'yŏng t'ongbo*, meaning "ever-constant treasure of commerce," became the coin of the realm. At times Chinese coins had been used, but now Korea had its own currency. The adoption of currency was not easy, and some barter trade continued, but eventually the coins became the medium of exchange in the latter part of the eighteenth century. For a time, use of the coins was hampered by hoarding, and the value of the coins themselves, rather than land, became the measure of wealth. But in spite of the hoarding, the government continued to mint the coins.

With the changes in currency and the market came changes in taxation. Taxes had previously been figured not so much on the amount of land one owned, but on the yield. Moreover, certain land was seen as more productive than others. In fact, there were five levels of fertility figured into the value of each parcel of land. Tax codes had become extremely complicated. However, in the late seventeenth century, a new tax code was implemented. Called the *taedong* reform, it simplified taxes. Later, in the mid-eighteenth century, the corvée labor system was revised under what was called the *kyunyŏk* reform, making work hours more evenly distributed and fair.

Thanks to the *taedong* reform, handicraft industries thrived. As tax payments, the government now collected rice, bolts of cloth, or currency, and no longer demanded necessary goods, such as weapons, paper, nails, ceramics, silks, brassware, and coins. Instead, it began to buy these items. Moreover, some of these articles were also in demand within the private sector. In the late eighteenth century, some handicraft industrialists maintained factories and hired paid laborers. Sometimes rich merchants invested in these to provide raw materials.

Mining industries began to also develop in the late seventeenth century when the government allowed private mining. In the initial stages, silver was a popular product, meeting a demand from Qing China, which had begun to cast silver currency. However, during the mid-eighteenth century, the government was again forced to ban private mining because many peasants deserted the fields in order to work in the new industry. Nonetheless, the merchant investors continued to illegally develop mines and hire laborers. In the late eighteenth century, they began to mine gold.

There were developments in agriculture as well. Transplantation replaced direct seeding, and the rice crop yield increased dramatically. And with more nutrition, the population began to grow. Studies on this growth have been not easy because of a lack of credibility in the censuses. Given that most of the censuses implemented in the Chosŏn period surveyed data for tax and corvée purposes, people often intentionally omitted real members of their families. For example, a census done in 1639 reports Korea's population as only 1,520,000. However, scholars believe the real number was likely much higher. In view of the number in the 1925 census, 19,020,000, they estimate Korea's population as 8–9 million in the mid-seventeenth century, and 13–14 million in the mid-eighteenth century.

SOCIAL MOBILITY

The Chosŏn kingdom is generally thought of as a status society where social mobility was almost impossible among the four social strata: *yangban, chungin* (middle people), *yangin* (commoners), and *ch'ŏnin* (base people). This latter class included the *nobi* (slaves). In the early Chosŏn period, these statuses were principally hereditary, and intermarriages were rarely seen. Particularly, the walls between the yangban and other statuses, or between the commoners and slaves or base people, were almost impenetrable. The *yangin* had opportunity to be educated if they were economically supported, and therefore they were technically able to become yangban if they passed the civil-service exam. But in fact, the commoners, who were mostly poor farmers, were unable to compete in the exam with the yangban, who could concentrate on their education without worrying about their livelihood. Moreover, to take the exam, one was required to enter genealogical information, of which the commoners were unable to keep records.

The base people had no opportunity whatsoever to change their hereditary status. However, the wars and later the industrial developments stirred the traditional social-status system, particularly that of the *nobi*. During the Imjin War, the government recruited slaves for the army, among whom many were freed for their service. Moreover, a new law, under which children of commoner mothers would be commoners despite their father's slave status, was implemented in 1731. This reflected a growth of intermarriages between commoners and slaves in this period. Moreover, an increasing number of slaves escaped from their masters and hid themselves as commoners. Thus, the *nobi* population decreased remarkably. However, the legal slave manumission would not be enacted until the 1894 reforms.

The yangban attempted to exclude themselves from the other statuses in order to maintain their privileges. Unlike China and other East-Asian societies, the Chosŏn kingdom discriminated against the *sŏja*, descendants of secondary wives or concubines. Politically, legal discrimination against *sŏja* was initiated in 1400 by King T'aejong, who had struggled with his half brother for the throne. Since the early period, the State Code recognized only one legal wife, although many legal submarital relations were allowed. Given that most of the *sŏja* were descendants of yangban, this effectively restricted the number of true yangban who competed for limited posts in the court. As the economy grew in the later Chosŏn period, rich commoners often bought yangban genealogies in order to take the *kwagŏ*. Therefore, the yangban, initially only 10 percent of the total population, continued to increase to more than 50 percent at the turn of the nineteenth century.

Chungin, or middle people, which included medical doctors, interpreters, astronomers, lawyer, and local clerks, were a marginal group between the ruling yangban and commoner *yangin*. Many *sŏja*, who were banned from entering the yangban class, often joined the *chungin*. Though their number was not significant in the total population, *chungin* played important roles in Chosŏn society due to their professions. In the nineteenth century, *chungin* emerged in the limelight for adopting Western civilization. For example, the local clerks in the bureaucracy, or *ajŏn*, aptly adjusted to the new paradigm in the early twentieth century, achieving landownership under the modern land-registration system enforced by the Japanese colonialists.

LITERATURE AND ARTS

This change in social mobility was well portrayed in the late Chosŏn literature. In the early seventeenth century, Hŏ Kyun (1569–1618) wrote a novel in hangul entitled *The Story of Hong Kiltong*, in which the protagonist, a *sŏja*, fights against corrupt yangban officials and, like Robin Hood, gives to the poor commoners. The author criticized not only the corruption of yangban politics but also the contradiction of *sŏja* discrimination. In the mid-eighteenth century, Pak Chiwŏn (1737–1805) exposed the hypocrisy of the yangban status in his short novel *The Story of Hŏ Saeng*. The yangban hero, disillusioned by social realities, engaged in commerce, a despicable job for his class. He thereby accumulated tremendous wealth by cornering the market.

Throughout the eighteenth century, many novels in hangul by anonymous authors became popular among the people. *The Story of Ch'unhyang*, which deals with a love story between a yangban and a *kisaeng*, or court lady, touched the audience of this period with the heroine's integrity toward her lover. Here, too, we can find a corrupt yangban official in the magistrate villain. The happy ending to the story, with an interstatus marriage, reflects the change of status consciousness in the eighteenth century. Later, in the nineteenth century, *The Story of Ch'unhyang* became one of the most popular repertoires for pansori, a unique traditional performance art in Korea. Pansori, scripts of which Sin Chaehyo (1812–84) compiled, is a musical monodrama performed by one singer-actor or actress with one drummer and is still popular in today's Korea. Unlike Chinese Peking opera or Japanese kabuki, the singer-actor or actress played all the various character roles with different tones and accents.

The eighteenth-century Chosŏn is often called a cultural renaissance period. New trends in philosophy and literature corresponded with new developments in arts. *Chin'gyŏng sansu*, or true-view landscape painting, was developed at this time. Painters began to draw native pastoral scenes in Korea rather than the commonly copied landscapes of south China, which they had never seen. Chŏng Sŏn (1676–1759) began to paint beautiful scenes of Korea's famous Mt. Kŭmkang, otherwise known as Diamond Mountain. However, true-view landscape painting was not created only in Korea. It had been earlier created by Chinese painters who wanted variety. Subsequently, it spread to Korea, Vietnam, and Japan.

According to Dr. Wen Fong, chief curator for Asian arts at the Metropolitan Museum in New York, landscape painting first appeared in world history in tenth-century Song China. In Europe, the first landscape paintings did not appear until the eighteenth century in the Netherlands. Kuo Xi's landscape in the tenth century depicted a pastoral scene in south China, which Song scholar-officials believed to be the most beautiful scene in the world. Consequently, scenes of south China began to spread throughout East Asia. Later on, various schools of landscape painting developed, but until the true-view fashion appeared, these consistently used south China as subject matter. Landscape paintings were first brought to Korea by diplomatic envoys in the thirteenth century. Korean painters meticulously copied the originals, and these precious works were shared among the Koryŏ scholar-officials. Through copying these works, the Korean painters developed their own technique.

In Chosŏn society, painters were treated as mere artisans, a lower social status. The yangban rarely engaged in painting, and instead practiced calligraphy as an art. Kim Hongdo (pen name Tanwŏn, 1745–?) was an unusual yangban in that he devoted himself to painting many inspired works, including genre paintings and true-view landscapes. Under King Chŏngjo's favor, he led the eighteenth-century court art in Korea.

PROS AND CONS OF CONFUCIANISM

Korea had achieved a kind of perfection in its acceptance of Confucianism. Although Confucianism had entered Korea in the Three Kingdoms period and had grown in influence and practice for more than 12 centuries, it was in the late seventeenth and eighteenth centuries that it reached its highest level of acceptance. Chosŏn Korea can be called the most Confucian of any state at any time on this planet. In the nineteenth century, the *sirhak* philosophers began to change Confucianism and adapt it to the times. But the Neo-Confucian form continued to dominate the thoughts and minds of Koreans.

Later scholars were to look back on this "perfection" of Confucianism and critique it for both its positive and negative points. On the positive side, Confucianism gave the state and society great stability. The Chosŏn dynasty was one of the longest and most stable of dynasties in the history of the world. Unfortunately, some remnant of the colonial-period rationalization for Japan's ending the dynasty, that it was "stagnant," still persists in the minds of some Koreans. The opposite of stagnant—vibrant, stable, long-lived, dynamic—is a better description of the dynasty. And much of that success is due to its Confucian underpinnings and Confucian transformations that continued to unfold throughout the 500-year history of the dynasty.

There were other critics, however. Confucianism was seen as relying too much on notoriety, to the exclusion of those who were not recognized. It is criticized for emphasizing family to the point of rampant nepotism. While loyalty is a positive attribute, critics said that group loyalty created cliques and factions that served their particular need more than the needs of wider society. And by idealizing the golden age of Confucius, critics have said that Korea failed to modernize and was left behind when the industrial revolution and modernization came knocking at the door.

However, modern social scientists began to rethink the Confucian tradition in East Asia when South Korea, Japan, Taiwan, Hong Kong, and Singapore exhibited impressive economic growth in the late twentieth century. The reoriented perspective in modern social sciences reevaluates the contribution of the Confucian tradition shared by these East-Asian countries. These arguments are reinforced by the recent economic success in China, the mother country of Confucius.

6

Modernization

CATHOLICISM AND CAPITALISM

Korea existed under the East-Asian world order until the mid-nineteenth century. The external policy of the kingdom of Chosŏn traditionally banned any open overseas relations not defined by the *sadae kyorin* doctrine. This meant that Korean external relationships were narrowly limited to China and Japan, and then only through controlled official channels. Since 1636, Chosŏn, under a nominal tribute relationship to the Qing court, practiced *sadae* in recognition of the empire's suzerainty. As for Japan, Chosŏn's diplomacy with the Tokugawa shogunate since 1609 continued via the Tsushima lord, who himself paid nominal tribute to the Chosŏn court.

In the mid-nineteenth century, however, this traditional East-Asian world order began to collapse. Qing suzerainty was damaged by the 1842 Nanjing Treaty, in which the Qing court accepted the loss of the Opium War with Great Britain, one of the "Western barbarians." Tokugawa Japan was forced to open its ports in 1854 to the United States after being impressed by Commodore Mathew C. Perry's fleet. In 1860, the Qing court had to cede the Maritime Province in Manchuria to Russia, thereby extending the Russian borders to Korea. However, because the Korean peninsula was buffered by the Japanese archipelago to the east and south and by the Chinese continent to the west and north, contact with the Western powers was delayed for a few more decades.

Unlike Japan, which had traded with the Portuguese and Dutch for centuries and was thus more prepared for extensive Westernization, Korea was lukewarm to Western influence, restricting outside contact with a maritime ban on its ports. To the Western powers that had already reached East Asia in the sixteenth century, Korea was indeed the last "hermit kingdom," its ruling yangban and people stubbornly adhering to orthodox Neo-Confucianism.

However, no matter how thoroughly the Chosŏn court isolated its kingdom, waves of Western influence began to seep into the Korean peninsula. Notably, much of this influence came from Beijing, where Western books and such conveniences as cotton cloth were in abundance, having been brought in by Catholic missionaries and merchants. Thus, Catholicism and capitalism were first introduced to Korea in the form of books and products. This is contrary to the typical progression of European imperialism into East-Asian kingdoms in the nineteenth century: first by missionary, then by cannon, and finally by merchandise.

Catholicism was first introduced in Korea during the late sixteenth and early seventeenth centuries by Catholic books translated into Chinese and brought back by Korean envoys to Beijing. However, Catholicism was not thought of as a religion but as "Western Learning." This new kind of thought influenced contemporary scholars to rethink orthodox Neo-Confucianism and to compare it with Buddhism and Taoism. In the late eighteenth century, some scholar-officials who had been politically alienated from the court began to take an interest in Catholicism. Therefore, Korean Catholicism is unique in the fact that it was not propagated directly by foreign missionaries but by native Koreans themselves. The first Korean Catholic convert, Yi Sŭnghun (1756–1801), was baptized in 1784 by a Western missionary when he accompanied his envoy father to Beijing. As Catholicism spread, it collected among its early followers an eclectic group of unfortunate yangban, clerks, interpreters, herb doctors, and some literate commoners.

As the growing number of converts increased, the ruling Neo-Confucian yangban urged the court to suppress it, citing a neglect of ancestor worship and violation of the law that banned contact with foreigners. In 1785, the court eventually condemned Catholicism as heretical to orthodoxy and outlawed the import of Catholic and scientific books. It even executed one of the converts who neglected to honor his deceased mother. The crisis-conscious Neo-Confucian yangban thereafter

launched a purist movement known as *wijŏng ch'ŏksa* (defending orthodoxy and rejecting heterodoxy). As the literati clique, known as the Pa-
triarchs, dominated the court at the turn of nineteenth century, Catholic
persecution exploded with the 1801 execution of more than 300 converts,
most of who belonged to the political opposition, the Southerner clique.
This slaughter also included Yi Sŭnghun and a Chinese priest.

The nineteenth-century Catholic persecution further isolated the kingdom of Chosŏn, and thus effectively prevented modernization, for a considerable period of time. In spite of the intermittent reform movements of
the Confucian statecraft, the ruling yangban were incapable of nurturing
the seeds of capitalism sown on the soil of growing commerce and agriculture. Discontent with socioeconomic rigidity and the decadent irregularities and corruption in the ruling class, the people began to rebel against
the incompetent monarchy. In 1811, Hong Kyŏngnae (1780–1812), a yangban who failed the civil-service exam, rallied people in the northwestern
province in an attempt to overthrow the throne. After five months, the
government army finally suppressed his rebellion. Fifty years later, another serious peasant uprising would occur in Chinju. Caused by the provincial magistrate's tax irregularities, the Chinju insurrection in 1862 was
organized by literate commoners in order to defend the people's interests
against the corrupt local functionaries. Thousands of angry people in the
neighboring countryside swarmed into the walled city of Chinju, arresting
the military commander and killing the clerks.

TAEWŎN'GUN

The 25th king of Chosŏn passed away in 1864 without an heir. At that
time, the Chosŏn court was dominated by a family of in-laws to the throne.
This family, part of the Patriarch literati clique, originated in Andong and
were thus known as the Andong Kims. However, the queen dowager, who
according to traditional practice was authorized to choose the heir, came
from the rival Cho family from P'ungyang. In order to circumvent the
Andong Kims, she unexpectedly picked as heir the 11-year-old son of
Prince Hŭngsŏn of the royal family. This resulted in an unusual transfer
of power within the authoritarian monarchy, as Prince Hŭngsŏn thereby
received the title of Taewŏn'gun (Grand Prince) and took charge of the
kingdom until his son came of age. Thus, Hŭngsŏn Taewŏn'gun (1820–
98), the de facto king of Chosŏn, led Korea into one of its most critical
stages in history, from 1864 to 1874.

Taewŏn'gun, born in the royal family and educated in Neo-
Confucianism, was a dedicated monarchist who lamented the corruption

and irregularities committed under the century-old rule of the Patriarch clique, the Andong Kims in particular. However, until he came to full power, he pretended to have no political ambition, avoiding the court and maneuvering behind the scenes. His advent as regent was a surprise to the established in-law family rulers. Afterwards, it was only natural for him to purge the Andong Kims from the court and abolish a large segment of the *sŏwŏn*, the political power bases of yangban in the provinces. His regime consisted of non-yangban clerks or commoners and formerly alienated literati cliques, such as the Southerners. Thus, sympathetic to the plight of the peasants, Taewŏn'gun endeavored to improve the grain-market system, which was a major cause of the rebellions. However, the chronic decadence of Chosŏn's authoritarian monarchy overshadowed most of Taewŏn'gun's attempts at reform.

In order to regain the people's confidence in the monarchy, he undertook the ambitious task of rebuilding the Kyŏngbok Palace, which had been burned during the Imjin War. Unfortunately, the kingdom's finances were not capable of supporting the costly burden of the construction. Nevertheless, Taewŏn'gun was bold enough to impose military tax on the formerly tax-exempt yangban. Besides taxes, he forced private donations from the people to cover the expenses. He mobilized a workforce from all of the provinces and used entertainers skilled in traditional music and dance to encourage the laborers. Interestingly enough, one can still see such entertainment performed at work sites in today's North Korea.

Taewŏn'gun's practical Confucian statecraft succeeded in tempering the people's discontent with decadent in-law politics. However, external powers were now seeking entry into the hermit kingdom. Contact with imperialist nations began in 1832 when an English merchant ship landed on the western coast. The crew was promptly sent on its way. Over the next two decades, appearances of Western warships, including those of the British, French, and Russians, became more common. These ships sailed around the coasts of Korea seeking contact with the court, but their overtures, which disregarded traditional East-Asian world-order diplomacy, were consistently rebuffed. In the early summer of 1866, the American merchant ship *Surprise* shipwrecked near the northwestern coast and was rescued by the local officials. The captain and crew, at first afraid of any hostility Koreans may have harbored toward foreigners, were surprised at their rescuers' unexpected hospitality. The Korean officials returned them to China without harm, believing that they did not intentionally violate traditional diplomacy. Two months later, another American merchant ship, the USS *General Sherman*, armed with cannons, penetrated the Taedong River as far as Pyongyang, seeking trade. This time, Korean soldiers, helped by the local people, burned the ship and killed its crew. Pak Kyusu (1807–77), then magistrate of Pyongyang, believed that they had violated the traditional world order by attempting direct contact with local Koreans without undergoing the proper diplomatic process of East Asia.

Taewŏn'gun was not informed enough about the Western world to understand the possible benefits, and inevitability, of opening Korea to outsiders. He was, as the nineteenth-century American missionary Homer Hulbert had observed, a leader of "commanding personality with inflexible will." Indeed, strictly adhering to the traditional East-Asian world order, Taewŏn'gun rejected any direct contact with the West without recognition from the Chinese sovereignty. His policy reflected the strong China-centered perspective among the ruling yangban as well as the commoners who were generally absorbed in Neo-Confucianism. Strengthening the military, Taewŏn'gun and the court were determined to fight against any inappropriate challenge from the Western barbarians. He ordered the erection throughout the country of many steles on which were inscribed, "To not fight against the invading Western barbarians and instead negotiate for peace is to sell the country" (author's translation).

At the turn of 1866, Taewŏn'gun, following strong suggestions from the Neo-Confucian court, decided to again suppress the spread of Catholicism. Thanks to 12 bold French Jesuit priests who had infiltrated the Korean peninsula, the number of Catholic converts had increased in this period to approximately 23,000. About 8,000 Korean converts and nine of the French missionaries were executed because the court feared that Catholicism propagated by the French priests might facilitate future external interference. Ironically, the execution of the French priests brought military intervention regardless. The diplomatic agency of Napoléon III in China, hearing from one of the French priests who had escaped, decided to retaliate against Korea. In the autumn of 1866, a French fleet of seven warships under the command of Admiral Rose invaded Kanghwa Island, which guarded western routes to the capital. The French forces landed, defeated the Korean garrison, and sacked the town. During the one-month occupation of the walled city, they demanded that the court punish those who had executed the French missionaries. Meanwhile, they pillaged gold and silver ingots; cannons and rifles; and books, including those printed with metal type. Much of this loot is now collected at the Bibliothèque Nationale of Paris. However, the French fleet could not subdue the rest of the Korean forces. These were armed with guns and cannons behind other fortresses stationed throughout the island. Eventually the French fleet withdrew without any diplomatic achievement. With this minor battle against the French empire, Taewŏn'gun and the court became confident they could resist the Western powers.

In 1871, five years after the burning of the *General Sherman* in the Tae-dong River, the U.S. government decided to use the incident as a pretext to force Korea to open its doors for trade. The U.S. minister to Beijing, Frederick F. Low, and the commander of the U.S. Asiatic Squadron, Rear Admiral John Rodgers, were ordered to proceed into Korean waters with a fleet of five warships. Overconfident, they entered into the Kanghwa Strait, where the shores were heavily guarded by strengthened fortifica-tions after the French invasion. The Korean batteries opened fire first. Although U.S. marines were able to capture two fortresses, the Korean defenders doggedly resisted and inflicted heavy casualties on the Amer-ican attackers. Thus, the short war between the United States and Korea ended without any political results.

Taewŏn'gun, encouraged by his recent victories over France and the United States, insisted on continuing the traditional *kyorin* relationship with Japan, which was now demanding a new diplomatic protocol ac-cording to international law. Since the Meiji Restoration in 1868, Japan had remodeled its political system after a Western-style constitutional monarchy. Therefore, the Tsushima lord was no longer in a position to mediate Japanese diplomacy with Korea. Taewŏn'gun thus began to cate-gorize Japan among the "Western barbarians" who lay beyond the East-Asian world order. His anti-Western policy was equally anti-Japanese.

However, Taewŏn'gun was soon forced to retreat from power as his son had grown older and was ready to assume the throne. The shift of power began with a denunciation by a bold scholar-official named Ch'oe Ikhyŏn (1833–1906), who criticized Taewŏn'gun's domestic despotism. Ironically, Ch'oe was a Neo-Confucian conservative whose ideology coincided with the prince regent's isolation policies. However, he was politically backed by the queen, whose family, the Mins, were to become rivals of Tae-wŏn'gun. Though hand-picked by her father-in-law to be the king's wife, Queen Min (1851–95) had been quietly nurturing her influence in the court. As a result, Taewŏn'gun's own influence soon waned. The king (1852–1919), known posthumously as Kojong, would eventually be dom-inated by his in-law family. But in 1873, for the time being, he emerged as an independent monarch who could personally rule his kingdom.

OPEN PORTS

The Japanese returned in 1874 with a renewed determination to break Chosŏn from the traditional East-Asian world order. However, after Taewŏn'gun had repelled the two Western challenges on Kanghwa Island, Koreans were eager to demonstrate to Japan the superiority of the Confucian state. Japan sent a letter to the Chosŏn court demanding trade. The letter was not written in the traditional *kyorin* format but with a new diplomatic protocol based on international law. This move was supported by the Meiji slogan of "rich nation and strong military" (*fukoku kyohei* in Japanese). Prior to this, certain impatient Japanese politicians advocated *seikanron*, a conquer-Korea policy. However, this radical policy was defeated by anti-*seikanron* advocates, who believed Japan's national power was not yet sufficient. Therefore, they chose diplomatic rapprochement instead.

King Kojong, who inherited a seemingly self-sufficient country from his father, Taewŏn'gun, was quite eager to reform the monarchy. In the early period of the young king's reign, he was relatively free from the Min in-law clan's influence. Thus he could appoint as his advisers more pragmatic officials like Pak Kyusu, a grandson of Pak Chiwŏn, the famous *sirhak* scholar-official. Known as the Pyongyang magistrate who ordered the burning of the *General Sherman* in 1866, Pak Kyusu later became a supporter of a more open foreign policy through his experiences as an envoy in Beijing. King Kojong was eager to know what was happening in the world beyond Korea's borders, listening carefully to the reports brought back from China. He was aware that China had begun to promote its "wealth and strength" policy by integrating Western science and technology with Chinese learning. Above all, the king knew that his kingdom lacked sufficient military strength to defend itself from foreign powers.

However, King Kojong's court was far from accepting the new world order that Japan sought to introduce to Korea. Only a few officials like Pak Kyusu, who understood the late-nineteenth-century reality in East Asia, were in favor of the king accepting the Japanese letter. Most of the court officials were conservative hard-liners who rejected the Japanese challenge to tradition. To the Korean people of this time, who had no idea or perspective on the world's capitalistic modernization, the collapse of the East-Asian world order meant a crisis of security. Thus, they could not accept this letter that went beyond traditional diplomacy. Meiji Japan eventually decided to use the same means to open Korea as the Western powers had used to open Japan: military intimidation.

On the 20th of September in 1875, the Japanese warship *Unyokan*, operating in Korean waters, approached Kanghwa Island, which was considered a "door to the capital." It was only natural for the Korean shore batteries to fire warning shots on the spying foreign warship. On the pretext of retaliating against these warning shots, the *Unyokan* attacked the

Korean batteries, landing on a neighboring island and killing many Korean soldiers. They also looted the island villages, capturing weapons and gunpowder. This resulted in the Kanghwa Treaty on February 26, 1876, Korea's first modern treaty with a foreign country. The Chosŏn court, intimidated by the demonstration of Japanese military might, had no choice but to accept, though grudgingly, the unequal treaty in the name of friendship, commerce, and navigation. Such is what Japan had experienced from the Western powers decades previously. And yet the two countries understood the treaty in different ways: Korea was complacent in resuming what they thought was a still traditional relationship with Japan, whereas Japan was proud of undermining one of the most crucial pillars of the old East-Asian world order.

Watching the Japanese initiative in opening Chosŏn, the Qing court felt its security threatened by future Japanese influence on the Korean peninsula and in Manchuria. Viceroy Li Hongzhang (1823–1901), the architect of nineteenth-century Chinese diplomacy, devised a strategy to curb Japanese ambition towards the continent by introducing Western powers into Korea. Given that the Chosŏn court was still practicing its nominal tribute diplomacy toward the Qing, he sent formal as well as secret messages to King Kojong and those of his officials who were more aware of the outside world. This was to promote "friendship and commerce treaties" with the Western powers. In 1880, Huang Zunxien, a Chinese diplomat in Tokyo, delivered a booklet entitled *Chaoxian celue* (*A Strategy for Korea*) to Kim Hongjip (1842–96), a Korean envoy to Japan. The author advised Korea herein to strengthen itself by implementing a foreign policy of "intimate relations with China, coordination with Japan, alliance with America, and caution toward Russia."

Meanwhile, Viceroy Li ordered his lieutenants in the Chinese office for external affairs to persuade Western envoys in Beijing to initiate diplomatic relations with Korea. However, most of the Western powers were not interested and, further, questioned Chosŏn's status as an independent kingdom with which they could even establish diplomatic relations on terms of equality. Li was rational enough to accept Korea's independence in internal as well as external affairs. However, he also wanted the West to recognize Chosŏn's special relationship with China as a nominal tributary.

The first Western power to succeed in opening Korean ports was the United States. After Commodore Robert Wilson Shufeldt's attempt at diplomacy through Japanese channels was rejected by the Chosŏn court in 1880, he engaged in a two-year-long secret negotiation between Beijing,

Seoul, and himself mediated by Viceroy Li Hongzhang. On May 22, 1882, Commodore Shufeldt and Korean representatives Sin Hon and Kim Hongjip signed and sealed the Treaty of Peace, Amity, and Commerce. This treaty, generally known as the Shufeldt Convention, was relatively fair compared to most of the unequal treaties Western powers had earlier established with East-Asian kingdoms, including Korea's Kanghwa Treaty with Japan. This treaty stipulated the trade tariffs Chosŏn could impose on commodities, whereas this stipulation was omitted in the Kanghwa Treaty, much to Korea's disadvantage.

The result of Li Hongzhang's secret efforts was an attachment to the treaty, "Dispatch from the King of Korea to the President of the United States of America," which asserted that "the king of Korea, as an independent monarch, distinctly undertakes to carry out the Articles contained in the Treaty, irrespective of any matters affecting the tributary relations subsisting between Korea and China, with which the United States of America has no concern." This is the first modern translation into Western concepts of Korea's traditional *sadae* relationship to China. This attachment recognizes the duality of the theory and practice of Korea's status with China. In theory, Korea is a tributary, but in practice it is an independent monarchy.

The U.S.-Korea Treaty was followed by similar treaties with Britain and Germany in 1883, Italy and Russia in 1884, and France in 1886. Moreover, like the treaty with the United States, each of these subsequent treaties was supplemented by communications from the king of Korea to the heads of these states, in which the Korean king acknowledged that Korea was a nominal tributary to China. It is notable that an article permitting Catholic missionaries to enter Korea was inserted in the Korean-French treaty.

THE MODERNIZATION INITIATIVE

Many historians agree that the opening of Korea's ports was the starting point of the challenges the kingdom faced in modernization under East-Asian power politics. Before the signing of the Kanghwa Treaty in 1876, King Kojong met with strong protests from the conservative Neo-Confucian scholar-officials against opening the ports to Japan. Ch'oe Ik-hyŏn once again led the traditional *wijŏng ch'ŏksa* movement among the rustic literati, opposing the Japanese economic invasion and the proliferation of Christianity. This time, his views coincided with the voice of the now retired Taewŏn'gun. King Kojong and his few officials who supported the open-door policy were unable to convince the court majority and the ruling yangban both in the capital and countryside of the need to accept Western relations. The king and these enlightened officials, impressed with the Chinese "self-strengthening movement" (*ziqiang yundong* in Chinese), turned their attention to external influences, Qing China in particular.

The first attempt at modernization in the kingdom of Chosŏn was initiated by King Kojong and these officials. In January of 1881, they created a new government office dealing with external affairs, the T'ongnigimu amun (Office for the Management of State Affairs), named after its equivalent in the Qing government. This new office was outside the traditional bureaucracy of the six ministries and was created in preparation for an expected increase in trade and diplomacy. Moreover, a newly formed military unit, called the Pyŏlgigun (Special Army) was trained under a supervising Japanese officer. These two organizations matched the Japanese idea of *fukoku kyohei* (rich nation and strong military), which the king and his officials sought to absorb.

However, members of the old army brutally disrupted these attempts at reformation. In July 1882, soldiers under the old military system, discontent over salaries delayed by the formation of the Pyŏlgigun, exploded in anger, killing the Japanese military adviser and attacking the Japanese delegation. Conservative officials and rustic Confucian literati supported the antigovernment and antiforeign emotions behind the riot. Making Taewŏn'gun their spiritual leader, they demanded his restoration to power. In the meantime, Queen Min was rumored to have been killed, but in fact she had escaped to the remote countryside. Given that Korea was still bound in its traditional ties to China as well as obligated under its new treaties with Japan and the Western powers, Taewŏn'gun and these rebels unwittingly created a situation that enabled Korea's neighbors to expand their influences on the peninsula. In response to the riot, China sent 3,000 troops, and Japan stationed one Japanese battalion in Seoul. To quote a common Korean expression that originated from this situation, the kingdom of Chosŏn had now become "a shrimp between two whales." Eventually, Taewŏn'gun was abducted by the Chinese forces and taken to Tianjin in China. Queen Min returned to the palace, and King Kojong restored his previous reform initiative, using the slogan "Eastern ethics and Western technology" (*tongdo sŏgi*).

With the presence of the Chinese troops, the Chosŏn court in 1882 fell under the far-off influence of Li Hongzhang. Li sent a former German diplomat, Paul Georg von Mollendorff, as an adviser to the king. However, Kojong, leery of Qing influence, instead turned to U.S. minister Lucius Foote for advice in diplomacy, defense, education, and agriculture.

Qing overlordship was not only unpopular among the people and yangban, who still harbored the centuries-old skepticism of the Manchu dynasty's legitimacy, but also among the reform-minded officials and the marginal group of *chungin* (middle men), who tended to be pro-Japanese.

A group of radical officials in the court, led by the reform-minded Kim Okkyun (1851–94) and Pak Yonghyo (1861–1939), staged a coup d'état on December 4, 1884. They took advantage of the opportunity created when the Chinese, in a war with France, withdrew half of their 3,000 troops in order to dispatch them to Indochina. Most of the leaders in this elite group of yangban had studied under Pak Kyusu, the *sirhak* descendent, and had been enlightened by their experiences overseas in Japan. Moreover, they were influenced by their contacts with intellectual *chungin* interpreters. Thus, they sought to progressively reform all political and economic institutions into a modern economy. This incident is known as the Kapsin Coup, named according to the year in the Chinese calendar.

The ambitious dream of the enlightened reformers lasted for only three days. Expecting Japanese military support that never came, they were overwhelmingly crushed when the Chinese forces again intervened. These young coup leaders were exiled to Japan under the protection of the Japanese legation.

EASTERN LEARNING

In the wake of the 1884 coup, China and Japan refrained from clashing but mutually agreed to withdraw troops from the Korean peninsula. Without consulting the Koreans, Li Hongzhang and Ito Hirobumi (1841–1909), the architect of nineteenth-century Japanese diplomacy, signed the Convention of Tianjin on April 18, 1885. Until 1894, the Korean peninsula thus experienced a decade of precarious peace under the balance of power between China, Japan, and Russia.

Since the opening of the ports, Western products and institutions, such as modern hospitals and schools, attracted the monarchy and the upper class in the capital. American and Canadian Protestant missionaries successfully gained entry into Korea by providing medical services. Dr. Horace Newton Allen (1858–1932), a young American Presbyterian missionary, arrived in Chemulp'o (now Inchon) on September 20, 1884, and opened a Western-style hospital in Seoul. Methodist missionaries such as Reverend Henry Gerhart Appenzeller and Reverend William B. Scranton, M.D., as well as the Presbyterian missionary Reverend Horace G. Underwood (1859–1916), were also interested in modern private educational institutions. Underwood founded the Paejae Boys' School in Seoul while

Scranton's wife, Mary, opened the Ehwa Girls' School. Besides these, Sunday schools run by the many Protestant missionaries now entering Korea played a great role in propagating non-Confucian education to the younger generations of Koreans.

However, imported products such as cotton clothes, matches, kerosene, dyestuffs, and chinaware began to undermine the conventional manual-labor-based industries. Tenant peasants in the countryside felt the worst of these effects, exploited by landowners and unable to profit with foreign merchants. Ironically, although Japanese demand was driving up the price of Korea's largest export, rice, the peasants who produced the rice did not benefit. Because of high tenant rates, they still earned less than they needed to survive.

A new religion, Tonghak (Eastern Learning), created by a yangban *sŏja* Ch'oe Cheu (1824–64), appealed to the peasants who suffered under both traditional exploitation and the new external market. Including some elements of Buddhism and Taoism, Tonghak rejected Neo-Confucian rigidity and turned instead to a more flexible, classical Confucian approach of respecting the will of heaven. Appealing to popular Korean xenophobia, Ch'oe Cheu named his new religion Eastern Learning, as opposed to Western Learning (i.e., Catholicism). The religion faced the persecution of the court because it advocated egalitarianism, which would abolish the social status of the yangban and discrimination based on sex and birth legitimacy. Moreover, with its promises of creating a new world, it offered redemption to the people suffering under a corrupt social system. Because of these radical ideas the orthodox Neo-Confucian court executed Ch'oe Cheu in 1864 for heresy.

As the number of Tonghak believers increased, a movement to vindicate the founder arose in 1892–93. While a grand-scale Tonghak congregation demonstrated in the countryside, two scores of representatives came to Seoul in early 1893 and appealed directly to the king, who eventually agreed to their demands that Ch'oe would be posthumously exonerated. However, the king failed to keep his promise, so a second demonstration followed the next year. The leaders of the Tonghak movement had intended to keep the demonstration peaceful and religious. However, Chŏn Pongjun (1853–95), a Tonghak district head, led a revolt of armed peasants in January 1894 and attacked a corrupt magistrate in the southwestern province. The rebels demanded liberation from restriction based on social status and the government's return to anti-Japanese and anti-Western policies as well as the restoration to power of Taewŏn'gun, who had always advocated these views. In April 1894, this Tonghak army defeated the government forces and in the end of May occupied most of the large cities in the southwestern province, including the provincial capital.

The court, dominated by the Mins, invited the Qing troops to quell the rebellion. However, pursuant to a clause in the Convention of Tianjin, neither China nor Japan could send troops onto Korean soil without the other sending troops as well. As a Qing force of 3,000 landed on the Korean peninsula in June, Japan immediately sent a force of 7,000. After a brief decade of peace, the shrimp was again threatened by tension between the two whales. The Tonghak resistance, demoralized by foreign troops, agreed with the government to immediately stand down. However, Tonghak influence continued over the provinces, and many of their reform programs were implemented.

In July 1894, Japanese forces in the capital provoked another coup d'état that overthrew the Min regime and installed a pro-Japanese reformist government. Interestingly enough, the Japanese this time invited Taewŏn'gun to become the symbolic head of the anti-Qing and anti-Min regime. While proposing a program of reform and modernization in Korea, Japan declared war against Qing China on August 1. On both land and sea, the rising Meiji Japan unilaterally defeated the old Qing dynasty. As a result, Li Hongzhang this time went to Shimonoseki, a port in western Japan, to sign a treaty in which China no longer recognized Korea as a tributary but as an independent kingdom.

THE KABO REFORMS

A new group of reform-minded officials, including some of the former members of the Kapsin Coup, now took power thanks to Japanese military support after the Sino-Japanese War. They began to implement their modernization program, which had been postponed for a decade. Historians called their series of modernization reform measures from 1894 to 1897 the Kabo Reforms. Kim Hongjip and Yu Kilchun (1856–1914), author of *A Travelogue of the West*, published in 1895, helped pass some 210 reform bills within the newly created Deliberative Council (Kun'guk kimuch'ŏ) nominally headed by Taewŏn'gun.

The first objective of the reforms was to establish Korea's independence as a nation, negating the nominal tribute relationship with Qing China and abrogating the unequal agreements made with the Qing between 1882 and 1894. Forbidding the use of calendars based on Chinese reign dates, the reform government substituted in official documents a Korean dating method based on the year of Chosŏn's founding. The title of the king was upgraded to His Majesty Great King (Taegunju p'eha), giving him the status of emperor. The Korean alphabet, hangul, was now used in major government publications, and Korean history began to be taught at all levels in the modern, newly established schools. From January 1895, the government began to print a new official newspaper in a mixed script of Chinese and Korean.

The next objective of the reforms focused on the reorganization of the government structure from the traditional institution into a modern cabinet-centered monarchy modeled after Meiji Japan. Abolishing the centuries-old State Council and six ministries, the reforms created the cabinet as an executive body with eight ministries. The Royal Household Department was created in order to separate palace from state affairs. This separation aimed at the restriction of royal power, shifting the fiscal prerogatives of the palace to the responsibility of the Ministry of Finance. Together with modern taxation, a new monetary system based on the silver standard was created. Moreover, a national bank was established for the first time, standardizing weights and measures.

A modern education system was introduced by establishing a number of elementary schools, high schools, and colleges. Accordingly, the traditional civil-service exam system was abolished. The government encouraged study abroad by sending some 200 students to Japan while consigning at its own expense the same number of students to the Paejae School, an American mission school in Seoul. The new elementary-school curriculum was aimed at expanding literacy in lower-level classes and stressed reading, writing, and arithmetic, while at the higher-level classes, the history and geography of Korea and other countries was taught along with sciences and an optional foreign language.

The most impressive objective of the Kabo Reforms was the modernization of social life. With the establishment of a modern judicial system, torture and the practice of extending punishment to the entire family for a single member's crime was banned. Moreover, the yangban, no longer a legally privileged class, were allowed to engage in commerce. Appointment within the bureaucracy was opened to all echelons of social status. Early marriage was prohibited, and widows were allowed to remarry. Sons of secondary wives were no longer discriminated against.

This enlightened cabinet and a new Japanese envoy, Minister Inoue Kaoru (1835–1915), enforced the implementation of the Kabo Reforms in a very short period of time. This was done under the scrupulous supervision of more than 40 Japanese advisers in the cabinet, who had experience from the reforms of the Meiji Restoration. However, unlike with the judicial and administrative measures, the Korean people needed time to accept the social and economic reforms. Taewŏn'gun strongly protested the reforms and attempted to replace the king with the help of the Qing forces and the Tonghak peasant army, who had ironically included some of these reforms in their demands. When the Japanese detected his plot, he was again forced to retire.

Minister Inoue Kaoru, a former foreign minister who was British-trained, modeled himself after Lord Cromer, Britain's nineteenth-century minister to Cairo and de facto regent of Egypt. Minister Inoue made Kojong reluctantly pardon the two leaders of the previous 1884 coup, Pak Yŏnghyo and Sŏ Kwangbŏm. These two joined Kim Hongjip's cabinet as home and justice ministers as soon as they returned from their exile. Moreover, Minister Inoue directed his Japanese troops to crush the Tonghak peasant army for its involvement in Taewŏn'gun's attempt at an anti-Japanese coup. However, with Western powers intervening in the Shimonoseki Sino-Japanese treaty, Japan changed its Korea policy from a model of the British protectorate over Egypt to a noninterventionist approach. Accordingly, the Japanese government decided to replace the diplomatic Minister Inoue. Nonetheless, his replacement, Miura Koro, was tactically chosen for his military background.

RESISTANCE

Not only did the Neo-Confucian yangban literati oppose the Kabo Reforms, but so did the people and the monarchy. King Kojong's power as well as Queen Min's influence had been reduced severely by the cabinet. For help, they looked to the Russians, who had effectively curbed Japanese ambition in Manchuria after the Sino-Japanese War. Japanese minister Miura Koro began to plot to rid the court altogether of in-law influence. At midnight on October 7, 1895, a group of armed Japanese, mixed with Korean soldiers trained by Japanese officers, snuck into the palace and brutally murdered Queen Min. To gain entrance, as well as legitimize their crime, they called upon the help of the old Taewŏn'gun, who was hungry as ever for power.

During the tumultuous period that followed, the Kabo Reforms continued. On December 30, 1895, the cabinet, headed by Prime Minister Kim Hongjip, adopted the Western calendar, beginning with the year 1896. On the same day, the king was made to issue an edict that decreed that all Korean males were to cut off their traditional topknots. In this, Kojong himself took the initiative. The order was immensely unpopular among Koreans, who had long since been indoctrinated with the Confucian teaching "One dare not damage one's body, hair, and skin received by one's parents, for filial piety begins there." The rustic yangban literati, already discontented over the removal of their privileges by the reforms, strongly protested. Ch'oe Ikhyon boldly exclaimed, "Cut off my head, but never my hair!"

Literati activists in the countryside began to rise against the pro-Japanese government. Playing off the xenophobia prevalent among the people, they waged armed struggles against Westernization in defense of the orthodox Neo-Confucian legitimacy of Korea in East Asia. This force, named the Righteous Army (ŭibyŏng), spread out all over the countryside. However, equipped with inferior weapons, they were a poor match for the Japanese and Korean government forces. Moreover, many of the peasants, by this time more educated by the egalitarian reforms, did not support the yangban's struggles for leadership.

In February 1896, King Kojong, a virtual prisoner in his palace since the assassination of Queen Min, secretly took refuge in the Russian legation with the help of his two officials, the pro-Russian Yi Pŏmjin (1853–1911) and the pro-American Yi Wanyong (1858–1926). Under the protection of Russia, Kojong escaped the grip of the Japanese and abolished the political system created by the Kabo Reforms. Kim Hongjip and the cabinet members were arrested but soon killed by an angry mob. Czarist Russia now held sway over the peninsula as a protector of the Korean monarchy. Japan, however, did not renounce its ambition toward Korea.

At the coronation of Czar Nicholas II on May 26, 1896, Russia was flooded by East-Asian emissaries seeking his favor. Expecting military and financial aid, Korea sent Min Yŏnghwan (1861–1905), a prominent official from the Min family. China's Li Hongzhang came to negotiate the laying of the Siberian railroad in Manchuria. Finally, Japan sent Yamagata Aritomo (1838–1922) to discuss the Korea issue. The Russian host, foreign minister Aleksey Borisovich Lobanov-Rostovsky (1824–96), could not satisfy the Korean and Chinese envoys. However, on two different days, May 28 and June 9, the Japanese envoy was able to secure an agreement called the Yamagata-Lobanov Protocol. Nonetheless, in the protocol, the Russians declined the Japanese suggestion to divide Korea on the 38th parallel in the event that Japanese and Russian troops were to occupy the peninsula. This concept, to which the Americans later unwittingly agreed, was resurrected in 1945 by Joseph Stalin, premier of Soviet Russia.

THE INDEPENDENCE CLUB

Having experienced Japanese dominance during the Kabo Reforms, the monarch and his court officials, along with anti-Japanese reformists, were eager to maintain the nation's independence. One of the most ardent independence advocates, Sŏ Chaep'il (1863–1951), exiled to the United States since the abortive 1884 coup, now returned to Korea as Philip Jaisohn, a U.S. citizen with a medical degree. He became a mentor of the Chŏngdong Club, a group of anti-Japanese, pro-American enlightened leaders located on Seoul's Chŏngdong Street in the vicinity of the American legation and their mission schools. After the king's flight to the Russian legation, Sŏ Chaep'il joined the new pro-Western government as an adviser. With its financial support, he inaugurated on April 7, 1896, the first modern newspaper, the *Tongnip Sinmun* (The *Independent*). The paper was published with the Korean alphabet, hangul, on one side and English on the other. On July 2, the Ministry of Foreign Affairs founded, through Sŏ's initiative, the Independence Club (Tongnip Hyŏphoe). Its first act was to demolish the special gate through which Chinese envoys were received according to traditional *sadae* protocol. In its stead, a new Independence Arch was constructed, a miniature model of the Arc de Triomphe in Paris.

With King Kojong under the protection of the Russian legation, the pro-Western Independence Club took advantage of the brief period of balanced power between Russia and Japan and aligned itself with the monarch's objectives to build a rich, independent nation with a strong military. In February 1897, Kojong left the Russian legation and moved to the Kyŏng'un Palace (today's Tŏksu Palace). Kojong and his pro-Russian officials attempted to institute active modernization programs that, unlike the pro-Japanese Kabo Reforms, would strengthen the kingship. In August 1897, Kojong changed his reign title to Kwangmu and in October of the same year named himself emperor, proclaiming his kingdom the Empire of Great Korea. A primitive constitution that stipulated the concentration of all legislative, executive, and judicial power in the czar-like emperor was announced on August 17, 1899. This Kwangmu Reform aimed to achieve conservative modernization by balancing both old and new. However, the rustic literati leaders of the Righteous Army opposed the concept, which conflicted with their views on the orthodox East-Asian world order. The Independence Club, which advocated the division of power among the three branches of government, disagreed with the Kwangmu Reform as well but was more passive in its opposition.

The Kwangmu government focused its modernization programs on establishing various economic reforms in order to secure the financial power of the monarch. Through a national land survey and population census conducted between 1898 and 1901, a modern landownership system was introduced with the creation of the Office of Land Contracts. The government directed the management of public industries such as the railroads, mining, telephones, postal system, and manufacturing. However, the financial base of the Kwangmu government was too weak to support all these ambitious programs. In order to raise money to modernize industry, the government granted special rights to foreign capitalist powers. These favors and franchises on modern business included gold mining, railroad and trolley-line construction, installation of electricity, and waterworks. Nationalistic officials in Seoul, prodded by the Independence Club, were unanimous in their criticism of the king's flight to a foreign legation and furthermore denounced the economic concessions to the external powers.

As the Independence Club began to criticize the Kwangmu Reform, high-level officials in the government, such as Yi Wanyong, began to leave the club in early 1898. Between April and July of the same year, the club initiated public discussion on creating a parliamentary democracy and constitutional monarchy. The club proposed the new system to Emperor Kojong, advocating the would-be benefits for Korea. At the same time, Sŏ Chaep'il, leader of the club, continued to criticize government policies from a democratic perspective in a series of editorials in the *Tongnip Sinmun*, which by this time had reached a circulation of about 3,000. Hated by those in power, he eventually became discouraged and returned to the United States in May 1898. Through the *Tongnip Sinmun*, Sŏ Chaep'il introduced for the first time in modern Korea the Jeffersonian concept of the newspaper as related to political power. He himself praised this contribution in an April 12 editorial:

> It is true that the people have been enlightened since the inauguration of the *Tongnip Sinmun*. Some who did not know the role of newspapers had blamed, laughed at, or neglected this strange thing. In these days, however, many people believe that a world without newspapers would be dark and unendurable. I dare to say that our *Tongnip Sinmun* did contribute in making people open. (author's translation)

SYNGMAN RHEE, A YOUNG RADICAL

In the vacancy left by Sŏ Chaep'il's reexile to the United States, a new generation of leaders rose within the Independence Club. Among these, Yun Ch'iho (1864–1946) and Yi Sangjae (1850–1929) were prominent. They had been influenced by American democracy through their education at the Paejae School and experiences abroad. Yun Ch'iho edited Korea's first commercial newspaper, the *Kyŏngsŏng Sinmun*. At this time, American

Protestant missionaries encouraged the publishing of vernacular newspapers in hangul such as the *Chosŏn Kŭrisŭdoin Hoebo* (*Korean Christian Bulletin*), the *Kŭrisŭdo Sinmun* (*Christian Newspaper*), and the *Hyŏpsŏng Hoebo* (*Bulletin of Mutual Friendship Society*). The *Hyŏpsŏng Hoebo* was a newsletter of a Paejae School student club, which Yi Sŭngman (Syngman Rhee, 1875–1965) had initiated as a leader. After graduating from the Paejae School, Syngman Rhee joined the Independence Club as a young radical member.

In October 1898, the Independence Club, with a membership of 4,000, organized at Chongno Plaza in downtown Seoul a mass assembly known as the Joint Meeting of Government and People. Attending the meeting were high-level ministers and officials from the government along with citizens of various backgrounds, such as literati, students, women, merchants, Buddhist monks, butchers, and so on. In this truly democratic meeting, the government representatives and citizens adopted a six-point proposal, which they submitted to the monarch. The proposal recommended transforming the Privy Council, a decorative office at the highest level of the bureaucracy, to a modern legislative body. Moreover, it sought a trial system that entailed due process. Thus the proposal aimed to shift the authoritarian monarchy to a constitutional one. Emperor Kojong, who accepted the proposal and promised to implement it, promulgated on November 4 a new set of Privy Council regulations, by which one-half of its 50 members would be chosen among the Independence Club.

Meanwhile, conservative royalists in the court began to plot the abolishment of the Independence Club, slandering its members and persuading the king that the club was attempting to establish a republic. Through the royalists' influence, Kojong abruptly ordered the arrest of club leaders. Yi Sangjae and 16 other leaders were immediately jailed. Club members protested the emperor's order of their dissolution, organizing among citizens of Seoul another mass assembly called the People's Meeting.

On November 29, 1898, Kojong appointed a 50-member Privy Council but included only seventeen Independence Club members. Young Syngman Rhee was one of them. Though the royalist group within the council, called the Imperial Association, outnumbered the Independence Club, these club members succeeded in passing a resolution to recall Pak Yŏnghyo and Sŏ Chaep'il from exile. Meanwhile, it was rumored that certain club radicals were plotting a coup to install a constitutional monarchy, thereby replacing Kojong with his son Prince Ŭich'in and inviting the exiled Pak Yŏnghyo to be prime minister. As a result, several club leaders, including Syngman Rhee, were imprisoned.

Finally on December 21, under orders of a strongly worded edict from the king, royal guards and mercenaries cracked down on the still ongoing mass demonstration of the People's Meeting and further arrested its leaders. Thus, the fledgling democratic movement of the Independence Club was brutally crushed by the police and the royalists in the Imperial Association.

7

Japanese Dominion

THE RUSSO-JAPANESE WAR

Military tension between the foreign powers gathered like storm clouds over the Korean peninsula. During this period, lacking in capital and modern technology, Korea continued to grant many concessions to foreign powers in developing modern industries, including mining, forestry, fisheries, urban trolley systems, and railroad construction. Among these powers, Russia and Japan were the most aggressive in expanding their interests in Korea. The situation was exacerbated in January 1902 when Britain recognized Japan's monopolistic privilege over the peninsular kingdom through the Anglo-Japanese Alliance.

In August 1903, the Japanese demanded that the Russians acknowledge Japan's special interest in Korea, whereby they would recognize Russian interests in Manchuria. However, Russia counteroffered in October to create a neutral zone on Korean territory north of the 39th parallel. As Russia had disregarded the Japanese offer of dividing Korea at the 38th parallel in 1896, Japan in turn rejected the Russian idea. It was then inevitable that the two whales would eventually clash over the Korean shrimp. In February 1904, Japanese forces landed on Korean soil and entered Seoul, intimidating the Korean government into renouncing its declaration of neutrality and signing the Korea-Japan Protocol, which mandated Japan's military occupation of Korean territory and the appointment of Japanese advisers to the king.

Japan aimed to dominate Korean politics, which was now quite active since the Independence Club movement. Japanese strategists searched out Korean collaborators and created behind the scenes a pro-Japanese Korean group known as the Ilchinhoe (Society for United Progress) led by Song Pyŏngjun (1858–1925) and Yi Yonggu (1868–1912). Song, an ex-official of the Korean government, had been exiled to Japan. However, he now returned home as an interpreter for the Japanese army. Yi, with his small group of Tonghak believers, branched off the main sect of the movement and joined with the pro-Japanese organization.

Financially supported by private Japanese activists, the Ilchinhoe included people of various backgrounds, such as former Tonghak leaders, reformist ex-officials, merchants, and so on. To show their loyalty, these members all cut off their traditional topknots and began to actively collaborate with the Japanese army in fighting against the Russians. They even volunteered labor service for insignificant wages in order to construct a railway. In spite of these Koreans' enthusiastic cooperation, the Japanese diplomats in Seoul were strictly ordered by Tokyo to deny any connections with the Ilchinhoe in order to give the organization an appearance of acting of its own volition.

In May 1904, Japanese forces crossed the Yalu River to attack the Russian army on the Liaodong peninsula. Although the Japanese army outnumbered the Russians in Manchuria, they paid a bitter price by suffering numerous casualties in order to capture Port Arthur (today's Lüshun). Fortunately for Japan, the victory was determined by sea. Thanks to the British obstruction of the Suez Canal in accordance with the Anglo-Japanese Alliance, the Russian Baltic Fleet in Europe had to sail the long way around the tip of Africa in order to join battle in Far East Asia. In May 1905, Togo Heihachiro, Japan's naval commander and an admirer of Admiral Yi Sunsin, crushed the Baltic Fleet while it attempted to slip through the Korea Strait to reach Vladivostok after a two-month journey.

After these unexpected victories, Japan strengthened its diplomacy with the United States and Britain before it started peace negotiations with Russia. The U.S. president, Theodore Roosevelt (1858–1919), who was more impressed by the rising constitutional monarchy of Japan than the autocratic czarist Russia, chose to cooperate with Japan in securing peace in East Asia. In July 1905, the pro-Japanese president sent then secretary of war William Taft (1857–1930) to Tokyo to sign a secret agreement with

Japanese foreign minister Katsura Taro (1848–1913). The Taft-Katsura Agreement mutually recognized both Japan's dominance in Korea and the American colonization of the Philippines. Furthermore, President Roosevelt volunteered to organize a peace negotiation between Russia and Japan in Portsmouth, New Hampshire. In August, thanks to U.S. arbitration in Japan's favor, the two parties finally signed the Portsmouth Treaty. In this agreement, Russia was made to hand over the southern half of the Sakhalin and Kurile Islands along with railways in Manchuria to the Japanese. More importantly, the Russians conceded Japan's dominion over Korea.

Meanwhile, Kojong and his officials sought American support in their struggle for independence from Japanese influence, naively trusting in the 1882 Treaty of Peace, Amity, and Commerce. In Article 1 of this treaty, the United States had pledged, "If other powers deal unjustly or oppressively with either government, the other will exert their good offices, on being informed of the case, to bring about an amicable arrangement, thus showing their friendly feeling." Because the Americans had previously intervened after the Sino-Japanese war, Kojong and his officials mistook the diplomatic words of the treaty for a more literal meaning. Therefore, Kojong attempted a last-minute appeal to President Roosevelt through Reverend Homer Hulbert (1863–1949), an American missionary. However, the president disregarded the monarch's letter. Kojong's officials attempted again through Syngman Rhee, who, having converted to Christianity while in prison, had journeyed by this time to the United States to study. Rhee, too, was coldly received by the pro-Japanese president.

Having persuaded the rest of the world of its dominion over the peninsula, Japan launched its long-prepared plan to conquer Korea. In November 1905, Ito Hirobumi, the former prime minister, hastily arrived in Seoul, where Japanese troops now occupied the palace. He demanded that the Korean government accept a new protectorate treaty by which Japan would control all the foreign affairs of Korea through a Japanese resident-general. Although Emperor Kojong rejected the treaty to the very end, the Korean cabinet, under threats from Ito and the Japanese military, signed it with his seal on November 17. A few cabinet members resisted, but most of them, including Yi Wanyong, collaborated with the Japanese and accepted the five-point agreement, which became known as the 1905 Protectorate Treaty. Thus, the Empire of Great Korea not only lost its independent sovereignty among the nations of the world but was also forced to hand over its domestic administrative autonomy to the control of Japanese deputy ministers.

On November 20, Chang Chiyŏn (1864–1921), publisher of the *Hwang-sŏng Sinmun* (the *Imperial Capital Newspaper*), wrote a deploring editorial entitled "Today, We Are Wailing":

> Never in a thousand dreams would we have conceived this five-point treaty! Its articles will divide Korea, Japan, and China into conflict; is this Marquis Ito Hirobumi's idea of keeping peace and stability in East Asia? Nonetheless, our Majesty has adamantly refused to sign it. Therefore, Marquis Ito knows full well that the treaty is invalid. Alas! Those so-called ministers of the cabinet, not unlike dogs or pigs, pursuing their own glory and interests . . . , sold our four-thousand-year-old territory with our five-hundred-year-old dynasty, and have thus made twenty million people slaves . . . My compatriots, shall we live or shall we die? Alas! What deep sorrow! My people, my people! (author's translation)

Protests arose. Grand Chamberlain Min Yŏnghwan, former envoy to the Russian czar, committed suicide, leaving behind appeals to the people and to foreign delegations for Korean independence. In the capital, many officials followed suit or left the court in protest. In the countryside, new waves of the Righteous Army surged, demonstrating against the 1905 Protectorate Treaty.

THE EGYPTIAN MODEL

Again modeling after the British protectorate in Egypt, the Japanese maintained the Korean monarchy, cabinet, and local magistracies as symbols of independence. However, they dictated Korean diplomacy at all levels and further controlled internal affairs through Japanese advisers. Political mandate in Korea fell on Ito Hirobumi, who was named resident-general in December 1905. His first action was to borrow 10 million yen from Tokyo to promote social infrastructure projects that were indispensable to efficiently rule the undeveloped protectorate. Taking Lord Evelyn Baring Cromer (1841–1917), the British agent and consul general in Egypt, as his role model, Ito attempted to convince Koreans of the protectorate's legitimacy with visible benefits. These included roads, hospitals, schools, and an increase in agricultural production. Furthermore, Ito built his residency-general headquarters on the slope of Namsan, a mountain overlooking downtown Seoul. The building, as a Western-style structure, was a reflection of Meiji imperialist mentality, a mimesis of nineteenth- and twentieth-century Western colonial powers.

Finding reliable Korean collaborators was vital for Ito Hirobumi, whose strategy ultimately aimed at ruling Korea without the use of force. Many of the old opportunistic elites, such as Pak Chesun (1858–1916), Yi Wanyong, and Cho Pyŏngsik, continued to survive within the cabinet. However, new collaborators, such as Song Pyŏngjun, Cho Chung'ŭng, and Ko Yŏnghŭi, joined in May 1907 under Ito's recommendation. With the kingdom having lost its sovereignty, the reformed government became a good opportunity for those in marginal groups who eagerly wanted to upgrade their social status. Among these, Song Pyŏngjun had previously adopted a yangban surname while serving the Min clan as a low-ranking military officer. Ko Yŏnghŭi was a *chungin* who had stayed in Japan since the first delegation sent there after the opening of the ports in 1876.

The Righteous Army waged sporadic military campaigns in the countryside, destroying local magistracies and attacking Japanese merchants or military branches. Yangban leaders like Ch'oe Ikhyŏn were willing to fight against Japanese forces but renounced any action against the Korean royal army, which the Japanese began to employ. Thus, new Righteous Army leaders emerged from among the peasants in the southern provinces.

Urban intellectuals, however, instead of joining in reckless armed resistance, launched a patriotic enlightenment movement. Having observed the results of the Sino- and Russo-Japanese Wars, they became social Darwinists, believing in the survival of the fittest. They concluded the solution to Korea's weakness lay in self-strengthening. Many conservative Confucians, who had criticized modernization as advocated by the reformists, now joined this campaign, establishing schools to which they could send their children for a modern education. They organized associations, such as the Chaganghoe (Self-Strengthening Society), and published newspapers and magazines to educate the public. One of their most successful projects in 1907 included a public donation movement to repay the national debt to foreign countries.

Meanwhile, Kojong continued to seek outside help, his only tactic since the influx of foreign powers. Again, at Reverend Homer Hulbert's suggestion, he secretly sent former officials Yi Sangsŏl (1870–1917), Yi Chun (1858–1907), and Yi Wijong (1887–?) to the second International Peace Conference held in The Hague, Netherlands, in June 1907. However, as Korea had lost its sovereignty to Japan, they were not recognized as official representatives and were not allowed to attend the conference. Nonetheless, Yi Wijong made a speech entitled "A Plea for Korea" at a press conference. Unfortunately, the Japanese resident-general used this as a pretext to remove the intractable Kojong from the throne. Indeed, Ito threatened Kojong through the Korean collaborators Yi Wanyong and Song Pyŏngjun. In July, Kojong abdicated, and his son, Crown Prince Sunjong (1874–1926), nominally took the throne as the last king of the Chosŏn dynasty. His first act as king was to sign a revised treaty, by which Japanese deputy ministers were appointed to all ministries of the government.

Kojong's forced abdication and the new protectorate treaty caused strong anti-Japanese sentiments among the Korean people. The Chosŏn military, now disbanded, joined the struggles of the Righteous Army, which intensified in 1908. Resident-General Ito, who had underestimated popular antipathy, now faced serious guerilla war in the countryside. Thus, he waged a large-scale military campaign against the resistance. In 1908 alone, the Japanese army killed 11,562 members of the Righteous Army.

As the Japanese authorities began to further suppress Korean public politics, An Ch'angho (1878–1938), a Korean nationalist formerly living in the United States, organized in 1909 a clandestine movement called the Sinminhoe (New People Society), whose purpose was to build armed resistance abroad. Other nationalist intellectuals engaged in the publication of newspapers and magazines in the capital while founding schools in the provinces. Sin Ch'aeho (1880–1936) was one of the more active journalists who criticized Japanese imperialism. His nationalistic writings would greatly influence many future historiographies, as well as Korea's first modern poet and historian, Ch'oe Namsŏn (1890–1957).

Powerless at home and internationally isolated, Koreans felt completely helpless. As a last resort, many turned to terrorism. In May 1908, Durham White Stevens, an American formerly employed by the Japanese foreign ministry and a diplomatic adviser to the Kabo regime, was shot by two Korean patriots at a station in Oakland, California, while on his way to Washington, D.C., to lobby for the Japanese position in Korea. His previous pro-Japanese activities in San Francisco had roused the Korean community on the West Coast. Thus he became the first victim of Korean terrorism.

In early June 1909, Resident-General Ito resigned as a political gesture after the advocates clamoring for direct rule in Tokyo criticized his gradual self-rule policy. In July, Japan's cabinet secretly adopted a policy to annex Korea when the moment was ripe. As his last diplomatic act, Ito Hirobumi visited Harbin, Manchuria, in October to meet with Russian finance minister Vladimir Kokovsoff and negotiate Russian approval of Korea's annexation, among other things. At the railway station where Kokovsoff was to receive him, a Korean patriot in the crowd, An Chunggŭn (1879–1910), shot and killed Ito. An, a descendent of a yangban family in one of Korea's northwestern provinces, was an independence fighter in exile, having once led a small group of guerrilla forces in southern Manchuria. Defeated by the Japanese forces, An and his comrades planned Ito's assassination in order to awaken the world to Korea's struggle for independence.

On the contrary, the murder raised international sympathy for Japan, though An Chunggŭn was considered a national hero among Koreans. The Japanese took advantage of the moment to push forward the annexation policy. Their idea was to start a grassroots campaign among the Korean people. In Seoul, Korean collaborators, led by Song Pyŏngjun and Yi Yonggu of the Ilchinhoe, circulated a petition that proposed to Emperor Sunjong the voluntary union of Korea and Japan.

By 1910, two Japanese army divisions occupied Korea, making the nation virtually a police state. After a sweeping military campaign against the Righteous Army in the southwestern region, the new resident-general, Terauchi Masatake (1852–1919), strengthened the police by employing the notorious *kenpei*, the Japanese gendarmerie. As of 1907, the *kenpei* numbered 2,369 Japanese, with 4,065 Korean helpers. In order to intimidate the Korean people, Terauchi ordered that all political and social organizations in Korea be dissolved, including the Ilchinhoe. Then, on August 22, 1910, Korean prime minister Yi Wanyong and Japanese resident-general Terauchi Masatake signed the treaty of Japan's annexation of Korea, thus ending the Chosŏn dynasty.

MILITARY RULE

After annexation, the office of residency-general was replaced with the Chosŏn Government-General, a colonial organization. However, unlike other colonies, the position of Chosŏn governor-general was unique in the Japanese empire. The office was invested with plenipotentiary powers, including some legislative authority and the command of the occupying army and navy. Therefore, only military officers were qualified for the post. Terauchi Masatake, a four-star general, doubled as the Japanese minister of army and the first governor-general of Korea. Japan's colonial policy of draconian military rule could be summed up in his quotation: "The Korean people must choose, either submit to our law or face death."

Why did Japan take such a brutal approach in colonizing Korea? First, it was unable to politically convince the Koreans with the promise to modernize their country. Even after most of the Righteous Army was crushed by Japanese forces, Korean antipathy toward Japan was not subdued, for Koreans had traditionally believed themselves to be superior to the Japanese within the East-Asian world order. Thus, only by intimidating Koreans with physical violence were the Japanese colonialists able to make them submit. Much of this violence was further instigated by the Japanese military, which had dominated the Japanese empire since its victory in the Russo-Japanese War.

Unlike the Western powers, Japanese capitalism was so fragile that it could not manage the Korean economy with a normal market system. Only by force was Japan able to exploit Korea as a supplier of rice and other raw materials, as a consumer market for Japanese industrial products, and as an irregular capital-investment target. Through its land survey, the Government-General nationalized vast rice paddies and woods traditionally unregistered but cultivated and used by the peasants. These lands were sold at inexpensive prices to Japanese investors, particularly the Oriental Development Company. In addition, Korean entrepreneurs needed a government permit to establish new companies. Tariffs were levied on Japanese exporters, but these taxes were so low that the inferior Korean manufacturing industries could not compete.

Through various legislations, the Government-General prohibited all political activities, preventing the Korean people from exercising freedom of speech, press, and assembly. In August 1911, the government issued a decree that discouraged Koreans from receiving a higher education and from studying the humanities and social sciences, including their own history and geography. However, they were encouraged to learn the Japanese language. Because of government regulations, the number of public schools in Korea began to rise while the more nationalistic private schools decreased.

In March 1912, Japanese authorities were given free reign in investigation. Particularly, they were permitted savage interrogation techniques and punishments. Ironically, the traditional Chosŏn method of flogging, which had been abolished since the Kabo Reforms, was revived at this time as a means of intimidation. The police abused their new authority against any Korean who resisted the Japanese.

THE MARCH 1 MOVEMENT

Under such harsh military rule, religion, though limited, was the only organized activity allowed to the Korean people. The government protected Western missionaries in particular in order to preserve Japan's international image. However, these missionaries, mostly from North America, spoke out from time to time in criticism of the colonial authorities, calling for human rights and other interests in Korea. Thus Christianity grew popular, as Koreans began to believe that it stood for Korean nationalism. In 1911, citing allegations of plots to assassinate Governor-General Terauchi, the Government-General arrested several Korean Christian leaders, including Yun Ch'iho. However, Koreans continued to receive Christianity with relative enthusiasm, particularly in the northwestern provinces, where yangban culture was not so deeply rooted. To counter Christian popularity, the colonial authorities supported Buddhism, which most Japanese practiced.

Meanwhile, the world was changing. When czarist Russia was toppled by the Bolshevik Revolution in November 1917, Vladimir Lenin's "principle of self-determination of oppressed peoples" did not immediately sink in among Koreans. However, this would soon become the mantra of the future communist movement in Korea. In 1918, the First World War ended with the defeat of Germany. In November, the exiled New Korea Youth Party in Shanghai, led by Yŏ Unhyŏng (1886–1947), decided to send a petition for Korean independence to the Peace Conference in Paris, dispatching Kim Kyusik (1877–1952) as a representative. At the same time, the Korean community in North America attempted to send a three-man delegation headed by Syngman Rhee. However, both attempts failed to rouse interest in the Western world.

Nonetheless, as the Peace Conference took place in January 1919, U.S. president Woodrow Wilson (1856–1924), using Lenin's principle, called for the self-determination of oppressed peoples everywhere. This inspired Korean students in Tokyo. On February 8, they organized the Korean Youth Independence Party and gathered for Korean independence in answer to President Wilson's call.

Many intellectual leaders in Korea believed that President Wilson's self-determinism would be applied to Korea. Song Chinu (1890–1945), Kim Sŏngsu (1891–1955), and Hyŏn Sangyun (1892–?) had earlier returned to Seoul from their studies at Waseda University in Tokyo to teach younger generations. Hearing the appeals of their junior classmates in Japan, they attempted to campaign nationally for independence. These young intellectuals appealed to prominent Korean patriots like Yi Sangjae, who on the contrary disagreed with their wild ideals, believing their movement might entail huge sacrifices without any realistic results. Thus, they turned to religious leaders. Fortunately, they found the support of another mentor from Waseda, Ch'oe Rin (1878–?), who was now secretary-general of the Ch'ŏndogyo sect, a new reincarnation of the Tonghak movement. Ch'oe Rin succeeded in persuading his superior, Son Pyŏnghŭi, leader of Ch'ŏndogyo, to head a committee of representatives in the national campaign. Meanwhile, Christian leaders, mostly from the northwestern provinces, including Yi Sŭnghun (1864–1930), had heard of the reactions of

Koreans abroad to President Wilson's call for self-determination and welcomed the campaign instigated by these youthful idealists.

Thus, on March 1, 1919, Son Pyŏnghi (1861–1922) recited the Korean Declaration of Independence in Pagoda Park, Seoul. It was signed by 33 national representatives, all of whom were religious leaders, consisting of 16 Christians, 15 Ch'ŏndogyo believers, and 2 Buddhists. Secretly authored by Ch'oe Namsŏn, the poet, the Declaration is still admired by Koreans today for its beautiful rhetoric and insight:

> We hereby declare Korea as an independent state and its people as free. This we declare to all the nations of the world in order to make clear the rightness of human equality. This we declare to our descendants that they may cherish their intrinsic right to national self-respect. Whereas we declare this with the precedence of a five-thousand-year history, whereas we proclaim this with the allegiance of twenty million people, whereas we affirm this for the everlasting freedom of the nation, whereas we submit this in accordance with the atmosphere of global reform through the manifestation of the human conscience, it is thus the solemn order of heaven, the tide of our age, and a just act of mankind's right to coexist. Nothing in this world dares to obstruct it!
>
> As a victim of outmoded policies of aggression and force, we have now suffered for a decade under the foreign shackle for the first time in the thousands of years of our history. How deprived are we of our right to live, how our spiritual growth has been hindered, how injured is our national glory, how oft we have lost our opportunity to make our own creative contributions to the stream of world civilization!
>
> Alas! If we are to wash off yesterday's rancor, if we are to shed today's agony, if we are to abolish tomorrow's menace, if we are to eagerly broaden our shrunken national conscience and state pride, if we are to achieve natural development of individual character, if we are to keep our poor children from inheriting anguish and shame, if we are to bestow everlasting blessings on our descendants—then our first duty is to secure the independence of our nation. If each and every twenty million of our people plant a dagger in their hearts, and if we are supported by our shared humanity and our conscience, as a just army and with the humanitarian weapons of today, can we not press forward and succeed? If we regroup and nurture our strength, can we not accomplish our will?
>
> Though it has frequently violated its promises since the 1876

treaty, we do not condemn Japan's untrustworthiness. Though scholars in their classrooms and politicians at their podiums claim our history began as a foreign colony and treat our civilization as primitive, and though they merely seek a conqueror's gratification and ignore our national psyche and social essence, we do not blame Japan's injustice. We are pressed to reprimand ourselves, and have no time for the reproaching of others. We are pressed to prepare today, and have no time for the chastisement of yesterday. Our duty now is to our construction and not the destruction of others. It is to explore our new destiny according to the solemn dictates of our conscience and not to squabble with others for old animosities and momentary grudges. It is to restore natural, rational veracity by improving and correcting the unnatural, irrational fallacy of the Japanese politicians who are bound by outdated thought and power. The annexation made without national consensus has naturally resulted in intimidation used as a temporary solution, inequality caused by discrimination, and statistics for show. Behold the result of the deepening gully of rancor that will never make peace between two peoples whose interests conflict. To boldly right old wrongs and open a new phase of friendship based on true and mutual understanding is undoubtedly the best way for the both of us to avoid grief and invite blessings. To forcefully bind twenty million bitter people will not secure permanent peace. Moreover, it will make four hundred million Chinese fear and distrust Japan and clearly result in the collapse of all East Asian countries. Today, Korean independence will permit Koreans to enjoy proper lives, will permit the Japanese to concentrate on their responsibility as supporters of East Asia and to free themselves from their mistaken path, and will permit the Chinese to escape from their waking nightmares of anguish and horror. Korean independence will be an indispensable step toward the stability of East Asia as well as be a part of world peace and human happiness. It is not merely a question of national animosity.

Ah, a new world is developing before us! The age of might has passed away, and the age of morality has come. The spirit of humanity nurtured throughout the past centuries now begins to shed the light of a new civilization on the history of mankind. A new spring has come, hastening the rebirth of every living thing. While we held our breath in the ice and snow, our pulse now stirs in the warm breeze and sunshine. The fortune of heaven and earth has returned to us and we ride the changing tide of the world. We neither hesitate nor flinch. By protecting our individual right to freedom our joy shall be full. By manifesting our creativity, our national essence shall be secured in the warmth of spring.

We hereby rise up! Conscience is with us, truth is our companion. Man and woman, old and young, by rising from decay, shall inherit a joyful resurrection with all of creation. The spirits of our ancestors throughout the centuries protect us and the tide of the world sustains us. To begin is to succeed. We only need to march in the light! (author's translation)

All 33 leaders as well as the young initiators were arrested. However, nonviolent demonstrations spread like wildfire all over the country. Their simple cry was *"Mansei!* (Long live) Korean independence!"*. This Mansei movement amplified nationally until 2 million people out of a population of 20 million enthusiastically participated. Originally initiated by moderates, the movement soon turned radical. As the demonstrations turned violent, colonial authorities began to retaliate with swords and rifles, mobilizing the police, the *kenpei,* and even the army. Over the course of a little more than six weeks, about 7,500 died, 15,000 were injured, and more than 46,000 were imprisoned and tortured. Yu Kwansun (1904–20), a young female Christian leader who was tortured to death while imprisoned for a year, is known by today's Koreans as a martyr for the independence movement. Moreover, 715 houses, 47 churches, and two schools were burned down. On April 15, in Cheamni, near Suwŏn, the Japanese forced every villager to assemble in the village church and massacred them by burning the building to the ground.

These savage violations of human rights attracted little attention in the contemporary international community. Although some American and Canadian missionaries went to the press to accuse the Japanese of atrocities, no nation, including the United States, would take notice at official levels of the inhuman suppression in Korea. The Western powers would not criticize a former ally during World War I.

CULTURAL RULE

The March 1 Movement did not succeed in achieving Korean independence. However, the Korean people demonstrated their capacity and will to resist Japanese colonialism. Compared with the various armed resistances of both right and left ideologies during the entire 40 years of Japanese dominion, no other political group ever made as crucial an impact as the March 1 Movement in terms of scale.

Surprised at the immense repercussions, Japan was forced to change its colonial policy from the primitive intimidation of military rule to the reconciliation of the so-called cultural rule. In 1920, the new governor-general, Admiral Saito Makoto (1858–1936), announced a set of measures that supposedly favored the Korean people. The notorious *kenpei*, the gendarmerie, were replaced with regular police, and Japanese officials and school teachers no longer carried swords as a symbol of the conqueror. Moreover, the measures allowed Koreans to publish vernacular newspapers and permitted the people to assemble. The wage discrimination between Korean and Japanese officials was reduced significantly, and the number of schools and school years was increased. The Japanese further made some effort to respect Korean tradition and religious freedom. However, in order to demonstrate Japan's colonial authority, Admiral Saito destroyed a traditional royal palace and constructed on that site an immense government building in Renaissance style, using a special budget he had personally requested from the Japanese emperor. Though it was destroyed in 1995 as a psychological catharsis of Korean nationalism, this was the largest building in the entire Japanese empire.

Of the three Korean-language daily newspapers founded in 1920, one was managed by the Government-General. The other two, the *Dong-A Ilbo* and the *Chosun Ilbo,* were privately owned by Koreans. The former was founded by Kim Sŏngsu, the educator-industrialist, who helped initiate the March 1 Movement. The two newspapers, which are now the two largest dailies in modern Korea, contributed not only in disseminating the Korean alphabet, hangul, but also awakened national consciousness among readers during the colonial period.

Despite the keen censorship of the Government-General, the papers resisted. The *Dong-A Ilbo* printed a modified picture of the Korean marathoner, Son Kijŏng (Kitei Son in Japanese, 1912–2002), who participated as a Japanese athlete in the Berlin Olympics in 1936, winning a gold medal. However, the *Dong-A Ilbo* doctored his picture by erasing the Japanese flag on his breast. For this incident, the paper was suspended for a time. During the 1930s, when the Government-General discouraged the use of the Korean language in favor of Japanese, the *Chosun Ilbo* published in installments a novel entitled *Im Kkŏkchŏng,* a sixteenth-century bandit saga. With this, the author and the newspaper intended to preserve the disappearing Korean language in a sophisticated form of literature.

By increasing educational opportunities, the colonial authorities hoped to maintain discipline, social order, and economic efficiency. Meanwhile, Korean educators sought to evoke modern nationalism among the people. While rapidly expanding public schools, Admiral Saito limited private schools, particularly those established by the Western missionaries, revoking licenses on the pretext that they were violating a prohibition against teaching religion in class. The Japanese authorities forced educators to teach a distorted history at the public schools, including the Mimana fallacy and the myth that Korea was historically dependent on external powers. This legacy of distortion persists, and the history-textbook dispute in Japan in recent years originated from this. The first university in Korea was established in Seoul in 1924 primarily for Japanese students. Koreans were allowed to enter, but only one-third of the total enrollment was allotted to them.

The domestic nationalist movement sought to train more Koreans through education, and, indeed, the number of educated among the younger generation grew. A prominent advocate of this gradual approach to nationalism was Yi Kwangsu (1892–?), a pioneer of modern enlightenment literature, who had earlier quit the provisional government in Shanghai along with his mentor An Ch'angho, a Protestant nationalist. Returning home in May 1922, Yi wrote a famous essay, "On Reconstructing the Nation" ("Minjok Kaejoron"), in a monthly magazine, *Kaebyŏk* (*Creation*). He argued that a moral reconstruction of the educated elites is a prerequisite of an independent nation-state. With this, he sought an evolutionary change within the colonial state. Eventually, this strategy was to be adopted by the majority of the Korean people for survival under ruthless Japanese oppression.

RESISTANCE AT HOME AND ABROAD

The March 1 Movement inspired many Korean freedom fighters to begin thinking about a future independent Korea. They had reached a broad consensus on the need to establish a modern nation, not as a monarchy but as a republic. During March and April in 1919, no less than five provisional governments for a future republic were organized at home and abroad, in Seoul, Vladivostok, and Shanghai. They were eventually unified in Shanghai on November 9, 1919, under the name of the Provisional Government of the Republic of Korea.

The provisional government in Shanghai aimed at a modern republic based on the democratic principle of three separate branches of government. During the provisional government's brief existence, various major Korean leaders participated. All of these represented different political backgrounds and included Syngman Rhee, a Christian democrat based in the United States; Yi Tongnyŏng (1869–1940), a former Righteous Army leader now exiled in Manchuria; Yi Tonghwi (?–1928), a former soldier of the disbanded Korean army turned early communist leader in Siberia; An Ch'angho, a moral self-reformer based in the Korean Protestant community; Sin Ch'aeho, a journalist who advocated a nationalistic Korean history; and Yi Kwangsu, author of the February 1919 student declaration in Tokyo.

However, this organization was a government in form only, and in view of these leaders' different backgrounds as well as their geographical distances, the provisional government's so-called unity was illusory at best. Syngman Rhee, its first president, was at serious odds with Yi Tonghwi, the communist. Other radical nationalists also criticized Rhee for his proposal to the League of Nations for an interim mandate over Korea. Finally, Rhee left Shanghai for the United States, where he continued his diplomatic campaign until 1945. After most of the leaders had left, Kim Ku (1875–1949) took control of the provisional government until after World War II. Today's South Korean constitution legitimized this organization by declaring in its preamble that the Republic of Korea succeeded the provisional government in Shanghai.

Syngman Rhee's diplomatic campaign in Washington, D.C., and Geneva did not attract the attention of the Western powers, most of which had their own colonies in Africa, Asia, and Latin America. Only the nascent Soviet Union, which ideologically advocated anti-imperialism, emerged as a substantial supporter of those colonized countries. Through the Communist International (Comintern), established in 1919, the Soviet Union supplied funds, arms, and advisers to independence fighters. Thus, the early Korean communist movement was created abroad with the support of Comintern among immigrated Koreans in Russia.

On June 26, 1918, Yi Tonghwi founded the Korean Socialist Party in Khabarovsk, Russian Maritime Province. However, a Korean immigrant group in Irkutsk, Siberia, had earlier formed in January 1918 a Korean section of the Irkutsk Communist Party while fighting against the czarist white army during the Bolshevik Revolution. The two factions competed for the hegemony of the Korean communist movement as well as the favor of Comintern. Whereas the latter laid emphasis on the proletarian revolution, the former underscored the national independence of Korea. Soon after failing to gain control of the provisional government, on January 10, 1921, Yi Tonghwi renamed his party the Koryŏ Communist Party, headquartered in Shanghai.

Meanwhile, the teachings of Marx and Lenin rapidly spread among Korean immigrants, exiles, and students in China Proper, Manchuria, Siberia, and Japan, spontaneously creating various communist groups. All of these groups attempted to infiltrate Korea and emancipate the masses from Japanese and capitalist dominance. However, Japanese police scrutiny in colonial Korea hampered the organization of any sort of proletarian revolution. Eventually, agents sent into Korea from the three communist factions of Irkutsk, Shanghai, and Tokyo agreed to cooperate in founding a domestic party. Thus, the first Korean Communist Party, supported by Comintern, gained a foothold in Korean territory in April 1925.

However, this party was soon crushed by the Japanese police, who arrested most of its members. The second party, which was reorganized in December, instigated a mass demonstration on June 10, 1926. Though it entailed another arrest of the party, the demonstration did have a certain impact on the anti-Japanese national resistance. The third party regrouped in September 1926 and changed its strategy to a "united front" policy with the nationalists, establishing the Sin'ganhoe (New Korea Society). However, colonial police surveillance was so effective that the party was still unable to survive. After the fourth party collapsed in October 1928, the Korean Communist Party ended its existence in Korea until 1945. Nonetheless, it continued activity under the various foreign communist parties (in Japan, Manchuria, and China Proper), as its cadres were exiled abroad.

Although the Korean communist movement in Korea failed politically, marxist thought attracted a growing number of Korean intellectuals, particularly literary artists. In July 1925, the Korea Proletariat Artist Federation (also known as the Korea Artista Proleta Federatio, or KAPF) was established, and "tendency literature," a genre that dealt with the class realities of colonial Korea from a socialist perspective, flourished. The proletariat artist movement was successful early on because it effectively formed a united front with other nationalist artists. Tendency literature, which blamed colonial exploitation for the miserable plight of the people, awakened readers to an appreciation of a more sophisticated realism than previous genres that had preached enlightenment.

As film and radio became more accessible to the Korean people during this period, a nationalist filmmaker, Na Un'gyu (1904–37), wrote, directed, and starred in a 1926 movie entitled *Arirang*. The story involved a student who came from a small village and studied in Seoul. After his arrest and brutal torture during the March 1 Movement, he returned home mentally unstable. His crazy shenanigans pestered the Japanese police and Korean collaborators. However, one day he saw the son of a pro-Japanese landlord assaulting his sister. He murdered the assailant with a sickle. When he was arrested by the Japanese police, he suddenly became normal. Aside from its comical portrayal of colonial authorities, the film struck a note of sorrow among Korean audiences for their lost country.

KIM IL SUNG

Japan sought a solution to the global economic panic from 1929 by strengthening its military fascism and invading China. In September 1931, the Japanese military in Manchuria wiped out the local Chinese warlord and established the puppet-state of Manchukuo, inviting the last emperor of the Qing dynasty to legitimize the secession of Manchuria from China. As the Japanese invasion of the continent began, Korea was used as a logistical military base. For Japan, the dream of Toyotomi Hideyoshi in the sixteenth century was now a reality. The Japanese military's advance in Manchuria threatened most of the Korean guerrilla fighters in northeastern Manchuria. During the late 1920s, Korean nationalist armed forces controlled the region's Korean community under an autonomous pseudogovernment directed by the provisional government in Shanghai. They often harassed Japanese forces in various guerrilla skirmishes but could not land any critical blows in their limited capacity. After several fierce battles with the Japanese army, most Korean nationalist guerrilla forces in Manchuria had collapsed by the late 1930s.

In order to support its invasion, Japan began to promote the metal, chemical, and textile industries in Korea, in addition to the previous emphasis on agricultural production. Under the Government-General's financial and various other favors, Japanese *zaibatsu* (large capitalist conglomerates), such as Mitsui, Mitsubishi, and Noguchi, were invited to Korea to produce military supplies. In the secured market in Manchuria they created monopolies by exploiting Korean labor with low wages. Statistically, industrial production in Korea increased remarkably due to these Japanese *zaibatsu*'s encroachment. A few Korean entrepreneurs were able to participate in this industrial boom. However, although their absolute value increased, their proportion to the total capital in Korea seriously decreased.

In July 1937, Japanese and Chinese militaries clashed in a suburb of Beijing. Taking this as an opportunity, Japan began the second Sino-Japanese War and conquered most of north China, which was ruled by warlords loyal to Chiang Kai-shek's (Jiang Jieshi) Nationalist government in Nanjing. Within five months, Japanese forces had captured Nanjing and massacred hundreds of thousands of citizens. However, the Japanese army occupied only the main cities of China and the railroads that connected them. In the vast countryside of the region, private bandits and ideologically organized guerrillas controlled the people. The latter was directed by the Chinese Communist Party.

In Manchuria, the Northeast Anti-Japanese United Army, established by the Manchurian Provincial Committee of the Chinese Communist Party on January 28, 1936, was one of these armed resistance groups against the state of Manchukuo and its Japanese army. During its peak in 1937–40, it became a serious burden to Manchukuo's security, though it did not pose any threat to its existence. Numerous Korean youths, who had no resistance army of their own in the region at the time, joined these Chinese Communist guerrilla forces.

One of the prominent Korean leaders in this bi-ethnic resistance army was Kim Sŏngju (1912–94). Like many others before him, he changed his name to Kim Il Sung, the name of a legendary Korean freedom fighter in Manchuria. With this name, he became the North Korean leader from 1948 to 1994. Chinese political commissars in the Northeast Anti-Japanese United Army encouraged their Korean fighters to raid the Korean territory that bordered with its operation area in southern Manchuria in order to enhance their morale. On June 4, 1937, Kim Il Sung, then a company commander of about 80 to 150 members, attacked Poch'ŏnbo in the northern border of Korea, killing Japanese policemen and burning the police station as well as houses of pro-Japanese Koreans. He then retreated to Manchuria, recrossing the Yalu River. In today's North Korea, the Battle of Poch'ŏnbo, together with his other military campaigns against Japanese troops, is politically eulogized as a symbol of Kim's fighting for independence. Beginning in early 1940, the Japanese military began a large-scale operation to subjugate the Northeast Anti-Japanese United Army. It is believed that Kim Il Sung and his followers retreated in January 1941 to Khabarovsk, where they were protected and trained by the Far Eastern Command of the Soviet Red Army.

TOTALITARIAN RULE

As the war in China expanded, the Government-General accelerated the extraction of both human and material resources from Korea to support Japan's military efforts. In order to do so effectively, Japan's colonial policy put Korea under the draconian rule of a totalitarianism that was unprecedented. Minami Jiro (1874–1955), the new governor-general appointed in August 1936, began to implement the policy of *Naisen ittai* (Japan and Korea as one body), which meant the total assimilation of the Korean people by the Japanese. Minami believed that abolishing the Korean identity would predispose Koreans to be effectively mobilized as well as militarized.

In 1937, the Central Information Committee was established in the

Government-General to police the Korean people. While the Japanese troops in Korea increased from two to three divisions, an increase of secret agents and gendarmerie remarkably strengthened the fascistic police force. In order to intimidate Korean intellectuals, the colonial authorities arrested Yi Kwangsu, the influential writer, and certain Christian leaders such as Yun Ch'iho, although they were soon released. The Government-General then launched in August 1938 an umbrella organization called the Korean Federation of Total Mobilization of National Spirit. Its branches formed along the provincial administrative echelons, the bottom units of which were "patriotic groups" of 10 households each. Living conditions became miserable as food and necessary goods were rationed. The people were forced to wear wartime uniforms. Menswear was designed similar to the Japanese military fashion, while women were forbidden to wear Western skirts or the Korean traditional dress, *ch'ima,* and instead were forced to wear brown trousers called *mompei.* Schoolboy uniforms were designed as a black cadet uniform, and schoolgirls were made to wear white sailor suits.

Governor-General Minami directed his assimilation policy in challenging Korean culture, religion, and tradition. His first target was the language. In March 1938, it was decreed that all schools use only Japanese in education and that students speak only Japanese, even at home. Korean-language newspapers, such as the *Dong-A Ilbo* and the *Chosun Ilbo,* were shut down. Koreans were forced to use Japanese as their national language in everyday life. Every morning, students had to bow to the east in the direction of the Japanese emperor's palace and recite a pledge in Japanese: "We are loyal subjects of the Great Japanese Empire . . . We swear wholeheartedly our allegiance to the emperor."

Every month people were forced to visit a Shinto temple and worship the shrine of Japanese historical hero-gods. This raised serious concern among Korean Christians. Worshipping at the Shinto shrine was at odds with the basic Christian tenet of the Ten Commandments. In 1938, 18 Presbyterian schools were closed. In 1940, more than 2,000 Christians who refused to worship at the Shinto shrine were imprisoned, and more than 200 churches were boarded up. Some 50 Christian leaders, including Reverend Chu Kich'ŏl (1897–1944), were martyred in prison. Later, after liberation, the Presbyterian church, the largest Protestant sect in Korea, split into two factions according to their past behavior of whether they worshipped at the Shinto shrine or not.

In 1939, the Government-General decreed that Koreans were to adopt Japanese-style surnames. To the Korean people steeped in the ages-old Confucian tradition of ancestor worship, changing their surnames was a serious insult and betrayed their beliefs in filial piety. To further encourage the name changing, the colonial authorities granted benefits to those who complied and burdened those who resisted with various disadvantages such as reduced rations, inadmissibility to higher education, and even a denial of mail services. Therefore, the majority of Koreans had no choice but to adopt Japanese surnames during the early 1940s. However, approximately 20 percent chose to keep their Korean names.

Joining World War II as an Axis power, Japan escalated the war with a surprise attack on Pearl Harbor on December 7, 1941. The colonial policy of mobilization in Korea drove the Korean people into a more direct participation in the Pacific War. The Japanese army had begun to accept Korean volunteers since 1938, and about 15,000 Korean youths had responded. Certain ambitious young men, including Park Chung Hee (1917–78), later the South Korean leader during 1961–78, entered the Military Academy in Manchukuo created by the Japanese and advanced to a higher echelon in the Imperial Army, becoming one element of the Korean elite during colonial times. From May 1944 to the end of World War II, Park served as a junior officer of the Japanese army in Manchuria.

As Japan suffered from a lack of manpower in the prolonged Pacific War, it instituted military conscription in Korea in 1943. About 187,000 were drafted into the Japanese army and about another 20,000 into the navy. Moreover, the Japanese military mobilized about 200,000 young Korean women into the notorious *Teishintai* (brigade of dedicated body). These girls, known as "comfort women," were sent to the front lines and forced into sexual servitude for the Japanese troops. In order to mobilize labor, Japan had been recruiting Korean laborers since 1939. However, the colonial authorities began in 1944 to forcefully draft men from the provinces. The total number of Koreans drafted for compulsory labor reached more than 1 million by the end of the war. They were put to work not only in mines and factories but also in the battlefield itself.

Until Japan surrendered on August 15, 1945, the Government-General's totalitarian rule completely silenced all Korean resistance on the peninsula and in Manchuria. The "December Theme" policy adopted in 1928 by Comintern had urged the Korean Communist Party to disband and hide as underground cells in industrial spots. Most of the prominent nationalist leaders, including Yi Kwangsu, Ch'oe Namsŏn, Kim Sŏngsu, and Yun Ch'iho, were grudgingly subdued under fascist suppression. Some of them were forced to write or speak as encouragement to Korean youths into volunteering in the war effort.

During the war years, Korean resistance to colonial rule could only survive abroad. However, it was fairly insubstantial. In China Proper, the provisional government, under Kim Ku's leadership, clung precariously to life in Chongqing, the temporary capital of the Chinese Nationalist government. In north China, Kim Tubong (1889–1958) and Kim Mujŏng (?–?) fought as members of the Chinese Communist Party in Yanan. In the Russian Maritime Province, Kim Il Sung and his followers were trained at the Far Eastern Command of the Soviet Army in Khabarovsk. In Washington, D.C., Syngman Rhee struggled for diplomatic recognition and financial support for Korean independence. However, the U.S. government would not seriously listen to his lonely cry, even after Japan became an enemy of the United States in the Pacific War.

8

House Divided

THE COLD WAR

Liberation

After Germany collapsed on May 8, 1945, the days of Pacific War were numbered. However, the stubborn Japanese military was determined to fight to the last, even if U.S. forces landed on their home islands. Emperor Hirohito (1901–89) finally decided to surrender only after Hiroshima and Nagasaki were struck by atomic bombs on August 6 and 9, respectively. Since Soviet Russia had declared war against Japan on August 8, the Red Army had already advanced to the northeastern provinces of Korea. However, the U.S. forces were at this time located on the Ryukyu Islands, some 600 miles away from the peninsula.

A few days before the August 15 radio announcement of Hirohito's unconditional surrender to the Allied forces, the secretary-general for political affairs of the Government-General in Korea, Endo Ryusaku, secretly approached Song Chinu and informed him of Japan's surrender, offering him a transfer of administrative power. The Japanese colonial rulers thought the Kim Sŏngsu party, of which Song Chinu was a leader, was one of the last groups of influential nationalists left on the peninsula, in spite of their reluctant cooperation. Thus, the authorities believed this group would control the expected disorder resulting from the stunning announcement of the surrender.

The Kim Sŏngsu group rejected the Endo offer, insisting that the provisional government exiled in Chongqing, China, was the only legitimate Korean political entity that represented the Korean people. Therefore, Endo turned at the last moment to his next choice, Yŏ Unhyŏng (Lyuh Woon-hyung). Since August 1944, Yŏ had been secretly forming a political party known as the Korean Independence League (Kŏn'guk Tongmaeng), the members of which were mostly moderate leftists. Yŏ accepted the Endo offer on condition that the Government-General free all political prisoners, release provisions of rice sufficient to feed the Korean people for three months, guarantee freedom of the press, and assure noninterference with Korean political activities, including labor and youth movements. In return, Yŏ promised not to dissolve the existing Government-General administration structure and above all to restrain Korean retaliation as much as possible. Yŏ, with his moderate colleague, An Chaehong (1892–1965), immediately organized the Committee for the Preparation of Korean Independence (Kŏn'guk Chunbiwiwŏnhoe), inviting all nationalist leaders regardless of ideological differences. Meanwhile, in Pyongyang, the Japanese governor approached a Christian nationalist, Cho Mansik (1882–1950), in order to organize a local committee that would maintain security of the region. Cho agreed to cooperate, uniting his organization with the Committee for the Preparation of Korean Independence on August 17. However, unlike the leftist-dominant committee in Seoul, Cho's group was led by right-wing nationalists, with only 2 communists among the 20 members.

The committee in Seoul started as a moderate group under Yŏ's initiative, but as the rightists hesitated in joining, it was soon controlled by the leftists. The Korean Communist Party was swiftly reconstructed in late August under the leadership of Pak Hŏnyŏng (1900–55), who returned to Seoul from hiding as early as August 17. As Soviet troops had already arrived in northern Korea, rumors that the Soviet army would soon occupy most of the peninsula encouraged the leftists. Moreover, the Soviet consul-general and his staff had stayed in Seoul during the war under the protection of a previous Soviet-Japanese nonaggression pact. As of August 1945, the Soviet Union was the only foreign power that had maintained its influence on the Korean peninsula. Taking advantage of the power vacuum, the committee rapidly created the Korean People's Republic, the name of which conveyed a communist influence. Indeed, the People's Republic, at least in its Seoul headquarters, was completely under a communist hegemony, despite the coalition with moderate nationalists. One hundred forty-five local committees were immediately organized, the majority of which were led by the solid core of the communist organization. In the provinces, a voluntary police group, called the Peace Preservation Corps, created by youth, undertook the deserted function of keeping public order.

Hearing that the U.S. forces would soon land on the Korean peninsula, Yŏ Unhyŏng and Pak Hŏnyŏng hurriedly held the Congress of the People's Representatives on September 6. Without any elections, over a thousand "delegates" from all over the country attended. The congress, with no mandate from the people, passed the Tentative Government Organization Law and elected 55 representatives for a People's Legislative Committee, chaired by Yŏ. Thus, the People's Republic of Korea was proclaimed. The Legislative Committee appointed a president and his cabinet members without consultation with their appointees. Syngman Rhee became president, Kim Ku became minister of the interior, and Kim Kyusik became the foreign minister. However, at that moment, these three were abroad and out of contact. Moreover, the majority of cabinet members were communists or extreme leftists. In other words, the People's Republic pretended to be a coalition government, decorating itself with independence-movement celebrities. Meanwhile, all of its decisions and programs were tightly directed by a cohesive communist core.

Occupation

The Allied countries had no clear consensus on postwar policy toward Korea. When Roosevelt, Churchill, and Chiang Kai-shek met in Cairo on December 1, 1943, they vaguely gave thought to a trusteeship in Korea under the tutelage of the Allied powers, declaring in a communiqué that "in due course Korea shall be free and independent" (U.S. Department of States, *Foreign Relations of the United States*, vol. 6, Washington, D.C., 1969, 1,098). The Allied leaders understood Korea as a country that had failed at self-rule during the early twentieth century. This was what Japan had promulgated in order to rationalize its dominion over the peninsula. However, Koreans, who had so ardently desired self-rule, largely misunderstood the phrase "in due course" as a promise for immediate independence. In early 1944, thousands of translated copies of the Cairo Declaration had been smuggled into Korea. Later, at the Yalta Conference in February 1945, Stalin, Roosevelt, and Churchill merely discussed the period of trusteeship without any firm conclusions. Even at the Potsdam Declaration in July, the United States showed a lack of interest in Korea, whereas the Soviet Union intentionally kept its responses on the matter ambiguous. Moreover, not one of the Korean independence fighters abroad had ever been invited by the Allied governments to discuss postwar policy toward Korea. U.S. indifference, in particular, led to the last-minute decision on August 10 at the Pentagon to draw a line at the 38th parallel as an occupation boundary between the United States and the Soviet Union. Because Japan surrendered earlier than expected, Russia, therefore, had no more excuse to advance further onto the peninsula. Stalin, who wanted to capture the northeastern ports of Korea as a part of his Manchurian campaign, was forced to accept Truman's demarcation line.

The Soviet 25th Army's occupation of the northern part of the Korean peninsula began on August 9, the day after the Soviet Union declared war against Japan. On August 15, Colonel General Ivan Mikhailovich Chistiakov, commander of the 25th Army, issued an appeal to the Korean people from his headquarters in Manchuria. He announced the establishment of a Soviet military command in Korea and pronounced Russia a liberator of the country from under Japanese dominion. However, the Korean people at first did not heartily welcome this "liberator," who often pillaged the towns and cities. Nonetheless, the Soviets attempted to establish local self-rule councils and police units in the region they occupied. When they arrived in Pyongyang on August 28, General Chistiakov and his political commissar, Major General Nikolai Georgievich Lebedev, reorganized Cho Mansik's local, primarily nationalist committee into a newly named People's Political Committee, which consisted of an equal number of nationalists and communists.

After the indecisive hesitation of the U.S. policymakers in Washington and Tokyo, Lieutenant General John R. Hodge, commander of the U.S. 24th Corps, was named commander of the U.S. armed forces in Korea. The only reason for his appointment was that his army had been located in Okinawa, the nearest U.S. force in the Pacific. When he arrived in Inchon by ship on September 8, a welcoming party of three English-speaking men from the People's Republic was waiting for him. Startled at being faced with a Korean "government," he refused to receive them. General Hodge indeed wanted to remain loyal to the Proclamation to the Korean People announced on September 7, 1945, by his superior in Tokyo, General Douglas MacArthur:

By virtue of the authority vested in me as Commander in Chief, United States Army Forces, Pacific, I hereby establish military control over Korea south of 38 degrees north latitude and the inhabitants thereof, and announce the following conditions of the occupation:

All powers of government over the territory of Korea south of 38 degrees north latitude and the people thereof will be for the present exercised under my authority. Persons will obey my orders and orders issued under my authority. Acts of resistance to the occupying forces or any acts which may disturb public peace and safety will be punished severely. For all purpose during the military control, English will be the official language. (U.S. State Department Bulletin, *Korea 1945–1948*, Washington, D.C., 1948)

Hearing this, the Korean people, who expected immediate independence after liberation, were greatly disappointed. A few of them well remembered the earlier Russian message in the "Appeal to the People of Korea by the Commander-in-Chief of the Soviet Troops in the Far East," which was made public on August 8 when the Soviet Union had declared war against Japan:

The dark night of slavery over the land of Korea lasted for long decades, and, at last the hour of liberation has come! . . . The powerful strikes of the victorious Red Army will be added to the strikes delivered against Japan from the sea and the air by the troops of America, England, and China . . . Koreans! Rise for a holy war against your oppressors! . . . Know that we will help you as friends in the struggle for your liberation from Japanese oppression. (Tikhvinskii, S. L., et al. (eds.), *The Relations of the Soviet Union with People's Korea, 1945–80*, Documents and Materials, 1981)

Although the appeal was mere war propaganda, its Soviet author understood at least what the Korean people wanted under the Japanese colonial rule. Meanwhile, the U.S. military authorities apparently regarded Korea as an "enemy country of the United States," bound in its duty to "abide by the terms of capitulation." Therefore, U.S. forces would not only continue to employ Japanese officials from the former Government-General but also preserve the laws enacted under Japanese colonial rule. According to MacArthur's General Order, the Korean people would only be politically protected "in their personal and religious rights," merely mentioning "the eventual reconstruction of political life on a peaceful and democratic basis" (Millikan, G. L., and S. Z. Kaplan, *Background Information on Korea: Report of the Committee on Foreign Affairs Pursuant to House Resolution 206*, Department of State Publications 7084, House Report 2496, Washington, D.C., 1950).

General Hodge, who had refused to see the welcoming delegates from the People's Republic, also refused to officially recognize the Provisional Government of the Republic of Korea in Chongqing, allowing the return of its leaders only on an individual basis and not as a political group. Thus, Kim Ku, chairman of the provisional government, returned home on November 23. The same policy was applied to Syngman Rhee, who represented the provisional government in Washington, D.C. The U.S. State Department, which had been troubled by Rhee and his stubborn requests for support for Korean independence during the Pacific War, went so far as to delay his return out of fear of adding to the political turmoil in Korea. Thus, Rhee, the most popular independence leader abroad in the 1940s, did not have the triumphant homecoming as was expected. Instead, he flew home in destitution on a U.S. military plane. However, the rightist nationalists in Seoul, particularly the Korean Democratic Party led by Song Chinu and Kim Sŏngsu, enthusiastically received him on October 16.

On October 14, at the Pyongyang Athletic Field, the Soviet military authorities arranged a Soviet-style hero's welcome ceremony for Kim Il Sung. The ceremony at first impressed the people. However, expecting an older, legendary freedom fighter, they were subsequently embarrassed when General Chistiakov presented them a 33-year-old man who had merely adopted the renowned name. While the old Korean communist leaders, including Pak Hŏnyŏng, struggled for their political hegemony in Seoul, where the Americans had established their military government, the Russians in Pyongyang found new blood in Kim Il Sung. He had served under General Terentii Fomich Shtykov, former commander of the 28th Military Group and now political commissar of the First Far Eastern Front, a higher command than the 25th Army and thus influential in Soviet policy in Korea. Incidentally, a few weeks before the welcoming ceremony, Kim Il Sung's most influential communist rival in Pyongyang, Hyŏn Chunhyŏk, was mysteriously assassinated.

In November 1945, the Soviet Civil Administration set up 10 administrative bureaus and once again reorganized the People's Committee into a mere Soviet-style executive organ. The Russians began to plant the Soviet political system within the occupied territory, in which all government organizations, such as the People's Committee, were controlled by the Communist Party. Thus, the way was prepared for Kim's future anointment as the leader of North Korea when in December he was appointed head of the new North Korean Bureau Branch of the Korean Communist Party, replacing all local leaders. This new branch was independent from the Communist Party led by Pak Hŏnyŏng in Seoul. The Soviets wanted to separate the two to keep Korea a divided entity.

Coalition Policy

The first serious consultation on the Allied policy on Korea took place in December 1945 at the Moscow Conference of foreign ministers from the United States, the Soviet Union, the United Kingdom, and subsequently China. The agreement made public on December 28 included holding a future U.S.-USSR Joint Commission to assist the formation of an interim democratic government "to guide the Korean people toward full independence" (U.S. Department of State, *Foreign Relations of the Unites States*, Diplomatic Papers, 1943–46), and discussing a four-power trusteeship over Korea for a period of up to five years. The superpowers now reconfirmed and materialized the idea of a trusteeship vaguely mentioned at the previous conferences in Cairo and Yalta.

The agreement made at the Moscow Conference unsurprisingly disheartened Koreans, who wanted independence as early as possible. Antitrusteeship movements exploded all over the country. Initially, all Koreans, Right and Left, opposed the idea. A few days later, however, the communist and Far Left parties, obeying Soviet direction, turned to support the Moscow Agreement. Nonetheless, on the right, Kim Ku, together with Syngman Rhee, continued to lead the antitrusteeship movement.

The Moscow Conference resulted in aggravating the conflict between Right and Left political parties in the south. The U.S. State Department's January 29 directive to the U.S. Army military government in Korea urged a political coalition between Right and Left parties in order to meet in the upcoming U.S.-USSR Joint Commission, which aimed to organize a provisional government for the trusteeship. This reflected the U.S. postwar policy on occupied countries liberated from the Axis in Europe and Asia. On February 11, 1946, rightist parties, despite their anti trusteeship position, assembled for the Representative Democratic Council of South Korea, organized by the U.S. military government. Syngman Rhee was elected chairman of this council, though General Hodge and his staff in the military government wanted to support moderate leaders, such as Kim Kyusik, who would better lead the coalition between Right and Left. Unfortunately, at the same time, communist and certain leftist parties rejected the council and instead formed the Democratic National Front.

The U.S.-USSR Joint Commission, first held in Seoul on March 20, 1946, was unable to reach a mutual agreement on the selection of Korean political parties that would take part in the future provisional government. The Soviet delegates insisted on excluding most of the rightist parties that opposed the Moscow Agreement, while the U.S. argued that the free expression of political opinion, including the antitrusteeship movement, should be respected. After a two-month stalemate, the Joint Commission was finally postponed indefinitely in early May.

The rightist camp began to wage an anti-Soviet, anticommunist mass movement, demanding immediate independence. During his provincial campaign, Syngman Rhee called on June 3 for the establishment of a separate independent government in the south if the Soviet Union would not cooperate with the United States in organizing a unified Korean government. Meanwhile, strongly supported by the U.S. military government, the rightist moderate Kim Kyusik promoted a coalition movement between Right and Left parties. In July 1946, the State Department in Washington, D.C., ordered Seoul to follow the January 29 directive to encourage the coalition of moderates as a first step toward establishing an interim government. While the leftist moderate Yŏ Unhyŏng joined this fragile coalition, Pak Hŏnyŏng's Communist Party opposed it.

Socialism in One Zone

In February 1946, the Soviet Civil Administration handed over its authority to a provisional administration in Pyongyang and stepped back as mere advisers. However, its influence remained while the Red Army continued to occupy the north. When Cho Mansik, the nationalist leader, had been arrested for his opposition to the Moscow Agreement in January, the Russians supported Kim Il Sung in heading the Interim People's Committee. Even before the U.S.-USSR Joint Commission held in March, the Russians and communists in the North renounced cooperation with the nationalists. The Communist Party and the People's Committee were now dominated by two loyal factions: the Manchurian partisans headed by Kim Il Sung, and the Russian Koreans who came with the occupying Red Army. Kim, supported by the Russian influence, urged the installation of a "democratic base in North Korea" before the establishment of a unified Korean government. This followed Stalin's Korean policy of "socialism in one zone," which meant an exclusive Soviet grip on the north, and this idea was loyally implemented by a group of political commissars of the Red Army in North Korea, particularly General Shtykov, chief of the Soviet delegation to the U.S.-U.S.S.R. Joint Commission.

In March and thereafter, Kim's provisional administration hurriedly pushed radical policies of land reform, by which the state confiscated all lands from owners without compensation and redistributed them to tillers without payment. At the same time, the administration nationalized key industries. In fact, the Korean communist revolution had begun, liquidating the system of landownership under the Japanese and the "parasitical" Korean landlords. Geographically, the North had a relatively small amount of arable land compared with the South. This land was shared by numerous small-scale landowners. Therefore, while many tillers were happy with the new distribution of the land, some anticommunist sentiment also arose. Uprisings of individuals against the Soviet Command and its People's Committee occurred in Pyongyang, mainly as personal attempts on the lives of the Soviet commander Chistiakov and Kang Ryang'uk, a procommunist relative of Kim Il Sung. Not only land owners, petit bourgeois, and intellectuals began to leave the North; anticommunist merchants, motivated students, and opportunity searchers did as well. Until 1949, approximately 2 million people immigrated south. However, free traffic over the 38th parallel was soon regulated.

The Interim People's Committee headed by Kim Il Sung was dominated primarily by the old Comintern group and the Korean communist faction previously serving under Mao Zedong in Yanan, China. However, Kim's group of Manchurian partisans and Russian Koreans, who had close connections with the Soviet authorities, obtained substantial power and occupied key organs, such as the party secretariat and the security services. Soviet policy in North Korea was more dictatorial than it was in Eastern European countries. Nonetheless, though favored by this policy, Kim Il Sung made a laborious effort to ally with the Yanan group in order to isolate the Comintern domestic faction. In August 1946, again under the directive of Soviet authorities, Kim created the North Korean Workers' Party, merging the North Korean Bureau Branch of the Korean Communist Party and the New People's Party of the Yanan group. Kim's party became an entirely independent body in the Soviet zone, completely separating itself from Pak Hŏnyŏng's South Korean Workers' Party. Thus, the communists' control over North Korea solidified quite rapidly compared to most Eastern European countries, which became Soviet satellites when their independent opposition parties became liquidated in the fall of 1947 or early 1948.

Meanwhile, in Seoul, the South Korean Worker's Party, led by Pak Hŏnyŏng, took a hard-line stance and turned to underground struggle in May 1946 when its forgery activities were disclosed and condemned. Following directions from Moscow and Pyongyang, Pak opposed the coalition movement and was determined to fight by mobilizing the masses against the U.S. military government. He demanded radical reforms of land, as in the North, and the transfer of power to a people's committee in the South. The communists instigated nationwide sabotage in September and an insurrection on October 1 in Taegu, a southeastern provincial capital. However, Pak's active struggle in the South did not impress Stalin, who had already established his "one-zone socialism" in North Korea.

Pak Hŏnyŏng and his communist followers pursued the establishment of an independent and unified Korean government in Seoul with a predominantly communist influence. The plan, which would hand over the already-secured North Korea to a government outside Soviet control, was not acceptable to Stalin. Eventually, under Shtykov's recommendation, Stalin chose Kim Il Sung as the future North Korean leader, discarding Pak Hŏnyŏng, who was supported by Russian diplomats in Seoul.

American Choice

On October 7, the coalition movement of Kim Kyusik and Yŏ Unhyŏng reached an agreement on seven basic principles for Korean unification, among which the Right and Left moderates decided to confiscate land while compensating the landowners and distribute it to the peasants without payment. Under U.S. suggestion, 45 members of an interim assembly were publicly elected and appointed to office. On December 12, 1946, Kim Kyusik became chairman of the Korean Interim Legislative Assembly, the majority of which included members from Kim Sŏngsu's Korean Democratic Party and pro–Syngman Rhee rightists. The U.S. military authorities, encouraged by the Interim Assembly, pushed a program of transferring administration to a South Korean interim government. In February 1947, An Chaehong, a sympathetic moderate, took office as chief civil administrator.

With the success of the coalition, the U.S. military government decided to try again for a trusteeship over the entire peninsula through a U.S.-USSR Joint Commission, unaware that the Soviets had already solidified their North Korean control. Meanwhile, the two rightist leaders, Kim Ku and Syngman Rhee, believing that the Joint Commission would give the Russians opportunity to gain control of the South, again resumed their antitrusteeship movement, embarrassing the U.S. authorities. However, the two nationalists had different dreams. Kim campaigned for the former provisional government in Chongqing to be legitimized by a unified rightist camp, while Rhee, who foresaw that the United States and Soviet Union would not solve the Korea issue, lobbied in Washington, D.C. for a separate anticommunist government in the South. Meanwhile, both Kim and Rhee welcomed the Truman Doctrine, declared by U.S. president Harry Truman in March 1947 to hinder communist activities in Greece and Turkey. Indeed, the Cold War between the United States and the Soviet Union had begun in Eastern Europe, where all coalition governments established by the Allies had become satellites of Moscow.

Nonetheless, the U.S.-USSR Joint Commission resumed on May 21, 1947. Again, the two negotiators were unable to reach any agreement by July. Given that the Soviet Union consistently opposed the inclusion of the rightist political parties on the pretext of their antitrusteeship position, it is generally believed today that Russian support for the trusteeship itself was a hoax strategy. Stalin's real intention was to secure his one-zone socialism in North Korea. Beginning in the fall of 1947 when Poland, Romania, and Bulgaria became satellite states of the Soviet Union, the United States started its containment policy to enclose the communist bloc. Thus, the United States dropped any illusion it harbored of a joint trusteeship over the entire Korean peninsula and began to distinguish North Korea as a part of the Soviet area that needed to be contained. As the Cold War escalated, the U.S. military government began to grudgingly cooperate with Syngman Rhee, from whom the United States had tried to distance itself. Therefore, the fragile coalition of Left and Right moderates in Seoul eventually collapsed.

Socioeconomic Panic

Liberation from colonialism caused immense population movement on the Korean peninsula during the next 4–5 years. In 1945, South Korea's population was estimated to be just over 16 million. However, it grew to 20 million the next year. While 630,000 Japanese were repatriated from South Korea, 1,108,047 Koreans, mostly drafted workers, returned home from Japan. Meanwhile, about 1,800,000 Koreans, including landowners, entrepreneurs, and other anticommunists, crossed the 38th parallel to the South, and about 12,000 Korean immigrants arrived from China and Manchuria.

The Korean economy, which was entirely based on the Japanese yen until the end of the war, now faced a crisis caused by the sudden withdrawal of its capital and management. Most of the industrial facilities run by the Japanese were abandoned and vandalized, while mines and railroads were deserted. Compared to 1944, the unemployment rate of South Korea's industries in September 1947 rose to about 60 percent. Though the rent of land was lowered in rural areas, the rice harvest decreased. The U.S. military government supplied flour, but as it was not the main staple of Korean food, the people soon became sick of it. Terrible inflation added to the chaos. From August 1945 to December 1946, retail prices rose to 10 times their normal amount, while wholesale prices rose to 28 times the normal amount. The average monthly cost of food per person rose from 8 yen to 800 during that first year.

Refugees and repatriates, though mostly young and employable, were excluded by the rural community and now joined the jobless mobs flooding into the cities. Some of these formed gangs of carpetbaggers and black-marketers; others were recruited as part of the police or constabulary; and still others became members of political youth groups, such as the Korean Democratic and Patriotic Youth Union (communist), the Great Korea Democratic Youth Association (rightist), the Northwest Youth Association (anticommunist), the Korean Independence Youth Association (pro-Rhee), the Taedong Youth Corps (nationalist), and the National Youth Corps (ultra-rightist). Dependent upon illegal funds, these youth groups instigated violence and disorder and were not above terrorism for the sake of their ideologies. Song Chinu, leader of the Korean Democratic Party, became the first victim to be assassinated by a left-wing terrorist, in December 1945. Yŏ Unhyŏng's assassination by a rightist followed in July 1947. Next came Chang Tŏksu (1895–1947), a founding member of Song's party, by a leftist in the same year. Finally, Kim Ku would be the last victim, in June 1949. Pak Hŏnyŏng's Communist Party mobilized its Youth Union into various demonstrations and acts of sabotage, including the September 24 railroad workers strike and the October 1 Taegu insurrection. Meanwhile, the police used several rightist and anticommunist youth groups to counter them.

Separate Governments

In September 1947, the United States took the Korea issue to the United Nations, where U.S. influence was now dominant. The rightist camp in Seoul welcomed this American initiative in the UN. However, moderate coalition leaders, foreseeing that the North would be uncooperative with the UN and thus render the American initiative impractical, called for an immediate assembly of political group representatives from the North and South in order to discuss a unified government. On November 14, the UN General Assembly adopted a resolution to hold a general election for a National Assembly no later than March 31, 1948. The election was to be "on the basis of adult suffrage and secret ballot to choose representatives," so that those elected "may establish a National Government of Korea" (Tewksbury, D. G. (ed.), *Source Materials in Korean Politics and Ideologies*, Institute of Pacific Relations, 1950). The UN Temporary Commission for Korea, organized to implement the resolution, was soon functioning in South Korea. However, the Soviet and North Korean authorities refused to let it operate within their zone. The North, furthermore, in February 1948 created the Korean People's Army and announced the draft of a constitution for a future people's republic.

Eventually, on February 26, the UN commission was directed to hold a separate ballot in the South, and the U.S. military government set the day for May 10. Moderate coalitionists and Kim Ku, who opposed the separate government, boycotted the election. Meanwhile, Pak Hŏnyŏng's Communist Party attempted to undermine the ballot by instigating a guerrilla insurrection on Cheju Island. However, the election was successful. Approximately 7,480,000 people, or about 75 percent of the eligible population, voted. The UN declared the election as "a valid expression of the free will of the electorate in those parts of Korea which were accessible to the Commission" (Tewksbury (ed.), *Source Materials in Korean Politics and Ideologies*, 1950).

A constitution leaning toward a presidential system was adopted on July 17 at the National Assembly. Among the 198 representatives, 83 of them, by far the largest group, were independents of no political-party affiliation; 56 representatives were pro-Rhee; and 29 came from the Korean Democratic Party. Furthermore, there was one member each from the pro–Cho Mansik group and Kim Ku's Korean Independence Party. However, Syngman Rhee, forming a coalition with the Korean Democratic Party, was easily elected president of the new government. On August 15, the Republic of Korea was proclaimed as the only legitimate government on the Korean peninsula on the basis of the UN-supervised election. This was confirmed on December 12 at the UN General Assembly. The United States and most of its Western allies promptly established diplomatic relations.

During the summer, a different type of election was held in the North, in which the voters had no other choice than those candidates recommended by the Communist Party's sister organization, called the North Korean Democratic Front for National Unification. In August, these elected representatives assembled at the Supreme People's Council and proclaimed the Democratic People's Republic of Korea. The new government of the DPRK was launched on September 9, headed by Kim Il Sung as premier and Pak Hŏnyŏng as vice premier and foreign minister. The Soviet Union and its allies in Eastern Europe quickly recognized this government.

Thus, Korea was divided into two houses. In late 1948, the Soviet occupation forces in the North withdrew. The U.S. withdrawal, however, followed later in June 1949, after a controversial debate on its military disengagement in Korea among the policymakers in Washington, D.C.

On the Eve of War

The South Korean Workers' Party with other furious underground activities seriously challenged Syngman Rhee's newly launched Republic of Korea. The antielection resistance organized by the communists on Cheju Island on April 3, 1948, soon extended into a yearlong guerrilla war between government forces and the communist fighters. Some 20,000–30,000 people became victims to this conflict. In October 1948, the communists instigated a revolt within another battalion of the South Korean army, which soon based itself in the Chiri Mountains, located where the borders of the four southern provinces meet. In the summer of 1949, the South Korean Workers' Party merged with the Korean Workers' Party in the North and reorganized as the South Korean Democratic Front for the National Unification, strengthening its activities of sabotage and guerrilla struggle in the South.

President Syngman Rhee, an uncompromising anti-Japanese and anti-communist statesman, now faced a dilemma of choosing one of his sworn enemies to fight the other. As the political leader of a divided nation under the Cold War, anticommunism took precedence over his anti-Japanese sentiment. Thus, he resorted to reemploying colonial police collaborators to crack down on the underground activities of the communists. His policy was controversial and criticized for shirking the responsibility of the new independent Korea to punish the Japanese collaborators who had oppressed Korean freedom fighters during colonial rule. Although a special law to this effect was adopted at the National Assembly, President Rhee did not enforce it as the people expected. Under his protection, the former collaborators in the Japanese police were free to crack down on the communist underground cells. By early spring in 1950, the core of the South Korean Workers' Party had collapsed due to efficient police investigation and large-scale military campaigns that had remarkably weakened guerrilla activity.

In China, Mao Zedong's People's Army drove Chiang Kai-shek's Nationalist forces from the continent in October 1949. The Korean Volunteer Army, recruited from Korean communities in Manchuria, helped subdue the Nationalist forces in the region and later performed a blitzkrieg operation on the Yangzi River. The fact that the U.S. military did not commit to the conflict in the Chinese civil war was duly noted by Stalin and Kim Il Sung. After the failure of the communist guerrillas in the South, Kim Il Sung and Pak Hŏnyŏng then planned to subdue the Republic of Korea by using North Korean forces. Beginning in early summer of that year, they requested military aid from Moscow and asked Beijing to supply the Manchurian-Korean volunteers. They believed that the United States would not engage in a civil war in Korea, as it had not involved itself in China. They were further encouraged on January 12, 1950, when the U.S. secretary of state, Dean Acheson, explained the American containment policy at the National Press Club. Mentioning the "defense perimeter" in the Pacific, he noted that "Korea was clearly left outside" (Chase, James, *Acheson: The Secretary of State Who Created the American World*, Simon & Schuster, 1998, p. 269).

In late January 1950, Kim Il Sung and Pak Hŏnyŏng visited Moscow and asked Stalin to endorse their plan of unification by military force. Stalin, who did not want the cold war with the United States to escalate into a hot war, decided to support them on the condition that the Soviet Union remain officially uncommitted to a "civil war" among the two Koreas. Mao Zedong sent 41,000 troops of the Korean Volunteer Army to North Korea. Soviet military advisers soon arrived with weapons and equipment. The North Korean forces now included 10 combat divisions, a tank brigade, and a motorcycle regiment. They were equipped with 1,600 artilleries, 258 T-34 tanks, and 172 airplanes.

Military buildup in the South was unable to catch up to the North. Approximately 100,000 men of the South Korean National Army were ill equipped. Of these, about 65,000 men were armed with unusable mortar and machine guns. Furthermore, they lacked tanks and air support. Despite all this, President Rhee continued to openly use phrases like a "northward march for unification" in his rhetoric, expecting U.S. military support to contain the communist bloc.

The War and Aftermath

From June 10 to 19, 1950, seven combat divisions of the North Korean People's Army moved to the 38th parallel on the pretext of maneuvering exercises. On the 23rd, their commanders were given the order to begin the war of liberation. They proceeded to march southward in the early dawn of the 25th. As an official excuse for its invasion, North Korea claimed retaliation against an imaginary full-scale South Korean attack. This excuse may have stemmed from frequent border clashes between the two belligerent armies along the 38th parallel. The tension had been further compounded by President Rhee's continued rhetoric.

The North Korean military, strengthened by Soviet aid, immediately overwhelmed the South Korean defense, capturing Seoul on the 28th, after only three days of war. However, against North Korea's expectations, the United States acted swiftly. On the 25th (New York time, a day after the invasion), the UN Security Council, urged by the United States, adopted a resolution to condemn North Korea's actions. Fortunately, the Soviet delegate, who could have blocked the resolution with his veto power, had been boycotting the council in order to protest mainland China's lack of representation in the UN. Soon afterwards, a second resolution was adopted to go to war, and President Harry S. Truman dispatched U.S. navy and air forces on the 27th and ground forces on the 30th. Sixteen UN member countries (Australia, Belgium, Canada, Columbia, Ethiopia, France, Greece, Luxembourg, the Netherlands, New Zealand, the Philippines, the Republic of South Africa, Thailand, Turkey, the United Kingdom, and the United States) sent forces to Korea under the UN Forces Command led by General Douglas MacArthur in Tokyo.

The U.S. and South Korean armies continued to retreat down the Naktong River line, which bordered the southwestern tip of the peninsula. After a brief stalemate, General MacArthur successfully launched his famous Inchon Landing operation on September 15, recapturing Seoul and cutting off the North Korean front lines to the South, which forced them to collapse. Following the U.S. Joint Chiefs of Staff directive issued on September 27, which approved of a military operation north of the 38th parallel in order to demolish the North Korean forces, MacArthur ordered his troops on October 2 to cross the border. On October 20, UN forces captured Pyongyang and continued to advance to the Yalu River. However, Mao Zedong had already sent 18 combat divisions of the Chinese Volunteer Army across the Yalu River on October 19. Against these new waves, UN forces again had no choice but to retreat and abandon Seoul.

In the early spring of 1951, UN forces returned and rolled the Chinese and North Korean forces back to the 38th parallel. On March 23, President Truman declared in a statement that UN forces had stemmed the communist invasion, and therefore the UN Forces Command was ready to negotiate a cease-fire. The next day, General MacArthur, while visiting the Korean front, disregarded the president's intention and urged the bombing of Manchuria to retaliate against the Chinese communists. Truman, like Stalin, did not want to escalate the conflict into a third world war, and relieved MacArthur from command of the UN forces in Korea on April 11. Thus, the Korean War remained a limited war.

On the advice of Moscow, the Korean and Chinese communists accepted the truce negotiation suggested by the United States, and talks started in July 1951. Until the two sides finally signed the armistice two years later on July 27, 1953, the prolonged war brought immense damages both in the North and South. The agreement was signed by General Clark (commander of the UN forces in Korea) on one side, and Kim Il Sung (commander of the Korean People's Army) and Peng Dehuai (commander of the Chinese Volunteer Army) on the other. President Syngman Rhee refused to sign it but tacitly approved of the truce after the United States assured him of its security commitment in South Korea. Thus, the Korean War of 1950–53 ended, and a border was formed that marginally followed the 38th parallel. This area became known as the Demilitarized Zone (DMZ).

The war cost a great number of human lives and affected all 30 million Koreans in the North and South, as well as about 700,000 Korean Chinese from Manchuria. Precise statistics were not available until recently. In the North, 2,720,000 were reported dead or missing. However, of that number, more than 1 million of the missing North Koreans are in fact assumed to have migrated south. About 500,000 North Korean soldiers are assumed to have been killed in battle, and the rest of the figure, more than 1 million, are believed to be civilian casualties. In the South, the military casualties in battle were 237,686. About 500,000 civilians were abducted or pressed into the North Korean army, and another 600,000 civilians were reported either dead or missing, making the total loss of human life in the South 1,330,000. According to official records, the U.S. casualties were 33,629 killed, 103,284 wounded, and 9 missing. As for other UN forces, excluding the South Koreans, the casualties were 3,143 killed, 11,532 wounded, and 525 missing. And last but not least, official Chinese records state that their casualties were 116,000 killed, 220,000 wounded, and 29,000 missing, making a total of 366,000. However, the actual number is now estimated to be about 900,000.

BUILDING THE NATION

Syngman Rhee

Syngman Rhee was the uncontested leader of the political scene in the late 1940s South Korea. His charismatic leadership originated from the simplicity of his patriotic beliefs, which disarmed not only the people in rural areas but also city dwellers and intellectuals. With an Austrian wife and no children, his political camp was free from nepotism, as he had no close relatives. Neither did he have special local connections, because of his long exile abroad. Receiving a Ph.D. earlier from the Princeton University, he was esteemed among intellectuals due to the Korean tradition of honoring the literati. Above all, he had saved the nascent Republic of Korea from the communist invasion by soliciting the United States with his prominent skills in diplomacy. He thus deserves to be respected as the founding father of South Korea.

Syngman Rhee's political ideology was strongly anticommunist and based on American democracy, which he had learned and experienced in the United States. His early tutelage under American missionaries in Seoul gave him ethical values based on the Christian conscience. However, South Korea's immediate importation of Western democracy and a market economy was in question. During the Japanese dominion, Koreans had no political life save forced obedience. In the short period before and during the Korean War, the South Korean economy depended largely upon agriculture and mining, as the modern industries that grew during colonial times were located mainly in the North. With the growth of colleges and universities, the population of highly educated elite increased remarkably in the ranks of the jobless. The United States provided aid, but the priority of its capital investment went to the armed forces.

After the war, President Rhee's leadership began to be challenged by his political opponents. Despite his old age, he still showed a strong desire for power and prolonged his one-man rule for 10 years, becoming somewhat of an authoritarian. He was criticized repeatedly for oppressing the opposition party in violation of the National Security Law adopted at the National Assembly in 1948. Along with the exploding population due to a high birthrate after the war, rapid urbanization and higher education could no longer tolerate Rhee's autocratic politics. During the March 15 presidential election in 1960, thanks to the earlier death of his strongest rival and the execution of another candidate, Rhee was reelected for the fourth time. However, most of the voters in the countryside, intimidated by police, were forced to support Rhee and his running mate.

Demonstrations to protest the unfair election began to arise in the provincial cities. On voting day in Masan, a southern port, a high-school student was killed by police fire. This instigated a large-scale student demonstration in Seoul on April 19. On that day, about 20,000 students, mostly from universities and high schools, took to the street, shouting, "Down with dictatorship!" The police fired on them as they marched toward the presidential office, killing more than 100. On April 26, President Rhee submitted to the pressure, stating, "If the people want it, I will resign." Soon after, he left for Hawaii, where he had once exiled himself during the independence movement.

Purges in the North

During and after the war, Premier Kim Il Sung concentrated his political power through a series of Stalinist purges. Accordingly, the balance of the four major factions in the Workers' Party was broken. In October 1950, Hŏ Kai (1904–53), a prominent Russian Korean, was censured severely for mistakes in rebuilding party organizations damaged during the retreat north. Later, it was reported that he committed suicide. In the same year, Kim Mujŏng, a leading general in the Yanan faction, was purged from the army for misfeasance.

However, Kim Il Sung's real target was Pak Hŏnyŏng and his faction of the former South Korean Workers' Party. When one member of the South Korean faction was arrested in early 1953, Pak was no longer seen at state occasions. After the war, 12 members of Pak's faction were indicted and condemned for activities as American spies and subsequently executed. Pak came to the same fate in December 1955. Pak and his followers were given the blame for the failure of the "unification war" and were therefore liquidated.

Nikita Khrushchev's criticism of Stalin's personal cult and advocacy of collective leadership at the 20th Congress of the Soviet Communist Party in February 1956 reverberated in North Korea. The Yanan faction plotted to change the one-man rule system to a collective leadership while Kim Il Sung visited Moscow during that summer. As soon as Kim returned home, they were immediately branded as antirevolutionary revisionists and purged. Moscow and Beijing intervened and strongly urged Kim to restore the Yanan faction's position. Nonetheless, the Korean Workers' Party declared in March 1958 that it had liquidated all dissension within itself. Kim now began to stress a policy of *juche* (self-reliance). This was an apparent attempt to break free of external influences from either Russia or China on domestic politics. Thus, the North Korean government and the Korean Workers' Party came under the sole direction of Kim Il Sung and his Manchurian guerrilla faction.

As his political power became more concentrated, Kim turned to the economy. Soon after the war, North Korea nearly restored its entire economy through its Three-Year Plan. In 1957, a Soviet-modeled five-year economic plan was started while Premier Kim launched a national campaign known as the Ch'ŏllima (Flying Horse) Movement, a North Korean version of Mao Zedong's Great Leap Forward. Although the achievements in the Five-Year Plan were reported to exceed expectations, in actuality it hindered further growth due to its abuses of raw materials and facilities. The aftereffect of the state-driven economic growth aggravated the situation as agricultural collectivization and industrial nationalization progressed. Nonetheless, by 1958, socialist reforms at various levels of production both in cities and rural areas were completed. Meanwhile, the Ch'ŏllima Movement, initiated from the economic drive, later transformed into a political campaign to consolidate the sole leadership of Kim Il Sung over North Korea.

Students and Soldiers

After the resignation of President Syngman Rhee, in June 1960 the South Korean National Assembly adopted a new constitution that stipulated a bicameral parliamentary system, heralding what was to be called the Second Republic. In the July 19 general election, the Democratic Party originating from the previous Korean Democratic Party dominated both of the houses of Parliament, with 175 out of 233 seats in the lower house and 31 out of 58 seats in the upper house. The parliament then elected Chang Myŏn (1899–1966), former vice president and ambassador to Washington, as the prime minister, and Yun Posŏn (1897–1990) as president. With the new constitution, the prime minister was now the chief of the government's executive branch with his own cabinet, while the president became a figurehead of the state.

Prime Minister Chang Myŏn, a U.S.-educated Catholic, attempted to plant American democracy on Korean soil, which was something President Rhee had failed at. Particularly, Prime Minister Chang encouraged a free press. However, Chang's Democratic Party, plagued by factional rivalries, was incapable of solving the serious unemployment in the cities and food shortages in the countryside. Moreover, the nascent Chang administration faced various difficulties in the forms of disputes and demonstrations by students, teachers, labor unions, and other social-interest groups. Among these various issues, the students' aspirations for national unification with the North prompted left-leaning politicians to stir on the political scene. The ideological adventurism of the students and the economic poverty of the unemployed and rural population created a sufficient pretext for certain ambitious soldiers to make a dash for political power. Though Prime Minister Chang had prepared his own modernization plan to solve these economic difficulties, it was too late. On May 16, 1961, a group of young officers, led by Major General Park Chung Hee (1917–79) finally staged a coup d'état.

As of 1961, the Republic of Korea's National Army had grown impressively to over 600,000 forces that had been trained, equipped, and maintained by U.S. aid and expertise. Modeled after the advanced American military administration, by the end of the Korean War the National Army had become more efficient than the government bureaucracy in South Korea. Moreover, in terms of solidarity, it was the strongest social organization. Park Chung Hee was a graduate of the Japanese-run Manchukuo Military Academy as well as the Japanese Army Cadet School in Tokyo. However, his young supporters, including Kim Jong Pil (1926–), were among the graduates of the Korean Military Academy in 1949. Most of them had started as junior officers during the war and by this time had reached lieutenant colonel.

In the early morning of May 16, 1961, the coup d'état forces broadcasted a six-point pledge of their revolution: anticommunism, strong ties with the United States, elimination of corruption, economic reconstruction, competition with North Korea, and a return to duties after completion of the stated mission. The military junta declared martial law and dissolved the National Assembly. The constitution's authority was suspended, and all political activities were banned. Moreover, the press became censored. Soon the junta named itself the Supreme Council of National Reconstruction, chaired by Park Chung Hee. The Korean Central Intelligence Agency, headed by Kim Jong Pil, was created under this council so that the military could control information at home and abroad as well as give themselves investigative power. The government ministries were thus headed mostly by military personnel.

The military regime enacted an anticommunism law that strengthened the National Security Law that had been prepared by Prime Minister Chang Myŏn's administration. This allowed the arrest of thousands of left-leaning politicians and intellectuals. The regime forced industrialists who had profited from their political collusions to pay back their ill-gotten gains by constructing firms with credit for foreign investments. The United States grudgingly supported the military coup, continuing to supply desperately needed grain on the condition that the military's clear commitment to return the government to civilian control would be implemented. Nonetheless, the regime launched its ambitious First Five-Year Economic Development Plan in 1962, thus demonstrating its political ambition to prolong its power.

In order to uphold its commitment to transfer power to a civilian government, the military merely prepared to take off their uniforms. In December 1962, the Supreme Council adopted a new constitution with a presidential system and a unicameral legislature. Soon, in January 1963, political activities resumed. However, Kim Jong Pil had already organized the Democratic Republican Party in secret. Presidential and parliamentary elections were announced for October and November, respectively. Park Chung Hee eventually ran as a presidential candidate of Kim's party. His rival candidate was the former president Yun Posŏn, who had formed an opposition party. In this carefully managed election, Park won over Yun with a narrow difference of 45.5 versus 45.0 percent. Park's party also dominated the National Assembly election. On December 16, 1963, Park Chung Hee was inaugurated as the fifth president of the Republic of Korea. Thus, the Third Republic was born.

Monolithic State

By early 1957, North Korean premier Kim Il Sung had almost completely purged the old factions from the Workers' Party. Even during the
ideological dispute between two giants in the communist world, China
and the Soviet Union, Premier Kim maintained neutrality. While he leaned
psychologically toward China, he made diplomatic gestures to the Soviet
Union at the same time. In North Korea, Kim Il Sung was now both the
party and the state itself. In February 1960, Kim, accompanied by high-
level cadres of the party, visited a collective farming community in
Ch'ŏngsan Village of the Kangsŏ prefecture near Pyongyang. There, he
pointed out the various problems caused by the leadership of the lowest
echelon of the party. Thereafter, a new policy line known as "on-the-spot
guidance" of the Great Leader (*suryong* in Korean) was launched and
spread over the whole country. The Ch'ŏngsan Village method aimed to
improve both political organization and economic productivity through
Kim's direct guidance.

In October 1960, the commemoration of the 15th anniversary of the
Korean Workers' Party started with the rewriting of Korean communist
history. From this point on, Kim Il Sung was depicted as the source of all
wisdom and truth in relation to the past, present, and future of the Korean
communist movement. The following is an excerpt of a recollection on
Kim's anti-Japanese struggle published in this period:

The Korean Communist Party occupied by petty-bourgeois intellectuals was founded in 1925. However, engaged in the incessant factional strife, the Party failed to root in the masses, became prey to
the oppressive Japanese colonial authorities, and finally was disbanded in 1928. While the opportunists deserted the movement, a
new group of communists under the leadership of Comrade Kim Il
Sung emerged. For the first time, a correct revolutionary line with
the principles of Marxism-Leninism being creatively applied to the
concrete practices and needs of the Korean revolution was established. Under Comrade Kim, the national liberation struggle against
the Japanese was upgraded to a higher level of the armed fight.
Beginning from the fall of 1938 to March 1940, the Korean revolutionary forces under Marshal Kim Il Sung imposed heavy casualties
upon the Japanese army; however, at that point the imperialists mobilized a grand-scale military campaign in order to exterminate us.
Despite our unutterable hardships, the Korean revolutionary forces
had to march and fight to break out of the enemy's encirclement

across snow-covered mountains and through dense jungles. Nevertheless, we performed a twenty thousand *li* [eighty thousand kilometers] Long March for our outstanding leader Marshal Kim Il Sung. In a jungle area, Kim taught the cadres with a brilliant, detailed analysis of the situation, local, regional, and international. (Yim Ch'un-ch'u, *The 20,000-ri Long March–A Recollection of April 1940, in Kŭlloja* April issue, Pyongyang, 1961)

This sort of political literature on Kim Il Sung's guerrilla past attempted to portray beyond historical fact the North Korean regime's legitimacy with its anti-Japanese independence struggle as well as its socialist revolution in colonial Korea. This would often attract certain intellectuals in the South, where Japanese police collaborators continued to be reemployed and Japan-trained military officers took power. Moreover, the indexes of economic growth in the late 1950s made North Korea confident. After the reports that the Five-Year Plan had achieved more than its goals, a new Seven-Year Plan was prepared to begin immediately in 1962. Under the strong confidence of the North Korean leadership, the Fourth Congress of the Korean Workers' Party was held on September 11, 1961, emphasizing a new socialist man armed with the monolithic ideology of the party, spurred onward by socialist patriotism, and equipped with advanced technical training. Thus, faith in the party and the science of productivity was combined.

The Third Republic

President Park Chung Hee's vision of building the nation targeted the economic modernization of the agrarian South Korea. As he was educated in the Manchukuo Military Academy in 1940, he saw how efficiently the Japanese military created a nation and industrialized it with the help of Japan's elite technocrats. Inspired by this, President Park attempted to build an efficiency-oriented government system. In order to implement a series of five-year economic development plans, he created the Economic Planning Board, headed by the deputy prime minister, giving him command of all economy-related ministries. Most of the military elites who joined the government gradually handed their posts over to the more efficient technocrats recruited at home and abroad, among whom were many U.S.-educated economists. The military satisfied itself in remaining within powerful security organs such as the Korean Central Intelligence Agency.

Like many underdeveloped countries, Korea desperately needed capital in order to drive its economic modernization. President Park saw that Japan had achieved a quick economic recovery and growth thanks to the demands of the Korean War, when the United States used the archipelago as a supply base. Supported by the United States, which wanted rapprochement between South Korea and Japan, he started normalization talks with Tokyo and negotiated compensation for Japan's colonial rule. Suppressing student demonstrations that opposed the hasty agreement, Park's government established diplomatic relations with Japan in June 1965, receiving only a compensation of 300 million dollars, with another 500 million in financial and private loans. In August of the same year, the South Korean National Assembly ratified the dispatch of military forces to Vietnam. This the government did in acceptance of a U.S. request, the basis of which was a pledge known as the Brown Memorandum. Under this memorandum, the United States agreed to supply modern military equipment to the Korean forces and assured the government of a loan for economic development. Thus, a total of 312,853 South Korean troops fought with the United States in Vietnam from 1965 to 1973.

During the First Five-Year Economic Development Plan (1962–66), the South Korean economy showed a 7.8 percent average annual growth rate, achieving a remarkable export increase due to the rise of labor-intensive industries such as textiles. The Vietnam War earnings, the Japanese compensation and loans, and other international commercial capital assured industrial investment for the Second Five-Year Plan (1967–71), despite poor domestic savings. Thanks to the economic growth, Park Chung Hee won again over Yun Posŏn in the May 1967 presidential election. Under his authoritarian leadership, South Korea transformed into a modern nation-state, engineered by efficient bureaucrats and adventurous industrialists. However, given that the government controlled the nation's economy, those industrialists' conglomerates, known as chaebol, built colluding ties with the politicians.

Park Chung Hee ran for another term in April 1971, removing the constitutional limitation on three terms in order to do so. He defeated the opposition candidate, Kim Dae Jung (1925–), a proponent of democracy who had persistently opposed Park's authoritarian rule. The chaebol contributed an immense amount of money through slush funds to Park's campaign, while the Korean Central Intelligence Agency kept a vigilant eye on any industrialist who supported Kim. Moreover, Kim's platform for the unification of the North and South, which seemed to imply a political compromise with the communists, came under attack. The results of the election showed that Park obtained 53.2 percent of the vote, while Kim received 45.3 percent. However, the votes were clearly divided by the two candidates' home regions. The southeasterners supported Park, whereas the southwesterners supported Kim. Despite his victory in the election, President Park faced student demonstrations and a riot of those still living in poverty, each protesting his one-man rule. He took a firm stance and suppressed both movements.

Juche, or Kimilsungism

The Soviet premier Nikita Khrushchev's irresolution during the Cuban Crisis in 1962 disappointed the North Korean leadership, who wanted to pursue orthodox Marxism-Leninism. Moreover, North Korea's relationship with China worsened when the Chinese Red Guard openly criticized Kim Il Sung in 1967 during the Cultural Revolution. The North felt threatened when a United States–Japan–South Korea security alliance formed after the diplomatic normalization between Seoul and Tokyo. To make matters worse, the South Korean army had been strengthened by the aid of the United States for its participation in the Vietnam War. In 1962, North Korea began stressing a defense policy along with its economic development, declaring a four-point policy slogan: all people armed, all territory fortified, all forces authorized, and all forces modernized. The defense budget abruptly increased to 30 percent of the total national budget from 1967 to 1971. However, this dulled the economic growth rate. Leading members of the Kapsan faction, a subgroup within the pro-Kim former guerrilla party, were purged in 1967 because of their opposition to Kim's defense policy.

When he visited Indonesia in 1965, Premier Kim Il Sung declared that the Korean Workers' Party would hold consistently to his *juche* philosophy, which meant political self-reliance, economic self-sufficiency, and military self-defense. *Juche*, or Kimilsungism, was created for the monolithic ideological system of Kim's personality cult. His birthplace, Man'gyŏngdae, became a holy national shrine, and his ancestors were depicted as nationalist fighters against foreign invaders throughout history. His grandfather was placed among the local people who burned the American merchant ship, the USS *General Sherman*, in 1866. The personality cult of Kim Il Sung is well expressed in the following poem, entitled "We Live in the Bosom of the Leader":

His love is boundlessly warm;
It is brilliant sunshine.
We live in the bosom of the leader.
We have nothing to envy in this world.

Oh, heavenly leader, Marshal Kim Il Sung,
We look to you and swear our allegiance. (author's translation)

In January 1968, a North Korean commando group snuck across the DMZ and infiltrated Seoul, attempting to attack the South Korean presidential office and kill President Park Chung Hee. Another commando group tested South Korean security by penetrating the eastern coast. Moreover, a U.S. intelligence boat, the USS *Pueblo*, was captured on the East Sea near the North Korean coast while in operation. However, these military provocations did nothing but spur President Park into strengthening his authoritarian grip over the democratic movements of students and oppositions.

Around 1970, Premier Kim Il Sung instigated another purge of certain radical military leaders, replacing them with technocrats and recruiting "second-generation revolutionaries" represented by his eldest son, Kim Jong Il (1942–). The North Korean core of political power was occupied by the Kim family and its in-laws, and this began to prepare a father-son succession.

North-South Talks

In April 1971, Premier Kim Il Sung announced a platform to unite the two governments in a confederation. Earlier in August 1970, President Park Chung Hee had also expressed his intention to initiate North-South exchanges. The South Korean Red Cross eventually suggested in August 1971 the discussion of the humanitarian issue of families separated since the division of the peninsula. To this, North Korea immediately responded. Red Cross representatives from both sides publicly exchanged one-way statements and made preparatory meetings while North and South authorities made decisions through secret contacts. Finally, on July 4, 1972, an intriguing agreement was made public between Kim Yŏngju (1922–), director of organization of the Korean Workers' Party and brother of Premier Kim, and Yi Hurak (1924–), head of the Korean Central Intelligence Agency, who had secretly visited Pyongyang. This North-South communiqué included three principles of reunification: self-reliance, peace, and national solidarity. The two sides agreed to establish the North-South Coordinating Commission, connecting a direct telephone line between Seoul and Pyongyang and promising to stop slandering each other in their rhetoric.

However, the dramatic July 4 Communiqué did not lead the two Koreas toward a reunification, but rather deepened the gap between the two different systems by consolidating each ruler's power. In order to create a more efficient political system to promote national solidarity against the North, Park Chung Hee again suspended the South Korean constitution, on October 17, by declaring martial law and dispersing the National Assembly. The draft of the Yusin (Revitalization) Constitution was adopted by an emergency cabinet and later approved by a national referendum. The new constitution maximized presidential power, including the authority to issue emergency decrees, disperse the National Assembly at will, and appoint one-third of the lawmakers, creating a six-year mandate without term limitation. The president was to be indirectly elected by 2,359 nonpartisan delegates from small districts that could be easily controlled. In December, these delegates of the new National Conference for Unification reelected Park Chung Hee as a virtually omnipotent president.

Meanwhile, in Pyongyang, the Supreme People's Council convened and adopted a new constitution that concentrated all political power into one person, changing the position of premier into president. The new Central People's Committee under the president controlled all legislative, executive, and judiciary powers of the state. North Korean President Kim Il Sung was now constitutionally bestowed with an unprecedented absolute power that the world had not yet seen. This monolithic rule in the North coincided with the Yusin Constitution in the South.

Beginning in August 30, 1972, the first talks between the North and South Red Crosses began in Pyongyang. South Korean delegations officially crossed the borders for the first time since the division. The next month, the North Koreans came to Seoul. However, the dialogue between the communists and capitalists never reached a substantial conclusion, as the latter proposed the discussion of practical issues, as in the time and place of reunions of separated families, while the former wanted first to resolve fundamental differences in political principles, like the abolishment of the south's anticommunist laws. Reciprocal visits among selected delegates and journalists remained mere ceremonial performances for the media, having no visible results like an agreement on the meeting of the separated families. However, the exchanges continued until August 1973, when Kim Yŏngju, the North Korean chairman of the North-South Coordinating Committee, announced the suspension of the dialogue in protest of the Yusin regime's abduction of Kim Dae Jung while he was in exile in Japan.

Park Chung Hee

Park Chung Hee and his followers believed in reserving democratic freedom in South Korea until its economy was strong enough to address

South Korea's widespread poverty. In fact, their motto was "Economy now, democracy later." As an answer to the widening gap of wealth distribution due to industrialization, in 1971 President Park initiated the Saemaul (New Village) Movement, a modernization program for the underdeveloped rural villages where he himself had grown up. Stressing moral slogans of diligence, self-help, and cooperation, the government extended the Saemaul Movement into a national political campaign by applying it to industrial firms, schools, and various social organizations.

However, the South Korean people were no longer docile like their other Asian neighbors in underdeveloped stages. On Easter 1973, liberal intellectuals, radical religious leaders, opposition politicians, and student movement leaders started an anti-Yusin political campaign. When Kim Dae Jung was abducted from Japan in August, student demonstrations protesting the Yusin regime began to occur incessantly. A petition campaign for a new constitutional amendment arose. President Park suppressed each of these with Emergency Decree No. 1, under which martial law could condemn violators to up to 15 years in prison. Nevertheless, the student demonstrations continued to spread. With the issue of Emergency Decree No. 4, 8 students were executed among 14 who were sentenced to death. Kim Chiha (1941–), an activist poet, became famous abroad for his struggle in prison, having violated the decree. On August 15, 1974, a Korean Japanese sent by North Korea attempted to assassinate President Park at an Independence Day celebration. However, he failed, instead killing the first lady, who had attended the ceremony with the president. Nonetheless, Park's Yusin regime continued to suppress the media and the anti-Yusin student demonstrations. The end of the conflict in Vietnam in April 1975, which brought more fears of the communist threat, further fortified Park's emergency decrees.

Park's draconian measures in dealing with the various protests provoked international attention for the suppression of human rights in South Korea. A South Korean lobbyist in Washington was accused of bribing a number of U.S. lawmakers in relation to his government's diplomatic effort to erase the international pressure. This scandal, known as Koreagate, was made public in the American press in 1976 and became a heated issue between Washington and Seoul. President Jimmy Carter, who had advocated the withdrawal of U.S. troops in Korea during his election campaign, put diplomatic pressure on President Park over the human-rights issue when he visited Seoul in 1978. Nonetheless, Park Chung Hee did not listen to Carter, who urged him to democratize South Korea to the extent of its economic development.

In May 1979, Kim Young Sam (1927–), a vocal activist against the Yusin regime, was elected leader of the opposition party. However, he was force-fully removed from the leadership by deliberate maneuvering by the no-torious Korean Central Intelligence Agency. In October, a serious student demonstration arose in Pusan, a southern port city and Kim's hometown. As the protest spread out to the nearby city, Masan, the government de-clared martial law under which Park's Special Forces were mobilized. However, the real enemy was in the inner circle of Park's authoritarian ruling structure.

On October 26, Kim Chaegyu (1926–80), director of the Korean Central Intelligence Agency, attended a private dinner party with Park to discuss the protest issue. There, Kim shot and killed President Park. Park's un-popular Yusin regime was substantially supported by "political armies," which included the Capital Garrison Command, the Special Forces Com-mand, and the Defense Security Command. Because control of the official South Korean army lay under UN forces in deterrence of North Korean invasion, Park created his own forces to suppress domestic rebellions such as insurrections or possible military coups. Ch'a Chich'ŏl (1934–79), though nominally chief of the presidential security guard, had become virtual commander of Park's phalanx of these political armies. Kim Chae-gyu, as head of the Korean Central Intelligence Agency, a powerful or-ganization also created by Park, was a rival of Ch'a, who had gained the president's trust in this period of insurrection. On that night, after dis-cussing the protest issue for some time, Park again favored Ch'a's argu-ments over Kim's. Kim left the room, obtained a gun from his aide, and returned. He first shot and killed Ch'a and then turned his gun on Park.

Despite his 18 years of authoritarian rule, Park Chung Hee did build a modern nation in South Korea, successfully industrializing the agrarian country that had neither capital nor technology to start with. Park's South Korea is often allegorized as "Korea, Inc.," where 51 percent of the shares were owned by Park himself, and the rest by the chaebol and the people. Indeed, he increased South Korea's GNP from a poor $2.3 billion in 1962 to $61.4 billion in 1979. Furthermore, the per-capita income increased from $87 to $1,597 at the same time. However, all this was at the cost of dem-ocratic development and thus bred social unrest. The next generation of the military subsequently inherited the profitable but increasingly volatile Korea, Inc.

Father-Son Succession

In September 1973 in Pyongyang, Kim Jong Il, the now 30-year-old eld-est son of Kim Il Sung, emerged as a powerful figure within the party.

Becoming a member of the party's Political Committee in February 1974, Kim Junior was then called "the Party Center," which implied the officially anointed heir of the Great Leader, his father. He began to wage a political campaign known as the Revolutionary Small-Group Movement, through which he promoted *juche,* or Kimilsungism, in three dimensions: philosophy, technology, and culture. By this, he controlled North Korea's younger generation of elites. A slogan, "Let us pledge allegiance to the son as we did to the father," appeared in the party paper. The father-son succession in North Korea was officially confirmed at the 6th Congress of the Korean Workers' Party in October 1980, when Kim Jong Il was appointed a member in two important organizations, the Executive Committee of the Party Political Bureau and the Military Committee of the Party Secretariat.

North Korea's *juche* policy demanded a self-reliance and self-sufficiency so absolute that its isolated economy remained stagnant during the 1970s. The Six-Year Plan (1971–77), and the subsequent Seven-Year Plan (1978–84), could not overcome the inherent economic difficulties. Moreover, North Korea's annual economic growth rate during these periods was less than 2 percent, while South Korea achieved a higher growth rate of around 10 percent. As of 1980, the South's GNP was four times larger than the North's. Due largely to the self-reliance policy, the North Korean economy was plagued by a lack of technological innovation, a decrease in foreign aid, trade inactiveness, and energy and crude-oil deficiencies. Despite this, the North Korean leadership continued to stress the monolithic *juche* policy in order to insulate its authoritarian system from any external influences.

After Park Chung Hee

Major General Chun Doo Hwan (1931–), head of one of Park Chung Hee's political armies, the Defense Security Command, became the chief investigator of the presidential assassination. In the judicial process of indicting Kim Chaegyu, Chun emerged as a strongman among the younger generation of military leaders in the vacuum left by the death of Ch'a Chich'ŏl, the top leader of Park's phalanx. While Prime Minister Choi Kyu-hah (1919–) succeeded the presidency in accordance with the constitution, Chun's Defense Security Command lieutenants, with the military support of Chun's close friend, Major General Roh Tae Woo (1932–), staged a coup in which they arrested the South Korean army chief of staff on December 12, 1979. Just as in 1961, the United States could do nothing to stop the coup. Thus, Chun and Roh took the first step toward political hegemony.

Once Park Chung Hee's 18-year authoritarian rule ended, the people began to hope for a democratization of political life in accordance with their improved economic life. Kim Young Sam, Kim Dae Jung, and Kim Jong Pil prepared to run for the upcoming presidential election. Nonetheless, the military, which still partially controlled the government, would not take the steps necessary to forward the political normalization process. On May 14, 1980, a large-scale student demonstration for democratization arose in Seoul. The next day, tens of thousands students filled downtown Seoul and protested against the military's political attempt to obstruct democratization.

However, this "Spring in Seoul" was short. On May 17, martial law was declared and all political activities were banned. The army proceeded to subdue the student demonstrations and occupy campuses. Kim Dae Jung and Kim Jong Pil were arrested on charges of insurrection and corruption, respectively. Furthermore, Kim Young Sam was placed under house arrest. Chun Doo Hwan established a military junta chaired by himself. On May 18, another large-scale student demonstration opposing the military's suppression arose in Kwangju, the southwestern provincial capital and Kim Dae Jung's home region. As the army's Special Forces brutally cracked down on the students, enraged citizens joined the demonstration, seized arms from the police, and fought back. The demonstrators succeeded in capturing Kwangju and maintained control over it for a week. Meanwhile, protests spread to other cities in the region. On the early morning of May 27, the army attacked the armed citizens and students with reinforcements, killing hundreds of them during the battle that ensued. Thus, the Kwangju democratization movement in May 1980 was bloodily quelled by the military. The United States, with 37,000 troops stationed in South Korea but following a noninterference policy, was again blamed by then South Korean dissidents for the military's Kwangju suppression.

In September 1980, Chun Doo Hwan was elected president by nonpartisan delegates of the National Conference for Unification, which Park Chung Hee had created in the Yusin Constitution. Before his election he revised the constitution to give himself a single seven-year term limit. Burdened by the December coup and the bloody suppression in Kwangju, President Chun chose appeasement policies, including abolishing curfew, softening security laws, and liberalizing overseas travel. To boost South Korea's international image, the government and the chaebol exerted themselves in 1981 to invite the Summer Olympics to come to Seoul in seven years.

Moreover, the next stage of South Korean economic growth, invested heavily in the chemical and other heavy industries during the 1970s by President Park, began to take off in the 1980s. Due to low prices of oil, dollars, and interests, shipbuilding, automobiles, and electronics began to be the leading exports. In 1986, the first South Korean car, the Hyundai Excel, landed in the American market. In 1987, the South Korean GNP reached $1.284 trillion, with a per-capita income of $3,098. However, the economic gap between rich and poor and the difference between urban and rural environments grew more serious as the scale of the national economy increased. Labor movements, initiated by student activists, began to grow, despite the Chun Doo Hwan government's suppression of trade unions.

Kim Jong Il

At the Sixth Congress of the Korean Workers' Party in October 1980, North Korean President Kim Il Sung proposed a new formula for reunification known as the Democratic Confederate Republic of Koryŏ. It entailed one state with two systems, under which a central government would take care of foreign and military affairs while each of the two local governments in the North and South would have complete autonomy over its own region. Interestingly enough, Kim chose the historical name Koryŏ for this confederation, which neither the North nor the South use as their state names in Korean. The North uses Chosŏn, the name of the last dynasty, while the South uses Taehan, the name of Kojong's short-lived empire. Although Kim Il Sung's idea sounded plausible, the question of who would control the central government remained ambiguous if the confederation were formed. In 1982, President Chun Doo Hwan countered the idea with his own Democratic Reunification Formula for National Reconciliation, under which delegates from both sides would adopt a constitution for a united democratic republic. However, in view of the difficulties of holding talks between the North and South, this idea also appeared unrealistic.

In October 1983, a North Korean terrorist set a bomb in an attempt to assassinate President Chun on a diplomatic visit to Burma. However, the bomb went off before Chun arrived, instead killing 17 high-ranking South Korean officials. Nevertheless, the North and South needed dialogue in order to ease tensions. The humanitarian issue of the separated families, in particular, became more and more desperate as the family members were getting older. The two sides finally reached an agreement to prepare a meeting of these families. In September 1985, for the first time since the Korean War, 151 people of divided families, carefully selected by the two authorities, crossed Panmunjom, the Joint Security Area of the UN and North Korean forces in the Demilitarized Zone. A group of North Koreans came to visit their families in Seoul, while another group of South Koreans visited their families in Pyongyang. Although their hearts were full of words, even communication between parents and children or brothers and sisters was difficult because of the decades-long schism between the two different systems.

As the Great Leader's monolithic system in North Korea had solidified, the personality cult campaign for Kim Jong Il started in the latter half of the 1980s. According to North Korean publications in 1987, Kim, born in a secret camp on Mt. Paektu, was a brilliant genius in all disciplines. To be sure, as Kim Junior began to take part in state affairs, he demonstrated that he had some bold ideas, including a sort of terrorist adventurism toward South Korea. Allegedly, he plotted the 1983 bombing in Burma as well as that of Korean Air flight 747 in 1987. However, Kim Jong Il's utmost task was to propagate his father's *juche* philosophy during most of the 1980s. With this meritorious service, he inherited from his father the supreme command of the Korean People's Army in December 1991 and the chairmanship of the National Defense Commission in April 1993.

Democratization

Beginning from the mid-1980s, the South Korean democratization movement demanded revising the constitution in order to institute a popular vote for the presidency. However, President Chun Doo Hwan persistently maintained the current constitution, under which he expected to easily pass on his presidency to his hand-picked heir through the indirect election by nonpartisan delegates. On June 10, 1987, the death of a student protester by police torture ignited a large-scale demonstration in downtown Seoul in which even white-collar citizens joined. President Chun and his heir apparent, Roh Tae Woo, grudgingly yielded to the people's demand and announced on June 29 their acceptance of a presidential election by popular vote.

In December 1987, an election for a single five-year presidential term was held under a new constitution that had been confirmed by referendum. In the first popular vote for the presidency in 16 years, Roh Tae Woo won over both Kim Young Sam and Kim Dae Jung with 36 percent of the vote, thanks to the two democratic rivals splitting the opposition votes.

In the subsequent general election held in April 1988, however, Roh's party failed to obtain the majority of the National Assembly. Thus, President Roh made a coalition with Kim Young Sam and Kim Jong Pil, thereby alienating Kim Dae Jung in order to get support from the National Assembly.

The 24th Summer Olympics were held in Seoul in September 1988. Thanks to Russian perestroika, the entire communist bloc that had boycotted the previous games in Los Angeles participated. North Korea was the only country to shun the occasion. The 1988 Seoul Olympics, organized by a city of a divided country, reflected the trend of world harmony at the tail end of the Cold War. At the same time, it gave modern South Korea an opportunity to show the world that the nation had achieved remarkable economic growth and democratic development. Taking advantage of the communist bloc participation, the Roh Tae Woo government launched a Northward Policy that broke down South Korea's long-standing diplomacy of isolating North Korea. Beginning in February 1989, South Korea established diplomatic relations with Hungary and subsequently with the Soviet Union in September 1990 and with China in August 1992.

Moreover, President Roh had earlier proposed an exchange of visits between the North and South in his July 7 Declaration in 1988. In this, he promised that the South would support the North in establishing diplomatic relations with the United States and Japan. Finally, in 1989, Roh presented a revised unification program known as the Korean National Community Unification Formula. Indeed, the two Koreas simultaneously entered the UN as individual members on September 17, 1991, after holding the first sports and cultural exchanges between Seoul and Pyongyang since the division. This same year, on December 13 in Seoul, the fifth North-South High-Level Talks signed the Basic Agreement on Reconciliation, Non-Aggression, and Cooperation of Exchanges. The two sides agreed to recognize the existence of each other's government body, respecting each other's different systems and autonomy in domestic affairs. Though each agreed to nonaggression toward the other, they still did not recognize each side as an independent state.

The Roh government, attempting in stages to liberalize its previous control over press and industry, faced aggressive trade-union movements not only among the blue-collar workers in industrial firms but also among white-collar work forces, such as schoolteachers and media employees. The number of trade unions increased from 2,742 in 1987 to 7,861 in 1989. Ever-present strikes and sabotages led to frequent wage hikes, which eventually dulled the growth rate of the South Korean economy.

Kim Young Sam

In the December 18 presidential election of 1992, Kim Young Sam and Kim Dae Jung, the two former democratic fighters under the authoritarian rule of Park Chung Hee, ran for the presidency. Here, Chung Ju Yung (1915–2001), chairman of the Hyundai Group, the largest chaebol in South Korea, joined in the election as a maverick. Kim Young Sam, who had earlier made a coalition with Roh's ruling party, won over Kim Dae Jung, in spite of this third candidate.

As the first civilian president in 32 years, Kim Young Sam wished to demonstrate the political legitimacy of his democratization career. President Kim's "Civilian Government" aimed to negate the past regimes of the three military presidents and place its roots through the Second Republic of Chang Myŏn, the First Republic of Syngman Rhee, and all the way down to the provisional government in Shanghai. Thus, he restored in Shanghai the original building of the provisional government. Furthermore, in November 1996 he demolished the former Japanese Government-General building in Seoul, despite the fact that it had been continued to be used as a capitol after independence and had later been remodeled into a national museum. President Kim's political purges of corrupt personalities from the previous military regimes, as well as "political soldiers" within the military in particular, demonstrated his tenacity for civilian democratization. Moreover, he pushed for elections on local levels in June 1995, where provincial autonomy had been absent since Park's coup in 1961.

Finally, Kim took the two previous presidents, Roh Tae Woo and Chun Doo Hwan, to trial. They were convicted for initiating the coup on December 12, 1979, and for the bloody suppression of the Kwangju democratization movement on May 18, 1980. They were also charged with corruption in relation to huge amounts of slush-fund money. Politicians and former generals involved in the coup and suppression, as well as the chairmen of certain chaebol groups, were also tried. The two former presidents and others were convicted, though all were later pardoned.

In the early 1990s, South Korea faced global pressure to liberalize its market. In August 1993, President Kim boldly reformed banking practices by adopting a real-name transaction system for financial transparency. In December, the government signed the Uruguay Round, opening most domestic markets, including commodities, finances, construction, distributions, and services. Finally, in September 1996, South Korea became a new member of the Organization for Economic Cooperation and Development, an international organization of developed countries. Indeed, South Korea's per-capita income reached $10,000 in December 1996.

The Death of Kim Il Sung

The North Korean *juche* philosophy, particularly its economic aspects, worsened the country's struggle for survival when the communist bloc collapsed in 1989. The need for two crucial resources betrayed Kim Il Sung's self-reliance policy: oil and food. It is difficult for a nation to remain self-sufficient with little arable land and no natural oil. During the Cold-War period, these two resources were supplied by the Soviet Union and China in consideration of North Korea's security alliance against capitalist countries. However, after the collapse of the Berlin Wall, the Soviet Union would no longer supply oil without payment to North Korea. They now demanded hard currency. Similarly, China would demand the same for their food supply when it eventually chose to build a market-economy system. Kim Jong Il, heir of the *juche* nation, was obliged to solve this vital problem for his father. Kim Junior found the solution in his own unique public diplomacy.

Yŏngbyŏn, a small town on the Ch'ŏngch'ŏn River where the Sui Chinese invaders were once defeated by Koguryŏ's Ŭlchi Mundŏk, became known to the world when the satellite picture of its nuclear power station and processing facilities was published in the *New York Times* in 1989. As plutonium cumulated from spent uranium fuel used at the power station might be used for making nuclear bombs, the United States began to monitor closely this otherwise insignificant town. Despite its obligation as a Non-Proliferation Treaty member, North Korea refused to receive a special investigation from the International Atomic Energy Agency, a UN organization that watches the proliferation of nuclear arms all over the world. As such, Kim Junior played a risky diplomacy of brinkmanship over the nuclear issue in order to obtain his desire to deal directly with the United States. Eventually, North Korea even used the withdrawal of its membership from the NPT as a threat. In 1994, this brought tension to the Korean peninsula when, after a series of tedious and unsuccessful negotiations with North Korea, the United States prepared to attack Yŏngbyŏn in order to destroy any possible nuclear arms. In June 1994, former U.S. president Jimmy Carter visited Pyongyang on a private mission to resolve the conflict, meeting personally with President Kim Il Sung. Carter returned with Kim's promise to abolish the Yŏngbyŏn program on the condition that the United States and its allies build light-water nuclear power stations in North Korea to help its energy problems. Such stations would produce no spent fuel to be used for nuclear weaponry. Furthermore, at Carter's urging for North-South talks, Kim Il Sung promised to meet Kim Young Sam.

President Kim Young Sam had earlier, in May 1993, proposed a North-South summit meeting to the North Korean leader, conceding to return to the North a communist convict imprisoned for decades in the South. Kim Young Sam, hearing from Carter Kim Il Sung's intention, hurriedly pushed for the North-South summit meeting. On June 28, 1994, a preliminary contact between two delegates was held. However, President Kim Il Sung died suddenly from a myocardial infarction on July 8. The negotiation was dissolved.

Kim Jong Il was well prepared to inherit his father's absolute power, since he had been anointed the official heir in the early 1980s. However, he did not take on his father's title of president, but merely maintained the position of chairman of the National Defense Commission. The position of president was to be posthumously occupied by his father, who would continue to rule through the injunctions he left behind to guide his son. For his own part, Kim Jong Il could now successfully employ his brinkmanship diplomacy over the nuclear issue in dealing with the United States. In October 1994, North Korea and the United States signed an Agreed Framework in which North Korea would freeze the Yŏngbyŏn nuclear station. However, in return, the United States would annually supply North Korea with 5,000 tons of heavy oil until the United States and its allies completed the construction of the two light-water nuclear stations in North Korea. The Korean Energy Development Organization, in which South Korea, Japan, and the European Union financially participated, began the construction of the light-water stations. Thus, Chairman Kim secured his desperately needed oil without payment.

The next problem was food. In 1995, China began to demand hard currency for its food supply to North Korea. The same year, Kim Jong Il appealed to the World Food Program, created by the UN for emergency aid to famine areas. To ask for aid, he claimed there was a famine in North Korea because of an unprecedented flood that had supposedly resulted in 5 million victims. The North Korean media publicized that millions were starving to death. However, the international inspectors from the World Food Program, who were only allowed to visit a limited area, could not confirm the fact. Given that the monsoon climate of the Korean peninsula brought both flood and drought almost every year, whether the North Korean "unprecedented" flood in 1995 really brought the "famine," or the starvation was caused by food shortage under a communist structure, is unclear. Moreover, the floods and the subsequent droughts in North Korea reportedly continued until 1997, when international humanitarian food aid had solved the problem.

Kim Dae Jung

After South Korea joined the OECD in the fall of 1996, President Kim Young Sam's government failed to organize global-standard institutions to safeguard free capital transactions in an international financial market. South Korean commercial banks liberalized by Kim Young Sam's government invested borrowed foreign capital with low interest into high-interest, risk-taking markets in Southeast Asia and Russia. When the international investors withdrew from the risky markets in Thailand and Indonesia, an Asian financial crisis hit in summer of 1997. South Korea, whose commercial banks had invested in those countries, was not an exception. President Kim's government hurriedly asked the International Monetary Fund to rescue South Korea's banks from declaring a moratorium.

Incidentally, the presidential election was expected on December 18. This time, Kim Dae Jung, the opposition, ran against Lee Hoi Chang (1934–), the incumbent-party candidate. On December 3, 1997, the government signed South Korea's first bailout package of $57 billion with the IMF, which stipulated strict conditions. The South Korean people, who had enjoyed their prosperity during the previous two decades, seriously suffered from the bitter layoffs caused by IMF's forced restructuring and high-interest finance. Dissatisfied, they chose the opposition, Kim Dae Jung, for the presidency. Thus, Kim achieved his long-standing goal to become president after trying for the fourth time.

President Kim Dae Jung acted immediately to solve the problem of the financial crisis. His international image as a democratization fighter greatly helped his diplomatic campaign to obtain financial support from the world. Under his leadership, the South Korean people were able to endure the crisis and overcome it in less than two years. In 2000, South Korea substantially paid back its IMF loan.

President Kim Dae Jung now turned his attention toward his decades-long aspirations on the unification issue. As a liberal opposition leader who had urged a more flexible policy toward North Korea under Park Chung Hee's authoritarian rule, Kim Dae Jung was often branded by South Korea's conservative mainstream as a marginal politician. Indeed, he proclaimed his Sunshine Policy toward North Korea, the term of which he derived from a famous Aesop fable. Under this policy, he would shine substantial economic assistance on North Korea instead of strangling it with military deterrence. This was to open the North to the international world and change its totalitarian system.

In June 1998, President Kim encouraged an intriguing idea by Chung

Ju Yung. Chung, the retired chairman and owner of the South Korea's largest chaebol, the Hyundai Group, wished to contribute some of his wealth to the North-South reconciliation. President Kim welcomed Chairman Chung's sentimental plan to cross the DMZ with 1,001 cattle to provide to his old home village in North Korea, despite the fact that it was legally prohibited for any South Korean citizen to enter North Korea without official permission. Thus, an old man, who had greatly succeeded in business, volunteered in support of President Kim's Sunshine Policy.

On the other hand, the South Korean mainstream establishment was skeptical of the effects of President Kim's reconciliation policy, given that the North Korean leadership under Kim Jong Il had never shown any inclination toward liberalization. However, the younger generation in South Korea, who had not experienced the bitter fratricidal war with the North, was easily persuaded by pro-North radical intellectuals who had led the student protesters against the authoritarian military rulers during the 1970s and 1980s. Thus, the Sunshine Policy incidentally brought an ideological division in South Korea at the turn of the century. However, President Kim remained a persistent suitor of North Korea, encouraging the Hyundai Group to invest in the Mt. Kŭmgang project, which allowed hundreds of South Koreans to visit North Korea as tourists. Finally, he himself visited North Korea, the first time the top leaders of the two sides ever met. He was received by Chairman Kim Jong Il along with a fervent mass of welcoming people at the Pyongyang airport on June 13, 2000.

President Kim Dae Jung and Chairman Kim Jong Il agreed upon a new cooperation between the two Koreas after the first North-South summit talks from June 13–15. The June 15 North-South Joint Declaration included agreements toward self-determination in the pursuit of national unification, acknowledgment of common ground between the two unification formulas of the North and South, resolution of humanitarian issues, pursuit of a balanced development of national economy, a promotion of exchange and cooperation in all areas, and a promotion of government-level dialogue. It further included a promise by Chairman Kim Jong Il to visit Seoul. Among these points, the common ground between the two different unification formulas acknowledged by the two leaders evoked controversy among the South Korean mainstream conservatives, who believed the North's confederation idea was a mere hoax to communize the South. However, President Kim Dae Jung accepted Chairman Kim Jong Il's assessment that the North's revised proposal of "lower stages of a loosened federation" was in reality not so different from the South's idea of a confederation of two different systems. Therefore, the June 15 Joint Declaration again motivated serious ideological controversy in South Korea. Nonetheless, for his contribution to inter-Korean reconciliation, Kim Dae Jung received the 2000 Nobel Peace Prize, something he had long dreamed of.

*   *   *   *   *   *   *

In view of Korea's millennia-old national history, a half-century division of the peninsula is a mere momentary event. Given that today's Koreans both in the North and the South have had so strong a desire for reunification, and that the Cold-War factors of the division have been removed since the 1990s, it is foreseeable that the divided house will be united in the future. In fact, the political division of the Korean peninsula in the twentieth century was a reflection of the ideological confrontation on the global front. During the last six decades, the two Koreas have respectively pursued the two different ideologies of communism and capitalism. We have seen such a divergence in principles, the conflict of idealism versus realism, throughout Korean history: Ich'adon versus Wŏnhyo, Sŏkkatap versus Tabotap, Choe Yŏng versus Yi Sŏnggye, Chŏng Mongju versus Yi Pangwŏn, Sayuksin versus Prince Suyang, rusticated literati versus meritorious subjects, Enlightened Party versus conservative royalists, coalition movement versus separate government, student versus soldier, democratization versus nation building. Nonetheless, these conflicting principles have always converged toward the integration of the nation. Therefore, Koreans will continue to shape a dramatic history when the house is again united in the twenty-first century.

Notable People in the History of Korea

Ado, or Mukhoja; Koguryŏ monk who introduced Buddhism to Silla.

An Chaehong (1892–1965), moderate nationalist; served as chief civil administrator for the U.S. military government in Korea in February 1947.

An Ch'angho (1878–1938), also known by the pen name Tosan; independence-movement leader; founded the morality movement, Hŭngsadan, in Los Angeles in 1913.

An Chunggŭn (1879–1910), independence fighter; assassinated Ito Hirobumi, former Japanese resident-general in Korea, at the Harbin railway station, Manchuria, in June 1909.

An Hyang (1243–1306), Koryŏ scholar-official; introduced Neo-Confucianism to the peninsula in the late thirteenth century.

Chang Chiyŏn (1864–1921), journalist in the early twentieth century who advocated nationalism; publisher of the *Hwangsŏng Sinmun,* a daily in the Korean language.

Chang Myŏn (1899–1966), prime minister 1960–61 under the parliamentary system of the Second Republic's constitution.

Chang Pogo (?–846), or Kungbok; maritime commander of Great Silla on Ch'ŏnghaejin Island, the southwestern tip of the Korean peninsula.

Cho Kwangjo (1482–1519), reformist leader of rustic literati in the early sixteenth century; purged in 1519.

Cho Mansik (1882–1950), Christian nationalist and chairman of the People's Committee in Pyongyang until he was dismissed in December 1945 by the Soviet military authorities.

Ch'oe Cheu (1824–64), founder of the religious sect Tonghak (literally "Eastern Learning"); martyred in 1864.

Ch'oe Ch'iwŏn (857–?), Silla Confucian scholar; served in Tang China after passing the Chinese civil-service exam.

Ch'oe Ch'unghŏn (1149–1219), Koryŏ military ruler; established the Ch'oe House, a Korean dynastic shogunate, in 1196.

Ch'oe Ikhyŏn (1833–1906), xenophobic scholar-official who led the anti-Western, anti-Japanese resistance; onetime leader of guerrilla volunteers.

Ch'oe Namsŏn (1890–1957), man of letters and the first modern Korean poet; wrote the Korean Declaration of Independence during the March 1 Movement.

Ch'oe Rin (1878–?), Ch'ŏndogyo leader; signed the Korean Declaration of Independence.

Ch'oe Yŏng (1316–88), loyalist general in the late Koryŏ period; failed to save the dynasty from the political coup of Yi Sŏnggye and his literati followers.

Choi Kyu-hah (1919–), career diplomat and president of the Republic of Korea from December 1979 to August 1980.

Chŏn Pongjun (1853–95), leader of the Tonghak Farmers Army in 1894; arose against the corrupt magistrate in a southwestern province.

Chŏng Chungbu (?–1178), leader of the Koryŏ military in the 1170 coup d'état.

Chŏng Mongju (1337–92), loyalist Neo-Confucian scholar-official in the late Koryŏ period; assassinated for his opposition to the shift of dynasties.

Chŏng Sŏn (1676–1759), true-view landscape painter; depicted native scenes in Korea, including Mt. Kŭmkang.

Chŏng Tojŏn (1337?–98), Neo-Confucian scholar-official who contributed to establishing the new Chosŏn dynasty.

Chŏng Yagyong (1762–1836), also known by the pen name Tasan; scholar-official of the *sirhak* (practical learning) school in the late Chosŏn period who designed the Suwŏn Hwasŏng Fortress.

Chŏngjo (1752–1800), posthumously titled sage-king of the late Chosŏn dynasty; established the Kyujangkak, a royal academy.

Chu Kich'ŏl (1897–1944), a Christian martyr who refused to worship the Japanese Shinto shrine during the Japanese colonial period.

Chumong (58–19 B.C.E.), posthumously named Tongmyŏng Sŏngwang; founder king of Koguryŏ.

Chun Doo Hwan (1931–), military man turned politician after the assassination of President Park Chung Hee; South Korean president 1980–87, after staging a coup and repressing the democratization protest.

Chung Ju Yung (1915–2001), founder of South Korea's conglomerate Hyundai Group; developed a tourism project of visiting Mt. Kŭmkang in North Korea.

Hech'o (704–?), Silla Buddhist monk who traveled twice to India; his travelogue was found in Dunhuang, China, in the early twentieth century.

Hŏ Mok (1595–1682), leader of the Southerners literati clique, stressing classical Confucianism.

Hong Kyŏngnae (1780–1812), leader of the 1811 rebellion in a northwestern province.

Hwanung Ch'ŏnwang, mythical heavenly father of Tan'gun, the priestking of Old Chosŏn.

Hyojong (1619–59), posthumously titled Chosŏn king; northward expedition plan against the Qing; debates over ritual took place in his court.

Hyŏn Sangyun (1892–?), modern historian of Korean thought; involved in the initiation of the March 1 Movement.

Ich'adon (503–27), Buddhist martyr in early Silla.

Im Kkŏkchŏng (?–1562), leader of brigands who was of base people.

Kang Kamch'an (948–1031), Koryŏ general who defeated the Khitan invasion in 1018.

Kija the Sage-King, legendary founder of Kija Chosŏn; its existence in history is controversial among today's scholars.

Kim Ch'unch'u (604–61), posthumously named King T'aejong Muyŏl; Silla leader who unified the three kingdoms on the Korean peninsula.

Kim Dae Jung (1925–), political leader of South Korea's democratization; South Korean president 1997–2003.

Kim Hongdo (1745–?), also known by the pen name Tanwŏn; painter of true-view landscape and genre paintings in the eighteenth century.

Kim Hongjip (1842–96), reformist official at King Kojong's court.

Kim Il Sung (1912–94), or Kim Sŏngju; former North Korean leader of personal cult.

Kim Jong Il (1942–), North Korean leader and chairman of National Defense Commission.

Kim Jong Pil (1926–), South Korean politician; initiator of military coup d'état in 1961.

Kim Ku (1875–1949), nationalist leader in post–World War II Korea and chairman of the provisional government in Chongqing, China.

Kim Kyusik (1877–1952), moderate nationalist leader in the late 1940s; the U.S. military government supported him as a leader of a coalition between the Left and Right.

Kim Okkyun (1851–94), leader of the Enlightenment Party in the 1884 coup.

Kim Pusik (1075–1151), Koryŏ civilian official who compiled the *Samguk sagi* (*History of the Three Kingdoms*) with a Confucian perspective.

Kim Sŏngsu (1891–1955), political leader of the Korean Democratic Party; vice president 1950–51; established the *Dong-A Ilbo* and Korea University; involved in initiation of the March 1 Movement.

Kim Suro, legendary founder and king of the kingdom of Kaya.

Kim Taesŏng (701–74), Great Silla prime minister who constructed the Pulguksa temple and Sŏkkuram grotto.

Kim Tubong (1889–1958), communist leader of the Yanan faction in North Korea; purged in 1958.

Kim Young Sam (1927–), political leader of South Korea's democratization; South Korean president 1993–97.

Kim Yusin (595–673), Silla general who contributed to unifying the three kingdoms on the Korean peninsula.

Kojong (1852–1919), posthumously titled king and later emperor; virtually the last monarch of the Chosŏn dynasty; eventually failed to maintain the independence of the kingdom in 1905.

Kongmin (1330–74), posthumously titled king; last reformist king in late Koryŏ.

Kung'ye (?–918), founder and king of Later Koguryŏ in 901.

Kwanch'ang (645–60), young Silla *hwarang* who fought bravely and died at the Hwangsan Battle in 660.

Kwanggaet'o (375–413), King Yŏngnak; posthumously titled Koguryŏ king who conquered the largest territory in Korean history.

Kwangjong (925–75), posthumously titled Koryŏ king who institutionalized the civil-service exam, or *kwago*, in 958.

Kyebaik (?–660), Paekche general who fought bravely and died at his last battle of the Hwangsan in 660.

Kyŏnhwŏn (?–936), founder and king of Later Paekche in 900.

Min Yŏnghwan (1861–1905), minister at King Kojong's court; protested with suicide against the Ŭlsa Protectorate Treaty in 1905.

Mun Ikchŏm (1329–98), Koryŏ envoy who brought cottonseed from China.

Myoch'ŏng (?–1135), Koryŏ monk adept in geomancy; rebelled in Pyongyang and was eventually suppressed by Kim Pusik.

Na Un'gyu (1904–37), Korean cineaste in the Japanese colonial period; in 1926, he wrote, directed, and starred in *Arirang*.

Onjo (r. 18 B.C.E.–28 C.E.), legendary founder-king of Paekche.

Pak Chiwŏn (1737–1805), also known by the pen name Yŏnam; scholar-official of the practical-learning school; authored a novel, *The Story of Hŏ Saeng*.

Pak Hŏnyŏng (1900–55), leader of the South Korean Workers' Party; North Korean vice premier in 1948; purged in 1953 in North Korea.

Pak Hyŏkkŏse (69 B.C.E.–4 C.E.), legendary founder and *kŏsŏhan* (shaman-chief) of Silla.

Pak Kyusu (1807–77), Pyongyang magistrate when the USS *General Sherman* was burned on the Taedong River; a grandson of Pak Chiwŏn; later became mentor of the Enlightened Party, led by Kim Okkyun.

Pak Yŏnghyo (1861–1939), member of the Enlightened Party; involved in the 1884 coup d'état.

Park Chung Hee (1917–79), leader of the 1961 military coup d'état; South Korean president 1963–79.

Queen Min (1851–95), King Kojong's queen; advised the king to lean toward China and Russia against Japan; assassinated by the Japanese in 1895.

Roh Tae Woo (1932–), military man turned politician after the December 12 coup in 1979; South Korean president 1988–93.

Sejong the Great (1397–1450), posthumously titled king; the most laudable Chosŏn monarch in Korean history; invented and proclaimed the hangul script; expanded territories to the Yalu and the Tumen Rivers.

Sin Ch'aeho (1880–1936), journalist historian advocating nationalism in the early twentieth century.

Sin Chaehyo (1812–84), compiler of pansori, the Korean traditional performing art.

Sŏ Chaep'il (1863–1951), or Philip Jaisohn; founder of the Independence Club and the newspaper in hangul, *Tongnip Sinmun;* involved in the 1884 coup as a young member of the Enlightened Party.

Sŏ Hŭi (940–98), Koryŏ official who stopped the Khitan invasion with diplomacy.

Sŏl Ch'ong (?–?), Silla Confucian scholar; invented *idu,* the old Korean script using Chinese characters; son of Great Monk Wŏnhyo.

Son Kijŏng (1912–2002), or Kitei Son; Korean marathoner and gold medalist in the 1936 Berlin Olympics.

Son Pyŏnghŭi (1861–1922), leader of Ch'ŏn dogyo (Tonghak); head representative of the 33 signers of the March 1 Declaration of Independence.

Song Chinu (1890–1945), leader of the Korean Democratic Party in 1945; involved in the initiation of the March 1 Movement.

Song Pyŏngjun (1858–1925), leader of the Ilchinhoe, a pro-Japanese collaborator group in the early twentieth century.

Song Siyŏl (1607–89), orthodox Neo-Confucian scholar-official, a leader of the Westerners literati clique in the seventeenth century.

Ssanggi (?–?), former Chinese envoy from Later Zou to Koryŏ; introduced the Tang-style civil-service exam.

Sundo (?–?), Buddhist missionary from the Earlier Qin to Koguryŏ in 372.

Sunjong (1874–1926), posthumously titled emperor; last monarch of the Taehan Empire.

Suyang (1417–68), prince, posthumously named King Sejo; usurped the throne of King Tanjong by a palace coup in 1455.

Syngman Rhee (1875–1965), or Yi Sŭngman; political leader of the independence movement who was exiled in the United States; South Korean president 1948–60; resigned after the student demonstration in 1960.

Taewŏn'gun (1820–98), or Prince Hŭngson; prince regent as the father of young King Kojong; ruled the kingdom 1864–74.

Tan'gun Wang'gŏm, priest-king and legendary founder of Old Chosŏn.

Tanjong (1441–57), posthumously titled king dethroned by his uncle, Prince Suyang, posthumously known as King Sejo.

Tosŏn (827–98), Late Silla monk known as a Sŏn master adept in Buddho-geomancy.

Ŭlchi Mundŏk (?–?), Koguryŏ general who defeated the Sui Chinese invasion on the Salsu River in 612.

Wang Kŏn (877–943), posthumously named King T'aejo; founder of the Koryŏ dynasty.

Wiman, (r. 194 B.C.E. –?) king and leader of the last wave of the Dong'yi migration; founder of Wiman Chosŏn.

Wŏn'gwang (542–640), Silla Buddhist monk; authored *hwarangdo*'s "Five Commandments for the Layman."

Wŏnhyo (617–86), Great Silla Buddhist master.

Yi Chun (1858–1907), one of the three secret envoys of Emperor Kojong to the International Peace Conference in The Hague in 1907.

Yi Hwang (1501–70), also known by the pen name T'oegye; one of the most prominent Neo-Confucian scholars in the Chosŏn period; advocated the primacy of principle.

Yi I (1536–84), also known by the pen name Yulgok; one of the most prominent Neo-Confucian scholars in the Chosŏn period; advocated the primacy of material force.

Yi Ik (1681–1763), also known by the pen name Sŏngho; scholar-official who suggested practical reforms of Confucian statecraft in his writings.

Yi Kwangsu (1892–?), writer of modern literature including novels and essays.

Yi Kyubo (1168–1241), Koryŏ civilian official under the Ch'oe House; authored *King Tongmyŏng*.

Yi Pangwŏn (1367–1422), posthumously named King T'aejong; scholar-official son of Yi Sŏnggye who contributed to establishing the Chosŏn dynasty; staged succession struggles against his half brothers until he himself obtained the throne.

Yi Pŏmjin (1853–1911), pro-Russian official at Kojong's court.

Yi Sangjae (1850–1929), one of the Christian leaders of the Independence Club.

Yi Sŏnggye (1335–1408), posthumously named King T'aejo; founder of the Chosŏn dynasty.

Yi Sŭnghun (1756–1801), first Korean Catholic convert.

Yi Sŭnghun (1864–1930), also known by the pen name Namgang; a Christian leader of the independence movement in the northwestern provinces; signed the March 1 Declaration of Independence.

Yi Tonghwi (?–1928), founder of the Korean Socialist Party in Khabarovsk in 1918.

Yi Wanyong (1858–1926), pro-Japanese collaborator in the cabinet of the Taehan Empire; involved in both of two treaties in 1905 and 1910.

Yi Yonggu (1868–1912), one of the leaders of the Ilchinhoe, the pro-Japanese collaborator organization.

Yŏ Unhyŏng (1886–1947), or Lyuh Woon-hyung; leftist leader of the independence movement; founded the Committee for the Preparation of Korean Independence and the People's Republic of Korea in 1945.

Yŏn Kaesomun (?–666), Koguryŏ autocratic ruler in the seventh century; fought against the Tang Chinese invaders.

Yŏngjo (1694–1776), posthumously titled king; longest-reigning monarch of the Chosŏn dynasty.

Yu Hyŏngwŏn (1622–73), also known by the pen name Pan'gye; off-court scholar of practical learning; criticized the established institutions and suggested reforms.

Yu Kilchun (1856–1914), enlightened scholar-official who studied in the United States; authored *Travelogue to the West*.

Yu Kwansun (1904–20), female Christian student fighter during the March 1 Movement.

Yu Sŏngnyong (1542–1607), prime minister of the court during the Imjin War.

Yun Ch'iho (1864–1946), one of the Christian leaders of the Independence Club.

Yun Posŏn (1897–1990), conservative politician; South Korean president under the Second Republic's constitution 1960–61.

Glossary of Selected Terms

ajŏn: Local clerks in the Chosŏn Dynasty; see *hyangni*.

ch'ach'aung: Name of earlier Silla kings.

chaebol: South Korean corporate conglomerates, which emerged in the late 1960s.

chaech'u: Council of High-Ranking Ministers of the two chancelleries during the Koryŏ period in which vital state issues were decided.

ch'ingje kŏnwŏn: To proclaim oneself emperor and establish one's reign title.

chin'gyŏng sansu: True-view landscape painting; depicts native scenes instead of the traditional Chinese landscapes from south China; in Korea, this school began in the early eighteenth century.

Ch'ŏllima Movement: North Korean economic campaign named after the Korean legend "Flying Horse"; modeled after Mao Zedong's Great Leap Forward, Kim Il Sung launched the movement in 1957, the first year of the North Korean Five-Year Plan.

chŏnsikwa: Field and Woodland Rank salary system in early Koryŏ; sizes of pre-bended fields and woodlands were scaled based on ranks in bureaucracy.

Chosŏn wangjo sillok: Annals of the Chosŏn dynasty for 25 kings from 1392 to 1863; the annals chronologically compiled policies and events in relation to each king's reign.

chungbang: Military junta in twelfth-century Koryŏ when the military staged a political coup.

chungin: Middle people, a social strata underneath the ruling yangban; various professions were included, such as medical doctors, interpreters, astronomers, lawyers, and local clerks (or *ajŏn*).

Dong'yi: Pejorative name used by the ancient Chinese for the "Eastern Barbarians," which designated the Han-Ye-Maek people in Manchuria and the Korean peninsula.

hangul: The Korean script or alphabet.

hwabaek: A system of tribal councils that ruled early Silla.

hwarangdo: A body of youth groups in early Silla; members trained in military arts, traditional values, and poetry; the leader of each of these groups was called a *hwarang*.

hyangga: Earliest form of Korean poetry written in *idu* script in the Silla period.

hyangni: Hereditary local strongmen during the Koryŏ period; degraded to clerks in the local bureaucracy (or *ajŏn*) during the Chosŏn period.

idu: Korean script that used Chinese characters to write Korean words and grammar; created during the Silla period.

juche: North Korean leader Kim Il Sung's policy of "self-reliance."

kenpei: Military police that the Japanese Government-General used to intimidate Korean civilians during the early colonial period.

kisaeng: Korean court-lady schooled in the arts; equivalent of the Japanese geisha.

kolp'um: Bone-rank system; a hierarchy of aristocratic ranks in the Silla period.

kongsin: "Merit subject," a title granted to yangban for exemplary services after the success of a political coup during the Chosŏn period.

kwagŏ: Korean civil-service examination; introduced in the tenth century; only by passing this exam could a yangban become a ranking official in the bureaucracy until it was abolished in 1894.

mangniji: Grand minister plenipotentiary; title of Yŏn Kaesomun, Koguryŏ dictator.

maripkan: One of the early titles of Silla kings.

Mimana: Japanese name for Kaya; old Japanese historiographies claimed ancient Yamato Japan established a military outpost in Kaya from the fourth to the sixth centuries.

munbŏl: Ruling hereditary class of literati in Koryŏ.

nangdo: Lay members of the *hwarangdo*.

nisagŭm: One of the early titles of Silla kings.

nongjang: A great estate owned by the aristocracy in the late Koryŏ period.

oeson: Grandchildren by one's daughters.

p'aedo: The Confucian concept of rule of might.

P'algwan: A Buddhist festival in the autumn worshipping the Spirit of Heaven in the Koryŏ period.

pansori: Korean traditional musical monodrama performed by one singer-actor or actress with one drummer; still popular in today's Korea.

pisaek: Secret color, a unique color of blue monochrome in Koryŏ celadon.

punch'ŏng: Chosŏn porcelain with gray-blue or gray-yellow engravings.

pungdang: Literati cliques for political hegemony in the Chosŏn court.

sadaebu: Neo-Confucian scholar-officials who dominated late Koryŏ and Chosŏn courts.

sadae kyorin: Traditional diplomatic policy of the Kingdom of Chosŏn in the East Asian world-system; *sadae*, or "attendance on the great," refers to Korea's relation to China, and *kyorin*, or "goodwill to neighbors," refers to the relationship with the Jurchen, Japan, Ryukyu, and Namman.

Saemaul Movement: National political campaign to modernize the underdeveloped rural villages launched by President Park Chung Hee of South Korea in 1971.

Saengyuksin: Six living loyalists who left the court and hid in the countryside to protest against the political coup by Prince Suyang, later King Sejo.

Samguk sagi: *History of the Three Kingdoms*, the oldest extant history book written by Koreans, which covered the period from Old Chosŏn to Great Silla; compiled by Kim Pusik in the twelfth century.

Samguk yusa: *Memorabilia of the Three Kingdoms*, authored by Buddhist monk Iryŏn in the thirteenth century.

sangp'yŏng t'ongbo: Korean copper coin minted in 1678.

Sanguozhi Weizhi Dong'yizhuan: Chinese historiography compiled in the third century, the oldest records on the Han-Ye-Maek people in Manchuria, the Korean peninsula, and the Japanese archipelago.

sarim: Rusticated literati educated under famous Neo-Confucian scholars; eventually dominated the court after severe literati purges in the sixteenth century.

Sayuksin: Six dead loyalists who failed to reinstate Tanjong, the king deposed by King Sejo, and were executed.

seikanron: Conquer-Korea policy advocated by radical nationalist Japanese politicians in the late nineteenth century.

sijo: Traditional Korean poetry of set-rhymed verse with three tightly structured lines; popular among the scholar-officials in the late Koryŏ and Chosŏn periods.

Sillabang: Korean communities on the mouth of the Yangzi River and the Sandong peninsula in Tang China in the Great Silla period.

sirhak: A new school of Confucian philosophy in the seventeenth and eighteenth centuries, which stressed the "practical learning" of statecraft.

sŏja: Descendants of secondary wives or concubines.

Sŏn: A Buddhist school of meditation (Zen in Japanese).

sŏwŏn: Private Neo-Confucian academies in provinces for rustic literati, or *sarim*.

suryŏng: Korean title of Great Leader for Kim Il Sung in North Korea.

t'angp'yŏng policy: Impartiality policy of eighteenth-century Chosŏn kings, maintaining a balance of competing literati cliques.

Teishintai: "Comfort women" forced into sexual servitude of the Japanese troops in World War II.

tongdo sŏgi: A slogan of King Kojong's modernization attempt in 1882, meaning "Eastern ethics and Western technology."

Tonghak: A new religion advocated by a Korean marginal yangban in the nineteenth century, based on the three religious sources of the Eastern Learning: Confucianism, Buddhism, and Taoism.

Tripitaka Koreana: More than 80,000 wood blocks used for printing Buddhist scriptures, laws, and treatises built as a devotion to solicit protection from the Mongol invasion in the thirteenth century; UNESCO designated it a World Cultural Heritage; now kept at Haeinsa Temple in South Korea.

ŭibyŏng: Volunteer guerrilla army under the leadership of yangban literati against Japanese military occupation since 1905.

wangdo: Confucian principle of rule of right advocated by Mencius.

wijŏng ch'ŏksa: Nationalist movement against Western influences among Neo-Confucian scholar-officials in the late nineteenth century, advocating "defending orthodoxy and rejecting heterodoxy."

yangban: The ruling class of the Chosŏn period; privileged to serve as scholar-officials at court through the civil-service exam; the word is derived from two wings of bureaucracy, civilian and military, in the Koryŏ court.

Yŏndŭng: A Buddhist festival in January worshipping Buddha in the Koryŏ period.

yŏyo: Popular verses mostly by anonymous authors in the Koryŏ period.

Yusin: A political coup by President Park Chung Hee in October 1972, suspending the constitution.

Bibliographic Essay

Ki-baik Lee's *A New History of Korea*, translated by Edward Wagner and Edward Shultz (Seoul: Ilchokak, 1984) is the most comprehensive survey history of Korea by a Korean historian. *A New History of Korea*, as the title says, was one of the most provocative interpretations of the development process of Korean history, although some of its aspects still remain controversial, particularly among non-Korean researchers. Despite its thorough translation by two eminent American scholars of Korean studies, it is not easy for English-speaking readers to access the unfamiliar cultural and political context of the East-Asian paradigm outside the original Korean.

Korea Old and New: A History (Seoul: Ilchokak, 1990), edited by Edward Wagner, is a condensed version of the premodern history taken from Ki-baik Lee's book, with new chapters on the twentieth century. Young Ick Lew, Michael Robinson, and Carter Eckert contributed their own parts on the nineteenth century, Japanese colonial period, and after liberation, respectively. Given that it merely condenses the premodern history of *A New History of Korea*, written in 1967, it is not updated to include the mounting volume of recent studies. Furthermore, the twentieth-century sections of the book mostly focus on South Korea, exclude North Korean developments, and do not include perspectives by Korean historians.

The *Sourcebook of Korean Civilization,* vols. 1 and 2 (New York: Columbia University Press, 1997), edited by Peter H. Lee, is meant to allow Korean-studies students access to primary sources encompassing political, social, religious, and literary traditions. The documents in the *Sourcebook* for Korea are well selected, categorized by period, and given brief introductions. However, the translations of the original texts, mostly from classical Chinese into English, are seldom satisfactory for a smooth read.

The history of premodern Korea has rarely been studied in learned circles in the West, except among a few American scholars: Edward Wagner, James Palais, Martina Deuchler, Mark Peterson, and John Duncan. Their works concentrate mostly on the Chosŏn period. Edward Wagner's *The Literati Purges: Political Conflict in Early Yi Korea* (Cambridge, Mass.: Harvard University Press, 1974) is a classic work done by an American Korean-studies scholar.

James Palais's recent masterpiece, *Confucian Statecraft and Korean Institutions: Yu Hyŏngwŏn and the Late Chosŏn Dynasty* (Seattle: University of Washington Press, 1996) challenges many Korean and Japanese scholars' ideas of modernization motivated by Korean Confucian statecraft in the mid-eighteenth century. In his mammoth work, Palais presents Yu Hyŏngwŏn's texts and the historical roots of Yu's reform ideas, analyzing the nature and degree of protocapitalistic changes. Palais has developed his interest in the political reforms of Confucian statecraft in the late Chosŏn period in his previous work, *Politics and Policy in Traditional Korea* (Cambridge, Mass.: Harvard University Press, 1975), which focuses on the reforms of Taewŏn'gun.

Martina Deuchler and Mark Peterson study the Confucianization process in the Chosŏn dynasty. Deuchler's *The Confucian Transformation of Korea: A Study of Society and Ideology* (Cambridge, Mass.: Harvard University Press, 1992) explains how Confucianism, and Neo-Confucianism in particular, transformed the traditional Korean society once it was introduced in the late Koryŏ period. She compares Koryŏ's pre-Confucian past with the Neo-Confucian legislation in Early Chosŏn using cultural-anthropological items such as marriage, ancestor worship, mourning rites, and inheritance. Peterson's *Korean Adoption and Inheritance: Case Studies in the Creation of a Classic Confucian Society* (Ithaca, N.Y.: Cornell University Press, 1996) focuses on cases found in the pivotal seventeenth-century Chosŏn when Confucianization in fact began to occur.

John Duncan's *The Origins of the Chosŏn Dynasty* (Seattle: University of Washington Press, 2000) portrays the political structure and function of premodern Korea, focusing on the Koryŏ-Chosŏn transition from the Great Silla period. The author attempts to refute a universal view that a new class of Neo-Confucian scholar-officials overthrew the capital-based aristocracy of Koryŏ. In this, he uses rich data compiled from primary sources like genealogies and tomb inscriptions to analyze the structure and composition of the central officialdom of the Koryŏ-Chosŏn transition.

Larger numbers of volumes of monographs and books in English on the modern period from the late nineteenth to the twentieth centuries have been published. The following deal with more general topics in modern Korea. Gregory Henderson's *Korea: the Politics of the Vortex* (Cambridge, Mass.: Harvard University Press, 1968) has been one of the most largely read by English-speaking audiences as far as modern political history is concerned. The author provocatively attempts to interpret Korean political culture in modern Korea after 1945, analyzing its political tradition in premodern history. While Bruce Cumming's *The Origins of the Korean War: Liberation and the Emergence of Separate Regimes 1945–1947* (Princeton, N.J.: Princeton University Press, 1981) criticizes the U.S. post–World War II policy in South Korea, Erik van Ree's *Socialism in One Zone: Stalin's Policy in Korea 1945–1947* (Oxford: Berg Publishers, 1989) describes the Soviet policy in North Korea during the same period. Dae-Sook Suh's *The Korean Communist Movement, 1918–1948* (Princeton, N.J.: Princeton University Press, 1967) explains the history of Korean communism at home and abroad and discusses Kim Il Sung's activities in Manchuria.

Don Oberdorfer's *The Two Koreas: a Contemporary History* (New York: Basic Books, 2001) portrays one of the most updated histories of Korea's travails and triumphs over the past three decades. The author explains the tensions between the North and South within a historical context that focuses on the involvement of outside powers.

Index

About the Author

DJUN KIL KIM served in the Korean government for more than two decades and was recently a visiting professor at Brigham Young University where he taught Korean history.

Other Titles in the Greenwood Histories of the Modern Nations
Frank W. Thackeray and John E. Findling, Series Editors

The History of Argentina
Daniel K. Lewis

The History of Israel
Arnold Blumberg

The History of Australia
Frank G. Clarke

The History of Italy
Charles L. Killinger

The History of Brazil
Robert M. Levine

The History of Japan
Louis G. Perez

The History of Canada
Scott W. See

The History of Mexico
Burton Kirkwood

The History of China
David C. Wright

The History of Nigeria
Toyin Falola

The History of Congo
Didier Gondola

The History of Poland
M. B. Biskupski

The History of Cuba
Clifford L. Staten

The History of Portugal
James M. Anderson

The History of France
W. Scott Haine

The History of Russia
Charles E. Ziegler

The History of Germany
Eleanor L. Turk

The History of Serbia
John K. Cox

The History of Holland
Mark T. Hooker

The History of South Africa
Roger B. Beck

The History of India
John McLeod

The History of Spain
Peter Pierson

The History of Iran
Elton L. Daniel

The History of Sweden
Byron J. Nordstrom

The History of Ireland
Daniel Webster Hollis III

The History of Turkey
Douglas A. Howard